DISCARDED

CHASING SPRING™
PRESENTS
Ray Eye's TURKEY HUNTER'S BIBLE

NWTF

Conserve. Hunt. Share.

CHASING SPRING™
PRESENTS

Ray Eye's TURKEY HUNTER'S BIBLE

The Tips, Tactics, and Secrets of a Professional Turkey Hunter

RAY EYE

Skyhorse Publishing

Skyhorse Publishing books may be purchased in bulk at special discounts for sales promotion, corporate gifts, fund-raising, or educational purposes. Special editions can also be created to specifications. For details, contact the Special Sales Department, Skyhorse Publishing, 307 West 36th Street, 11th Floor, New York, NY 10018 or info@skyhorsepublishing.com.

Skyhorse® and Skyhorse Publishing® are registered trademarks of Skyhorse Publishing, Inc.®, a Delaware corporation.

Visit our website at www.skyhorsepublishing.com

10 9 8 7 6 5 4 3 2 1

Library of Congress Cataloging-in-Publication Data is available on file.

ISBN: 978-1-62873-812-4

Printed in China

I dedicate this book to our country's brave men and women in uniform, past, present, and future.
I would like to thank America's warriors for their service to our great country, for without these great American heroes' tremendous sacrifice, this book and the many freedoms we enjoy today just would not be possible.
God bless our troops, and God bless America.

Ray Eye

Contents

Contents

About the Author

What others in the hunting industry say about Ray Eye

Major League Baseball has greats such as Babe Ruth, Mickey Mantle, and Harmon Killebrew. The NFL has standouts such as Vince Lombardi, Fran Tarkenton, and Joe Montana. And what would NASCAR be without Dale Earnhardt or Richard Petty?

Each and every sport produces those special icons whose names withstand the test of time and become synonymous with the sport itself. And those names belong to people who've dedicated their lives to the betterment of themselves and their sport and, most often unintentionally, touched the lives of thousands of people along the way. Turkey hunting has Ray Eye.

Mr. Turkey, Ray Eye, and Peanut.

Born in St. Louis, Missouri, in the early 1950s, Eye entered the world of turkey hunting when neighbors were tight-lipped and books or magazines on the subject were scarce. Ray had to learn his hunting know-how the hard way—in the turkey woods.

Eye credits much of his early turkey hunting success to his grandfather. In his book, *Practical Turkey Hunting Strategies*, Eye states, "A little later, he [Grandpa] gave me what became my most prized possession—my own turkey call. Grandpa had made it by hand, using a piece of slate from the chalkboard at on old one-room schoolhouse. For a striker he'd cut a piece of cedar from a fence post and fit it in the bottom of a hollowed-out corncob."

Eye's grandfather gave him the roots he needed to begin growing into a full-blown turkey hunting fanatic, and he has grown to the point where many claim he has reached legendary status.

Humble Beginnings

Ray Eye was born the son of an auto body man, along with five brothers and one sister. The Eye family was steeped in turkey hunting tradition from the beginning. Eye's grandparents owned a farm in the Missouri Ozarks and as Eye states, "I didn't graduate from a college, but I earned a degree in Turkeyology from Johnson Mountain University in the Missouri Ozarks!"

That degree has served him well during his climb to the top of the turkey hunting totem pole, but Eye has paid plenty of dues along the way.

Eye's first job in the outdoor industry came by working a promotions gig in a new Wal-Mart store in 1977 selling his turkey calls—the original corncob slate and several mouth calls—under the name of his new call company, Ozark Mountain Turkey Calls.

Eye also guided turkey hunters for pay from 1978 to 1986, and began giving seminars at sporting goods stores, high schools, and colleges. He would trade turkey calls for gas and meals while he traveled from place to place—telltale signs of an up-and-coming turkeyholic. During this same time, Eye was heavily involved in competition calling—taking first-place honors at many local or regional contests and several national and world calling titles. A career highlight includes winning the Levi Garrett All-American Open turkey calling championship and NWTF Grand National Championship, Owl Hooting Division.

Eye then began working for H. S. Strut in 1986, building mouth calls. When asked how many mouth calls he's personally made, Eye smiled and said, "Over the years, I've made hundreds of thousands of mouth calls." When asked how many turkeys he's killed, he smiled even bigger and simply said, "A lot."

Today, Eye works harder than ever; still learning about turkey hunting while giving back to the sport that has given him so much. He spent the past eleven years educating hunters on his outdoor radio show, has presented and spoken at countless national seminars and major sports shows, he works closely with several conservation groups, organizes media hunts, hosts a national television show, belongs to the pro staff of several outdoor companies, is an outdoor writer, a professional TV cameraman, a field producer, pro staff member for H. S. Strut, and the list goes on and on.

But through it all, Eye has remained close to the roots of turkey hunting and has continued to live the lessons about hunting and the importance of family that his grandfather instilled in him many years ago.

What Ray's Friends Say

It's obvious that Ray's family continues to come first, and that he gives much more than he takes, in every aspect of his life. But as Theodore Roosevelt once said, "You can tell a lot about the character of a man by what his friends say about him when he's not listening."

So, what do fellow hunters say about Ray Eye when he's not listening?

"I've known Ray for more than thirty-two years. Because Ray hunts them in spring and fall, all of his hard-hunting experience is what really makes him knowledgeable. Ray *knows* how to hunt turkeys.

"Plus, he's a great teacher. He comes across easy, understands people, and can relate well to anyone—young or old.

"I bet there isn't a turkey in the woods that can humble Ray Eye. He's the real deal."

—*Harold Knight, outdoor personality and founder of Knight &*
Hale Game Calls

"Every time I see Ray he has a big smile on his face. We shake hands and actually give each other a hug. Ray is the kind of guy you are going to have fun with, no matter what.

"Ray has hunted enough to know when you have to be aggressive or back off and have patience. He knows when to call and where the turkey might be headed so he can cut him off.

"The best thing about Ray is that he's able to promote the sport he loves in a fun, positive, and safe way, whether talking to kids or seasoned veterans. He's been instrumental in keeping the sport of hunting alive. I'm proud to call Ray Eye my friend."

   —Ernie Calandrelli, director of PR for Quaker Boy and expert hunter

"Ray is a good public promoter of the wild turkey and turkey hunting because he's friendly to everyone he meets. He's upbeat, likes having fun, and that makes people feel comfortable around him.

"Ray Eye still has one of the most realistic hen yelps I've ever heard. Back when Ray was calling in turkey calling competitions in the 1970s and 1980s, I was fortunate to be running in the same circles, and we had some great times. When I was finally lucky enough to win a qualifier to my first Grand Nationals, Ray was as excited as I was . . . he had been there and done that. He came to me and told me that if I was going to be competitive, I was going to have to make a few changes to my calling style. He made sure I had the right calls and equipment and helped teach me the ropes along the way.

"I will never forget that and will always be thankful to him. The only sad thing about this is the fact that after all these years in the outdoor industry, we've only been able to hunt turkeys together one time . . . that has got to change. Thanks again, Ray!"

   —Walter Parrott, outdoor TV personality and champion turkey caller

"I've known Ray Eye for probably more than thirty years, and have hunted with him in such diverse locales as New York, Hawaii, Missouri, and Wyoming. I'm proud to call Ray Eye (I call him RayJay, he calls me JayRay—long story—"You can call me Ray, you can call me Jay…") my friend. I've got two things to say about RayJay.

"First, I know Ray has hunted all over the planet, with a bazillion different people—from celebrities to regular, run-of-the-mill folks. And there's no question that Ray Eye is one of the best, most innovative turkey hunters ever. But what's cool about Ray, and what I respect him for, is the fact that he treats everyone the same, no matter who you are, or what you do for a living. Ray puts on no airs, has no ego, and doesn't expect you to have one either; when you're hunting, you're hunting, period, let's do it right, let's get the job done, let's have some fun while we're doing it. And when the hunt is over, then it's time to wind down, shoot the bull, have some good food somewhere, simply relax, and probably watch some turkey hunting videos. And that brings me to my second observation. . . .

"If you've ever hunted with Ray Eye, you know that he has an obsession with clowns. Walk through the woods in the early morning with Ray, and he's likely to stop and point his green light at some jelly beans that have mysteriously appeared on the trail. 'Clown sign,' he'll say quietly. Or maybe you'll see a clown footprint in the dirt. 'It's clown mating season,' he'll whisper in a hushed voice. 'Move slowly—they can be dangerous now.'

"Once, Ray told me that he was hunting with a father and teenage son. The son, it seems, didn't believe Ray when he said they were in clown country and had to be careful. The next morning, Ray put on his favorite clown mask—a macabre-looking thing—and got to the ground blind ahead of the teenager, whom he had told to just meet him in the woods. When the boy came through the woods in the dark, just before daylight, he carefully opened the blind flaps and eased into the tent. 'I've been waiting for you,' Ray whispered into his ear, while shining a light to his clown face. Rays laughs hard when telling that story. 'I don't think I've ever seen anyone move out of a tent so fast in my life!'

"The stories go on. Imagine going to the beach in Hawaii, after a morning hunt, and turning around to see that Ray is wearing not only his bathing suit but his clown mask on the beach! There are many more.

"It's all about enjoying life when it comes to Ray Eye. He loves to hunt turkeys, loves to spend time with people—and it shows, which is why it's so much fun to hunt with him, and which is why it's an honor to call him a friend."

—*Jay Cassell, Editorial Director, Skyhorse Publishing*.

"It's hard to describe Ray because he's multifaceted. On the surface he's a modern-day mountain man. I honestly believe you could drop Ray off about anywhere in the world with only a pocket knife, come back a week later, and he would have an animal hanging in the nearest tree with a fire going and would be no worse for the experience. Leave him alone for two weeks and he'd probably have a log cabin built as well.

"While his woodsman skills are legendary, there is another side to Ray that few see. One year I was at one of the last of his spring outdoor writers' events. When everyone left, Ray finally had a chance to relax. Being hunted to death for the last two months, he decided to stay in on my final afternoon. I figured he was going to catch up on some much-needed sleep so I went fishing.

"When I returned at nightfall, the cabin smelled wonderful. Not only did Ray make an awesome steak, but he had made a homemade peach pie that afternoon. He delivered it to the table wearing a white chef's apron—it was quite a sight!

"Yes, Ray is an expert caller. But to kill a turkey, it takes more than just sounding good. Ray spends way more time in the field than anyone else I know, learning all he can about the turkeys that live there. By spending a ton of time scouting, both pre- and post-season, Ray has a good idea where he can find birds on any given day."

—Mike Schoby, book author and editor of Petersen's Hunting magazine

What Others Say

"Within the hunting world, Ray Eye is a national treasure. He doesn't just call turkeys, he talks to them. Ray Eye is the turkey whisperer.

"Not only is Ray Eye the name most associated with turkey hunting and consistently killing turkeys, he has become one of the premier professional cameramen of all time.

"Eye's archive of film footage rivals that of *National Geographic*, and his expert woodsmanship, along with national-championship calling skills put him at the top of his profession. If I didn't know better, I would swear his DNA is pure wild turkey.

"As a professional outdoor communicator, I have had the opportunity to hunt with many "name" hunting personalities during hunting industry media hunts all across America.

"I'm not taking anything away from any of them, but in the turkey hunting World Series, bottom of the ninth, two outs and two strikes, or the final seconds of the Super Bowl and down by one touchdown, Ray Eye is the man you bet on to kill a turkey, when no one else can."

—Bobby Whitehead, Editor/Publisher, Outdoor Guide Magazine, St. Louis/Southern Illinois Labor Tribune

"I am very fortunate to spend a lot of time with Ray Eye, and to have the opportunity to see the real Ray Eye, and he is the real deal. His passion for the outdoors and his love for helping young hunters with their first deer or turkey are off the charts.

"I also have an opportunity to review raw video footage from his hunts, and it is always incredible. You will not see better anywhere, and his still camera photos are a work of art. Put this all together—his seminars, this book, his magazine articles, and his DVDs—and what you have is nothing more than the confessions of a wild turkey serial killer.

"Ray has hunted throughout America, across Canada and Mexico, and in extremely wild areas of Africa. You'll enjoy his teaching style as he helps walk you through a wild journey of his tactics and information for turkey hunting, with wit, humor, and his incredible storytelling.

"He's one of those rare people born with the 'Daniel Boone gene' . . . you could drop him out of an airplane in the middle of the night in a remote place, and the next day he'd be sitting over a fire cooking what he hunted down. Then—if he felt like it—he'd walk out to civilization.

"I have read the stories in this book and I have to say thanks for the trip to the Ozarks; Ray is such an artist with the camera and with the pen that I felt like was there; I could see it in my mind. I could smell the woods, and the wood fires in the distance. I could hear the wind in the trees, the birds singing, and turkeys gobbling. I could see the dinner table, and when he says; 'blackberry cobbler,' I felt like Pavlov's dog. I was drooling for the food like your grandma prepares.

"Some of us are not as fortunate to have such a rich history as you share, so you, Ray Eye, introduce all of us to Ozarks history and the true spirit of hunting. More people need to reinforce the rich heritage of the outdoors, and I thank you for teaching me so much about the outdoors, tradition, and honor."
—*Chris Vogler, KFNS Radio, Head Optician,*
SafeVision Hunting Glasses

"If wild turkeys had brains larger than peas, they would fear Ray Eye as their apex predator. Simply, Eye possesses an uncanny ability to locate and kill wild turkeys.

"Having been born to a Missouri Ozarks country farm family, Eye began his turkey hunting career at an early age, and was taught by all his older kin how to go about it. Fancy camo, calls, magnum shells, decoys and extra-full turkey chokes didn't exist then. Instead, the Eye clan utilized their knowledge of the land and woodsmanship skills to hunt and kill all types of wild game, including wild turkeys. Ray Eye fell in love with the notion of studying wild turkeys all year round. As the decades passed, Eye accumulated more film footage of wild turkeys than perhaps any human being. His studies have put him in the know about turkey behavior at any time of the year. His knowledge and understanding of the pecking order gives him exceptional insight into the social order of wild turkeys.

"Eye has film footage of wild gobblers strutting, gobbling, and fighting every month of the year. It is the constant struggle for dominance among flocks of birds that Eye uses to his great advantage, while many other hunters continue to argue that turkeys only gobble and fight in the spring. It quickly becomes obvious to students of Eye's techniques that those other guys haven't spent as much time in the woods as Ray Eye has.

"Eye has taught and helped more hunters about hunting wild turkeys than any other personality through his thousands of seminars, presentations, appearances, articles, TV shows, and DVDs. He is far and away ahead of all others with his teaching, information, tactics, and turkey hunting knowledge, and is especially far beyond what anyone else produces with DVD video productions.

"Some turn their noses up at Ray's aggressive techniques, but they work, period. Ray Eye is the consummate caller, hitting his calls loud, hard, and long. His calling skills are second to none and he goes after gobblers with a confidence that is infectious. A legend in his own time, Eye has consistently called what other hunters say are uncallable gobblers.

"Hunting turkeys eight months a year, Eye is the purest of real turkey hunters out there, and calls and kills as many gobblers in the fall as in the spring season. All over the country, in all kinds of terrain, Eye consistently kills the unkillable gobblers hunted by other "professional hunters." He has literally left a pile of feathers everywhere he has hunted.

"An icon of the turkey hunting world, Eye absolutely loves teaching others about hunting wild turkeys. He holds crowds spellbound with his slap-happy, matter-of-fact, vivid presentations at his seminars. His spectacular film footage of wild turkeys and the hunts to get them makes every hunter want to be there.

"Ray began his long-running, entertaining outdoor communications career in the late 1970s at local turkey calling contests. I know, because I was there. His Ozark charm and truly spectacular story telling abilities mesmerized audiences everywhere he traveled. His outdoor communications career literally exploded across the land. He became a pioneer in outdoor TV programming, promoting hunter safety, outdoor skills, outdoor ethics, and sound conservation principles as far back as 1983. Some of his first articles and photographs appeared in *Outdoor Life* magazine back in 1983. In 1987

Eye appeared on both radio and TV programs all across Missouri on PSAs for the new concept of turkey hunting safety. These programs later went national through the National Wild Turkey Federation.

"Ray began conducting outdoor media hunts in 1983 for outdoor communicators. At these camps, writers, editors, and radio and TV media personnel used and promoted the latest in outdoor equipment and the safety issues surrounding them. Ray continues this tradition to this day by hosting spring and fall media hunts every year. And even though he is a busy man, he gives back regularly through his volunteer efforts of appearing at fundraisers for conservation organizations and running youth hunting camps. He has also volunteered seminars for the NRA, NWTF, US Sportsman's Alliance, and various school districts and sports clubs. He also volunteers his services for fundraisers for Saint Jude's Children's Hospital. Eye never passes up the opportunity to mentor a young, up-and-coming hunter.

"Ultimately, Ray Eye has become a conservation communications giant. His accomplishments could fill volumes. He has generated and created an awareness of our great outdoors and the issues surrounding them in millions of Americans. Few individuals in the history of the conservation movement have generated the quantity and quality of outdoor-related media materials over a span of several decades. Yet, Ray remains humble, down to earth, and a friend to all he meets. He is a friend of the wild turkey, conservation, the outdoors, and America's hunting future. Above all, Eye is a lover of life. I've been fortunate enough to spend time with him in many turkey hunting camps. His exuberance for the camp life, for turkey hunting, and for having friends around to spin yarns to is unequalled.

"My life is much richer for having known the turkey hunter of all turkey hunters, Mr. Ray Eye. As for those turkey hunters who still won't follow Ray Eye's methods for locating, calling, and killing wild turkey gobblers, well... those guys will be light-years from figuring it all out, if they ever do.

—*Bill Cooper, freelance outdoor writer*

"Ray Eye is so good at hunting turkeys that for years we have suspected he secretly goes into a room at night and flies up in the rafters to sleep. How else can you explain him being the last one awake at night, and no matter how early you get up, he's already dressed and drinking coffee and yelling at the rest of us about how we need to be out in the yard doing wind sprints?

"He sounds so much like a real turkey on any type of call that you can be fooled even when you are sitting there watching him make the sounds. This is especially true when it comes to mouth calling, an art that is so difficult to master, but that he makes appear so easy that it becomes a source of amazement and jealousy for all who hear it.

"I will never forget the first time I heard him call. It was in northern Missouri, years ago. The only reason I got to go hunting with Ray is because Gary Clancy, a big-time writer, couldn't go. So I drove down there, arriving at about midnight, and knocked on the door of the old schoolhouse. Ray yelled, 'Who's there?' through the door, and I explained who I was. He opened the door, and said something about the only reason he was letting me in was because Clancy asked him to, and he said, 'Throw your [stuff] over there; we're getting up in two hours.'

"In the pitch black, Ray woke me up. 'Come on, Clancy replacement . . .' We got into this extremely old red pickup and drove off into nasty-looking weather that kept getting worse by the minute. There were tornado warnings left and right. We're driving over single-lane river bridges older than the truck, and we're out there trying to make turkeys gobble. This was a guy after my own heart. You're there to go hunting, so you go. Who cares about the weather?

"The nasty weather hung around long enough that every other writer expected in camp didn't make the trip, so Ray was stuck with me for four days. At times it was raining so hard you couldn't see from the road to the ditch, but Ray kept driving around, rolling down the window on the old pickup, and calling, and calling. The sound was like nothing I had ever heard from a call, because it didn't sound like a call. I asked him, 'How are you doing that?' In classic Ray fashion, he said, 'I'm just making the same sounds I hear the turkeys make.'

"The weather stunk, but being shipwrecked with Ray Eye was the best thing that ever happened to my turkey hunting career. I kept hitting him with questions until it bordered on waterboarding, and just from his answers I could tell he was the real deal, the guy that other guys look to for the 'rules.'

"Up until that point, my years of turkey hunting had been a blur of personal experiences and conflicting advice from so-called experts. The purity, simplicity, and consistency of Ray's answers was readily apparent. He lived with turkeys, he lived for living with them, and he is almost one of them. He hunts them, but he loves them.

"It's so obvious once you see it up close.

"He hunts with tenacity and focus, every day, all spring. But he also has a great sense of humor and wants to have fun out there. When the weather cleared enough for us to hunt on that first trip, I did my best to keep up with him through the woods for about four hours, his legs chugging without rest, seeking out a 'ready Freddy' as he calls them. I never saw him eat or drink anything. After my fiftieth swig of water, I asked him why he didn't have any with him. 'I'm not usually out here this long,' he said. 'I'm usually with somebody who can kill a turkey.'

"When it was time to leave, Ray told me to get my camera. 'Take a picture of the schoolhouse,' he instructed. 'It's the only way you'll ever see it again.'

"When the spring season is over, Ray goes on hunting turkeys, following them around with his ever-present video camera, documenting their life cycle. He has incredible footage of baby jakes displaying, fighting, and flying up into low branches of trees. He has footage of calling up big toms, gobbling and strutting, in July and August and pretty much every other month of the year.

"When fall arrives, he's back out there hunting, calling up gobblers on purpose, without busting up flocks. 'Why would I scare 'em away first, when I want to call 'em up and shoot 'em?' he asks, in typical Ray fashion. Everything he says makes sense, and you don't have to think about it.

"When he was young, Ray loved to 'dog turkeys,' as he called it, following them through the Ozark hills all day long, from the time they flew down until they flew back up. He'd bring a few cans of Vienna sausages, drink water out of the streams, and lie down to sleep near the turkeys after they flew up. In the predawn gray, Ray and the turkeys would wake up and begin another day, Ray watching them and slinking along behind. He says he learned everything about how to hunt turkeys from the turkeys themselves, and it's absolutely true.

"Since those days, he has traveled essentially everywhere there are wild turkeys, proving in every corner that his methods are consistently effective, resulting in a 'trail of blood and feathers' that now flows into Mexico and the Yucatan.

"Now, after all these years of hunting turkeys all year long, he has come to a point in his life where he wants to tell it all, just lay it out there, the full details of how he calls and kills turkeys. He no longer concerns himself with whether others think his tactics are 'too aggressive' (whatever that means). He says, 'Turkeys just call how they feel, and when they want to get together with other turkeys, they call excitedly, and a lot.' We have joked that it's better that he tells us now, rather than saving his best stuff for the nurses in the nursing home.

"He's not ready for a rocking chair anytime soon, though, having completed his first season of *Chasing Spring*™ for *Outdoor Life* magazine and its website, and planning more of the same.

"Wherever he goes, turkeys respond, because he sounds for all the world exactly like they do, and he knows where they're likely to be, and he knows how to hold still at the critical points. Oh, look, we're all out of time. I was just about to tell you what he says about head-bobbing outdoor writers.

"I am both happy and excited Ray made a decision to share with you his secret of a professional turkey hunter. I feel very fortunate to have experienced while hunting with Ray much of what's within this book, and after reviewing several chapters, there is no question in the archives of turkey hunting history, it will be spoken that Ray Eye 'wrote THE book on turkey hunting.'

"Enjoy Ray's stories and soak up his hunting tactics, for you can take them to the bank and cash 'em in for your own trail of blood and feathers."

—*Mark Strand, freelance outdoor writer, President/Founder,*
School of Outdoor Sports

"So, what else can I say about The TurkEye Legend? Geez, Harold Knight, Ernie Calandrelli, Walter Parrott, and Mike Schoby, all hunting legends in their own rights, gushed quite a bit over Ray.

"Well, I can say this: If you sit down and talk to Ray Eye, like I have, you'll realize immediately that he's an honest, hardworking, down-to-earth man who simply and absolutely loves turkeys and turkey hunting. He gets frustrated and tired too, just like all of us, though I think he just 'recovers' faster than anyone else—and that's what keeps him in the woods so much.

"During my interviews with Ray, I could tell he was having a great time reminiscing about the people he's met, jobs he's accomplished, friendships he's earned, and outdoor adventures he's shared with family, friends, and strangers alike.

"I imagine Ray kneeled down on the ground to admire the beauty of a big Ozark Mountain gobbler that he'd just harvested, one spring or fall day. Then he looked up at the sky, closed his eyes, and whispered, 'How can I make this experience my lifetime career?' Then with absolute determination, unparalleled calling capabilities, a great personality for networking, and a tremendous effort amassing an incredible amount of turkey hunting knowledge, *he did.*"

—*JJ Reich, Freelance Outdoor Writer, Copywriter, and NWTF Columnist*

Acknowledgments

AS WITH ANY ACKNOWLEDGMENTS, IT IS IMPOSSIBLE TO thank everyone—my family, my wonderful friends, my hunting industry family, and especially every turkey hunter across this great country—with whom I am privileged to share a campfire in hunting camp.

However, there are three individuals I have to mention: Jay "JayRay" Cassell, Mark Strand, and Gerry Bethge. They are my turkey hunting brothers, my friends, and are all incredibly talented outdoor media specialists. Without their tireless effort, encouragement, skill, and motivation, this book would have never been possible.

But a special acknowledgment goes out to each and every turkey hunter across America, turkey hunters everywhere who attend seminars, support outdoor radio programming, read our writing, line up for autograph sessions, and purchase our books and DVDs.

As an outdoor spokesperson, even after all these years, I realize how fortunate I am to have an opportunity to continue working with the hunting public. I remain flattered, honored, and proud, because only you make this possible.

Because the truth is, without all of you, without your support, I and others could not and would not do what we do for a living: have a career in the hunting industry as we do today.

From my early seminars some thirty years ago, to today, those close to me know I never quite understood why anyone asks for my autograph, or to have their photograph taken with me, as I am no different or better than any of you. However, please don't take this the wrong way; I am both honored and flattered as well, and more than happy to do this for all of you.

To my amazement, during my 2011 Chasing Spring™ national seminar tour, turkey hunters after all these years continue pouring into my seminars, hundreds stand in long autograph lines to visit with me personally, and everyone asks great calling and tactics questions.

Everywhere during my travels, so many of you offer encouragement, and express how you appreciate everything I do for hunting. Then there are the hundreds of incredibly humbling letters thanking me and encouraging me to continue what I'm doing. So to all of you, I would like to personally thank you—and say how much I really appreciate each and every one of you.

With today's mass media coverage with outdoor television, national seminars, DVD production, radio shows, national magazines, and websites, celebrity status is off the charts like never before for today's professional hunting personalities.

Well, I have to say, I am honestly not any type of rock star, or even a celebrity for that matter, simply because the real hunting celebrities are my turkey hunting brothers and sisters all across this great country. Yes, America's turkey hunters are the real hunting superstars of today's hunting world.

Introduction

RAY EYE'S TURKEY HUNTER'S BIBLE IS A COLLECTION OF THE tactics, tips, and information I have developed over the years that help me to consistently call and kill turkeys for TV shows with limited time, too many people, under extreme pressure, in places I've never seen before, and without any time for scouting. From my many travels on the seminar and hunting circuits, I find that today's turkey hunters are hungry for new, aggressive tactics, and *Ray Eye's Turkey Hunter's Bible* will deliver exactly what they want.

Ray Eye's Turkey Hunter's Bible offers information on how to hunt today's henned-up, pressured turkeys, so hunters everywhere can develop the skills needed to call the wild turkey consistently under all conditions. My highly developed turkey tactics in this book will arm hunters with the knowledge they'll need to enhance their turkey hunting success, no matter the conditions, including hunting with limited time, without any preseason scouting, and in hunting early season, late season, pressured gobblers, and much more. After years of turkey hunting professionally, I've condensed my calling and hunting tactics down to my most important, most utilized, and most successful tactics, namely calling, roosting, and setup. I have found these to be the most important keys to success in consistently killing spring gobblers in all kinds of situations, during any turkey seasonality or type of weather.

After my early years on my grandpa's farm, my turkey hunting experience for many years came from hunting turkeys on public ground, in the Ozarks national forests. I earned my degree in turkey hunting in my home state of Missouri, down in the trenches, so to speak, battling with public land turkeys, with plenty of interference from other hunters.

I earned every bird I killed, hunting in all kinds of conditions: wind, rain, and even snow. One of the reasons is that I hunted harder and longer than most, never gave up, and was willing to keep an open mind and adapt to many different hunting situations. I firmly believe my early days of public-ground hunting under extreme pressure made me the turkey hunter I am today, and without question enhanced my success everywhere in America.

I've hunted turkeys now for more than forty-eight years and in forty-three states and in Mexico. Even with these years and years of experience, I continue to make mistakes and I still learn something new every time I hunt turkeys. And when it comes to making mistakes, I have made them all—that's how I honed my skills as a turkey killer, by learning from my mistakes.

I share with you in this book my time-proven techniques and tactics to help hunters everywhere with tactics, tips, and information so they too can be successful in "chasing spring."

For the record, it's not my intention nor the purpose of this book in any way to imply that I am a better caller or hunter than others, but rather to share what I have learned and what has worked for me throughout my professional turkey hunting career. I will give you guidelines, but it is up to you to form your own opinion, with an open mind, and maybe implement some, or all of my tactics under different situations to see if they might improve your success in turkey hunting.

—*Ray Eye*

1

The History of the Missouri Ozarks, Return of the Wild Turkey, and My Family's Hunting Heritage

FOR ME, THIS CHAPTER IS A WONDERFUL GLANCE BACK IN time to early life in the Ozark Mountains, my family's Ozarks history, and the return of the wild turkey in my home state of Missouri and their later spread across the Midwest. All are important ingredients in my turkey hunting heritage, and had a direct effect on my hunting style and calling tactics detailed later in this book, tactics that served me well back in the early days and as a professional turkey hunter, and continue to serve me well today.

Around 1830, my ancestors came to the Missouri Ozarks from Pendleton County, Virginia, and settled just west of Potosi, Missouri, bringing with them turkey hunting skills honed from generations of hunting in the Virginia mountains.

Sometime in the 1860s my great-grandfather moved his family deeper within the Ozarks from the Eye settlement, to homestead up a remote "holler" at the base of Johnson Mountain. Years later, my grandpa, one of eleven kids, moved back to the same home—the place where my dad was born and raised.

The rugged landscape of the Ozarks made travel difficult in the early days of settlement. Roads were few and poor, usually little more than wagon ruts. Unlike most

At the head of the creek bottom holler, among the oaks and pines, a rustic two-story farmhouse nestles against the base of one of the highest mountains in the Ozarks.

The rugged landscape of the Missouri Ozarks.

other areas, the Ozarks also lacked centralized towns and cities. People tended to live on widely scattered homesteads, farming and hunting for their needs, only rarely going to commercial centers for trade goods they couldn't make on their own.

My family's remote Ozarks farm was part of a self-contained hill-country community, a place where people lived, worked, and raised their families. It wasn't until more modern times, after many generations, that residents traveled outside the valley to an established town for supplies. The Ozarks was a place where most residents were related. Many never ventured away from the Ozarks for an entire lifetime, without any thought of what type of world might exist out beyond the hills.

It was a time when families raised their own food, grew corn and vegetables, and raised chickens, pigs, and milk cows. Those provided the main sources of food, but food and income were both supplemented by hunting and trapping, as well as by gathering nuts, berries, wild edible plants, and digging roots in the Ozarks hills.

My great-grandma dried fruit in the sun on the tin roof of an outbuilding; some of this fruit was used to make the finest fried pies in the world. It was a time when vegetables were buried in the ground for later use during the winter months, and root cellars were filled with canned jellies, meats, and vegetables.

Wild berry picking was a family event. Some of the most important berries that were gathered were the wild gooseberries, dewberries, and blackberries, all forming an important component of the family diet. Wild grapes were picked in the fall for jelly, and hickory and walnuts were gathered for wintertime baking.

Trapping provided not only part of the family's yearly income, but helped to safeguard valuable chickens from predators. Digging ginseng and other roots helped to supplement an income as well. There was a smokehouse for the family supply of meat; a pig was sold in the fall to supply the money for winter shoes.

Hunting was a very important part of life. A great quantity and wide variety of wild game always filled the smokehouse during the long winter months, and my family especially took advantage of the always abundant population of wild turkeys within those hills. Wild turkeys were taken for Thanksgiving and Christmas, and deer were also taken in the fall for meat to help the family make it through the long, cold winter.

Special occasions were celebrated with horse-drawn wagons circled on a high ridge around a big campfire. Basket dinners of fried chicken and a jug of the area's finest locally-grown corn were always present. Men, women, and

In a grove of oaks near the old church house is a 200-year-old graveyard.

children alike would listen to the music of foxhounds as they chased a coyote throughout the night. Those were places and occasions with the finest storytelling, and there was always a heated argument late into the night about whose hunting dog was the best in the hills.

Several miles downstream from the family homestead, where the valley widens, in a place where a spring-fed stream joins the river for its long journey to the outside world, is a grove of oak stands. In those stands is a 150-year-old church house, complete with an ancient community family graveyard.

Community families worked their fields and livestock in remote hollers during the week and would not see anyone from outside their families, so from miles around on Sunday morning they would meet at the old church. Generations of my family went to that church house in a horse-drawn wagon

on an old roadbed that no one knows the age of across the hills through a timbered saddle on the main ridge.

After church service and during the Sunday basket dinner, they would visit with neighbors, catch up on the latest gossip, and maybe hear some of the latest news from the outside world. This

The old church is still standing, and this is how it looks today.

Near to the old church runs a bubbling, ice-cold Ozarks spring.

church building was utilized not only for Sunday morning worship, but was the local meeting place as well.

Throughout the years hundreds of weddings and funerals were held in this old church building. It's a wonderful place, complete with a spring with bubbling ice-cold water, a hitching post for horses, and large handmade oak tables under 200-year-old oaks. Basket dinners covered the tabletops for fellowship gatherings after church.

Just a little farther down the holler, and along the same stream, is the community's one-room schoolhouse where my dad, uncles, and aunts all attended grade school. The building of the school was often the first "community" development in an area. The first schools were haphazard affairs, built by local labor and financed by "subscription." Under the subscription system, parents paid the costs of their children's education directly.

Once a school was established in an area, it became sort of a focus. Children from the local area could meet each other and mingle. As they grew to know each other, a sense of belonging to a particular area grew. They were developing a sense of community. In some early settlements, the school was often the only community building; it quickly evolved into a community center of sorts. Elections were held there, church services and even weddings regularly took place in the one-room schools.

Downstream from the one-room schoolhouse is a combination post office and grocery store and a blacksmith shop. Just a little farther downstream, where the river narrows and the current increases, stands one of the most important hubs of the community, the

The community's one-room schoolhouse as it looks today, as a private home.

A central element of any rural Ozarks community was the water-wheel gristmill.

old water wheel gristmill and feed store.

The Missouri Ozarks is a unique place and rich in history; let's take a look at how the name "Ozarks" and many others used today originated, and a closer look at Ozarks history from far back in the past, and then let's move forward to more modern times.

Many names in the Ozarks came from early French explorers and trappers in the river hills area. They trapped in "La Rivière Courant," the "Running River." According to local legend, the Jacks Fork River is named for a Shawnee Indian named Captain Jack who camped along the river with his tribe.

Encyclopedia Britannica states that "Ozark" is probably a corruption of *Aux Arcs,* a French trading post established in the region in the 1700s. Others say Osage Indians hunted with longbows made from the wood of a tree known to the French as *bois d'arc,* known today as Osage orange.

The Osage and Shawnee Indians in the Ozarks made the Current and Jacks Fork River valleys their home. An Osage chief named Cardareva is said to be buried on top of the mountain known as Cardareva Bluff. In the early 1800s, trappers brought animal hides to the river to process into leather. The hides were soaked in a "tan vat" filled with tannic acid. Later, the hides were removed from the vat and submerged in the deep water of what is known to this day as Tan Vat Hole.

Troublesome Hollow got its name during the turbulent Civil War years. Lawless guerril-

Approximately 80,000 acres along the Jacks Fork and Current Rivers form the Ozark National Scenic Riverways.

Scotch-Irish settlers began to filter in to the Ozarks in 1804, and by the 1850s most lands in the river valleys were occupied by subsistence farmers.

...las known as "bushwhackers" used the hollow as a base to cause nearby settlers grief and trouble during an unsettled time. Meeting House Cave also takes its name from the Civil War period. According to legend, the cave was used as a hideout during the war. Marauding bands from both sides of the conflict used the cave as a place to meet. Nearby Hospital Cave was supposedly used as a hospital during the war.

The southeastern Ozarks were long isolated from outside influence due to the rugged nature of the environment and the lack of improved transportation routes into the region. Scotch-Irish settlers began to filter in shortly after The Louisiana Purchase in 1804, and by the 1850s most lands in the river valleys were occupied by subsistence farmers. The Civil War brought devastation to the region, and economic recovery was slow to come.

It was not until the 1880s that major change began to occur, with the coming of the railroads and large lumber companies moving into the hills. Railroads provided economical transportation for goods into and out of the southeastern Ozarks. Lumber companies established large mills, and millions of board feet of native pine lumber were sawn and shipped out, mostly to rapidly growing towns on the Great Plains. Timber was quickly stripped from the Ozark hills, and wildfires consumed most of the rest, reducing the Ozarks to a barren wasteland hardly capable of supporting the people who stayed behind when the lumber companies left. As a result, rains and snowmelt washed topsoil into the rivers

In 1933 large tracts of land in the region were purchased to form the Clark National Forest, which today is part of Mark Twain National Forest.

and gorged them with gravel. The region became poverty-stricken, and only the sheer determination of the Ozark people kept them on their farmsteads to eke out a meager living.

In 1933, large tracts of land were purchased in the region for the Clark National Forest, which today is part of Mark Twain National Forest. In 1936 the Missouri Department of Conservation (MDC) was established, and game laws became more rigidly enforced in the region. In 1956, The National Park Service conducted a study and issued a report calling for the

In 1962 President Kennedy endorsed the formation of Ozark National Scenic Riverways.

establishment of a corridor park along the Current and Jacks Fork Rivers, and in 1960 momentum grew when Congress appropriated funds for a feasibility study for the establishment of an "Ozark Rivers National Monument," which would include the Eleven Point River.

There was stiff resistance to the formation of such a park from many local residents, particularly landowners who did not want to lose their family farms, and county officials who did not want to lose a large portion of the tax base.

In 1962 President John F. Kennedy endorsed the formation of Ozark National Scenic Riverways, and Secretary of the Interior Stewart Udall and other officials visited the region and floated the Current River.

Following Udall's strong endorsement, a bill was submitted and passed by Congress for the formation of the park. President Lyndon Johnson signed it into law, and Ozark National Scenic Riverways became a reality. A formal dedication ceremony was held at Big Spring in 1972, presided over by Patricia Nixon Cox, who cut the ribbon. This offi-

The southeastern Ozarks were long isolated from outside influence due to the rugged nature of the environment and the lack of improved transportation routes into the region.

The Ozarks Scenic Riverways area provides thousands of acres of public hunting land in the Missouri Ozarks.

cially opened the park to millions of visitors to enjoy all that it offers.

Only in the last forty years has there been a national park that manages and protects these natural and cultural resources. This river corridor sustained many families from the time of initial settlement in the early 19th century to the mid-1960s, when it became a national park. Today, approximately 80,000 acres of rugged Ozark land along the Jacks Fork and Current Rivers form Ozark National Scenic Riverways, a riparian corridor through Shannon, Carter, Dent, and Texas Counties in the southeastern Missouri Ozark Highlands.

Hundreds of thousands visit this scenic park each year, including hunters who enjoy the solitude and natural beauty of the river. Forested hills, soaring bluffs, caves, springs, plants, animals, and historic buildings combine to create a memorable experience.

Just as historic and important as the creation of the Ozarks Scenic Riverways is a place called Peck Ranch, where the long road to modern-day turkey hunting throughout the Midwest began many years ago. Peck Ranch Conservation Area in eastern Shannon County consists of 23,048 acres of rugged, forested hills and hollows, with nearly 1,500 acres in glades, along with old fields, savanna, cropland, and some wetlands.

Limestone and rock glades provide natural openings among the oak and pine forest that dominates the region. The area's highest point is Stegall Mountain, 1,348 feet above sea level. Two spring-fed streams wander through the area, Rogers Creek and Mill Creek, which eventually flow into the Current River.

Peck Ranch began as the dream of George Peck, a wealthy Chicago businessman. After acquiring 19,000 acres

Limestone and rock glades provide natural openings among the oak-pine forest that dominates the region.

along Mill and Rogers Creeks, he established the Mid-Continent Iron Company. Peck's dream included clearcutting Peck Ranch to supply the 100 cords of fuel per day needed to fire the smelter's blast furnaces. Peck employed 200 families and installed his own mule teams to haul cordwood.

During World War I, the area continued to boom. The U.S. government spent $3.5 million to install a wood alcohol distillery to be used in making ammunition. This period of prosperity was brief. The low-grade iron ore mill folded after the end of the war, and a flu epidemic ravaged the Ozarks. Peck returned to Chicago. The workers who remained in the area tried to eke out a living on the abused land.

When Prohibition ended, the demand for white oak barrels surged. Griffith Stave Company bought the remaining timber rights on Peck Ranch and revived the area's timber industry. The boom was short-lived, and Peck Ranch was once again for sale.

In the early 1900s, the Mid-Continent Iron Company had smelted low-grade iron ore and made wood alcohol seven miles away from the ranch, which led to the region's timber being cut down. In 1945 the Missouri Department of Conservation (MDC) bought Peck Ranch, in part through the Pittman-Robertson Wildlife Restoration Act administered by the U.S. Fish and Wildlife Service, mainly for purposes of wild turkey restoration. Today the hills and hollows of this area are much quieter than they were ninety years ago.

This is where the return of the wild turkey for the rest of Missouri and for more than a dozen other nearby states began more than fifty years ago. When the MDC began turkey restoration efforts, Peck Ranch was center stage to provide turkeys for trapping and relocation. The area also served as a vital research site for understanding the ecology of Missouri's remaining wild turkeys.

Today, diverse management techniques continue, including the introduction of elk to Missouri, ongoing wild turkey research, prescribed fire and forest products harvesting methods, all being used to maintain and restore the diverse natural communities on Peck Ranch.

Wild turkeys have specific habitat needs in order to thrive. Cover for nesting and brood rearing was as vital as places for turkeys to forage for nuts and browse green plants. Peck Ranch was a great place to find forest and grassland habitats with appropriate soil and moisture. Turkey nesting cover is found in the mature grasslands or thick forest cover, and the tender growth of grasses and wildflowers make for a great place to rear a brood as they search for insects.

The woodland forest at Peck Ranch isn't a typical forest. The rugged Ozark landscape of Stegall Mountain contains a cross-section of Ozark natural communities of the Current River Hills region. The ground is exceptionally rocky, the soil is thin, and often the south or western hillside exposure bakes the soil to release its moisture faster than it would on other slopes.

The canopy here is mainly shortleaf pine, along with post, blackjack, and chinquapin oaks. The ground is lightly leaf-covered, with a strong component of sedges, grasses, and other plant types that tolerate conditions varying from filtered sunlight to shade. A unique feature of the area is the forty-foot cascade of Rocky Falls, a scenic shut-in where Rocky Creek tumbles downslope.

Research conducted on fire scars (recorded in tree rings) shows that in the 1800s, fires swept through the area on average every five years. Thinning and prescribed fires are now being used to manage the glades and their associated woodlands, resulting in a more diverse landscape and wider variety of wildlife, including whip-poor-wills, tanagers, warblers, and many other bird species. But even more important to me is the history of the wild turkey comeback in Missouri, because without the restoration of the wild turkey in Missouri, including cannon-net live trapping and the work of pioneer turkey biologist John Lewis, this book—and my career—would not exist today.

During the 1800s, the North American continent was home to an estimated ten million wild turkeys. However, destruction of habitat and unregulated market hunting reduced the North American population to approximately 300,000 birds by 1950. In Missouri, wild turkeys were found in large numbers throughout the state from around 1840 until about 1900. Some sixty years later, the Missouri turkey population had been reduced from 250,000 to approximately 3,000 birds, and most were limited to remote Ozark regions, including the area around my family's homestead. With the destruction of timber by fire and ax, open grazing of the forest, and market hunting, the wild turkey in Missouri was near extinction.

Rocky Falls, a scenic shut-in where Rocky Creek tumbles down a forty-foot cascade.

From around 1925 to 1943, an effort was made to halt the decline in numbers, with approximately 14,000 game farm turkeys being released as breeding stock. However, turkey numbers continued to decrease, and these early efforts proved futile.

In 1938, research studies were conducted to determine why the game farm turkeys failed to establish themselves as a breeding population. Though interrupted by World War II, these studies resumed after the war, in 1951. Researchers eventually learned that only a true wild bird could survive in the wild, and also that restocking of wild turkeys to unoccupied range, suitable to their survival, was the answer. But first, a source of native wild turkeys was needed, along with a method of effectively trapping birds.

To ensure an ongoing and reliable source of wild birds, the MDC bought a large tract in the southern Ozarks that still contained a few native wild turkeys, providing protection to the birds, as well as restoring food sources and cover to ensure their survival and support this small breeding population. By 1954, numbers on what was now known as Peck Ranch Wildlife Area had increased from only nine turkeys to thirty-two, and in 1957, trapping began on an 11,000-acre plot that had been intensively managed and that now supported about 100 birds.

These restoration and management practices, carried out first on Peck Ranch, demonstrated that turkeys could also potentially be restored in other areas of the state. However, an efficient method of turkey trapping still needed to be developed. The answer was an adaptation of the cannon-net trap used for capturing waterfowl, with the turkeys being lured to the trap site by baiting. Finding suitable release sites for the birds involved gaining public support for the project, and communities were encouraged to submit requests for restocking, with these requests evaluated dependent on the existing habitat conditions.

Because of the great number of acres required, residents also had to agree to protect the birds post-release. MDC personnel held town meetings to explain the program and also to outline these community responsibilities. A "gentlemen's agreement" was then made between the MDC and the involved communities, to help protect these fledgling populations. The restoration program began in 1954, and by the spring of 1979, the program was terminated. By this time, total of 2,611 turkeys had been trapped and placed in 142 areas in eighty-seven counties. The normal stocking situation was two hens to each gobbler, with twelve to twenty-four birds usually released at each site.

In testament to the overwhelming success of these habitat and population restoration programs, all 114 Missouri counties now have turkey populations for hunters and everyone else to enjoy, with 101 of these counties having populations directly as a result of restocking. Missouri has also made important contributions to restoration programs in other states as well, by swapping Missouri-bred wild turkeys for other wildlife species. Since the early 1960s, Missouri has traded for ruffed grouse, otters, pheasants, and prairie chickens. Descendants of Missouri's original Ozark wild turkeys now gobble in more than a dozen other states.

As research continues and populations expand further, understanding of the wild turkeys of Missouri improves. The highest turkey densities now occur in agricultural regions of the state, where crop fields, swaths of timber, and even old fields intermix, with higher turkey populations typically in those counties with less than 20 percent timber. Prospects for continued high populations are excellent, and flocks restored in many other states from original Missouri wild turkey stock are prospering as well. Obviously, the wild turkey is much more adaptable than was previously thought.

The return of the wild turkey continued across America during the 1980s and 1990s with the help of the National Wild Turkey Federation (NWTF). Through dynamic partnerships with state, federal, and provincial wildlife agencies, the NWTF and members have helped restore wild turkey populations throughout North America, spending more than $372 million to conserve nearly seventeen million acres of habitat.

The National Wild Turkey Federation is dedicated to the conservation of the wild turkey and the preservation of our hunting heritage. NWTF volunteers introduce about 100,000 people to the outdoors through these programs every year. Founded in 1973, the NWTF is headquartered in Edgefield, South Carolina, and has local chapters in every state and many Canadian provinces. According to many state and federal agencies, the restoration of the wild turkey is arguably the greatest conservation success story in North America's wildlife history.

2

The Formative Years

IN CHAPTER 1 I WROTE OF THE HISTORY OF MY ANCESTORS in the Ozarks and my family homestead. Now let's talk about later years, the time Grandpa raised his family—my dad, his four brothers, and two sisters—and how I too became part of my family's rich hunting history as a young boy roaming those same hills and hollers as my ancestors before me.

I am blessed to have experienced so many wonderful times as a young boy, including having a loving family in a two-parent household, parents in a busy world of working and raising a family, yet taking the time to teach me about the outdoor world and to take me hunting. Fortunately I hailed from a big family rich in turkey hunting tradition and was lucky enough to experience turkey hunting at a very early age. I grew up during good times for Missouri turkey hunters, when turkey hunting in the Ozarks was improving. I hope this chapter gives you a better understanding of my perspective of turkey hunting as well as my calling tactics.

In those days, neighbors and family alike would pitch in and help each other, whether it was building a barn or harvesting the crops in the fall. Neighbors would help with the slaughtering and butchering of winter meats, and women would help each other can food for the winter. It was also a common practice that if someone killed a deer, shot a number of ducks, killed a turkey, or caught a mess of fish, they should share the bounty, especially if they hunted on someone else's land. This community heritage was a major influence in making me the turkey hunter I am today, and also shaped the hunting methods and tactics I continue to use to this day.

The Eye homestead in 1973. Ray Eye is seen in the lower left corner, and the high hill in the background is Pruitt Mountain.

A young Ray Eye in 1967 with an Ozarks buck, while holding his daddy's Browning 5, the same gun the author also used for turkey.

After my dad and mom married and began raising a family of their own, my dad had to leave the family home to find work in St. Louis to support his growing family, but we returned to the Ozarks on weekends, and as kids we spent summers on the farm. But the most exciting and memorable trips back to the hills were always at the holidays, and during fall and spring hunting seasons.

It was always quite an adventure to just make it back to my family's isolated home in our 1957 Chevy. Miles of muddy, rutted roads and swollen creeks were always a challenge. One Sunday evening when I was a small boy, my dad had to return to the city for work, but our car stalled in the rising creek, and a huge logging truck rescued us, and our car, by towing us to safely to the other side.

For a small boy, traveling down to the farm for hunting season was always another adventure. The most exciting part of this annual journey began where the winding state highway blacktop ended in a narrow gravel road that continued to follow the base of Pruitt Mountain. When the gravel road turned to dirt—or mud, depending on the weather—and the deeply rutted road met the junction of two spring-fed streams, the two-track dropped off into a low-water creek crossing, then turned south alongside a granite outcropping.

It was a rough ride following the old streambed as it snaked up the valley to where the narrow rutted road intersected at a fork. The right fork would take you across the stream at another low-water ford, and then straight up a steep, rocky incline, then disappear out of sight across an rocky glade straight to Johnson Mountain. The left fork led to Grandpa's farm, following the streambed until it intersected another spring-fed stream, and then turned left, following the ancient stream-carved valley up to the base of Pruitt and Johnson Mountains. A little farther up the road, just past the old sawmill and across several smaller streams, was a remote world where families were stranded for days during spring rains when the creeks rose.

After fording the second low-water crossing, a rough two-track dirt road twisted and turned as it followed alongside a rock-strewn stream. When you

The typical outdoor hand pump used for water for the farmhouse.

finally ran out of dirt road at an abrupt dead end at the head of the isolated holler, you spotted the rustic, two-story farmhouse nestled among the oaks and pines against the base of one of the Ozarks' highest mountains.

Electricity didn't make it up to this isolated holler until the mid-1960s, and telephone lines never have. Plumbing consisted of a hand pump in the kitchen, a yard pump, a springhouse, and a recently remodeled outhouse. In a clearing between a steep ridge and the creek sat a log woodshed, smokehouse, chicken house, and a fruit cellar.

The rutted old roadbed now dead-ends at my family's home, but in the old days it continued upward over the mountain, twisting its way down the other side until it ended in a small town called Banner. During the 1940s and early 1950s, Banner was not only the closest town, but the *only* town that provided supplies for families living in this remote corner of the Ozarks.

Today, the old road past the house is just a faded two-track through the mountains, but is still the only route from Banner and the outside world to Grandpa's farm. No one really knows just how old the Banner road really is—my family traveled it by horse and wagon at least as far back as the Civil War. It is said the road is much older that that, and some of my ancestors traveled that very route when they arrived in this valley from Virginia.

The old Banner road is rich with history, and for years was the only way in or

Generations of my family rode in horse-drawn wagons to church on an old road that probably dates to the 1700s. This two-track road is known as the "Banner" or "Eight-Mile" road, and is pretty much the same today as it was way back in the old days.

out of this remote, almost inaccessible valley. Stories were told of buried treasure from a stolen Wells Fargo shipment, and another about gold hidden by a Confederate cavalry unit from the Battle of Pilot Knob, among other legends. Treasure hunters from far and wide have scoured those hills trying to find instant wealth. I remember both distant family members and strangers asking questions about possible treasure. There was the story of a man who supposedly knew where the gold shipment was buried, but he was hanged in a tree in my great-grandpa's front yard for robbery and for stealing a horse. A sheriff from another county arrived in the valley the day after the hanging, searching for the now very dead robber because he was the only one who could have told the sheriff where the gold was buried.

I have so many wonderful memories from my formative turkey hunting years, and vividly recall the long-ago sights, sounds, and smells. When I was barely old enough to walk on my own, my dad would carry me piggyback into the hills to go hunting, teaching me how to read turkey sign, how to move in the woods, and what to listen and watch for on the hunt. I can remember as if it were just yesterday the ringing of church bells on Sunday mornings, the dinner bell at the farm, and the cowbells hanging from the necks of cattle grazing in the field at the base of the mountain. I clearly recall unmistakable aroma of the outhouse, the creaking sound of the spring as the door opened, and the constant buzzing of insects I heard while looking at the pictures in a Sears Roebuck catalog.

Another element of my memories is the engine resonance of what could only be a 1940s John Deere tractor and the creaking of the harness on my grand-

pa's workhorse, Ole Bill, and the aroma of fresh-plowed furrows of dirt alive with the fragrance of Ozarks wildflowers. Nothing reminds me of those early years as much as the aroma of a big breakfast cooking on a wood-fired cookstove. I vividly remember waking in the old farmhouse to the smell of breakfast cooking on Grandma's woodstove, hearing the whip-poor-wills and owls calling amid the sounds of the adjacent

An afternoon at Grandpa's farm, 1970. Missouri only allows half-day hunting in the spring, so the afternoon is filled with napping, fishing, mushroom hunting, and just goofing off.

Dawn breaks over the Ozarks.

spring-fed stream rushing down the valley. Early on Saturday mornings, in the glow of a kerosene lantern, my grandma appeared in my bedroom wearing a bright-colored dress and stained apron, the scent of freshly baked bread filling the room. Her fingers ticked my ribs, and a warm, familiar voice asked if I was playing possum, then she would giggle and say, "You had better get up because those old gobblers will be hollering before long."

The smells of freshly split firewood, kerosene lamps in an old farmhouse, and kerosene lanterns in the spring woods are a just a few more impressions that come to mind. Anytime I smell wood smoke, it takes me back to yester-year when I was a little boy back on the farm for turkey season.

No sounds are more reminiscent of the Ozarks in the springtime than the roar from the granite "shut-ins" as water rushes down the valley from spring rains, the rumble of thunder in the distance, and the early morning songs of whip-poor-wills. Then, as dawn finally breaks through the morning mist rising from the mountains, the mystical gobble of an Ozark Ghost greets a new day.

My turkey hunting past from later years is filled with special memories from old-time turkey camps. In those early days, wilderness turkey camps were special places where everyone in camp was related, and practical joking ran rampant. Our Ozarks turkey camps were worlds filled with wood smoke, and where on early April mornings the aromas of fresh coffee and frying bacon filled the mountain air. I vividly recall climbing the mountain with Grandpa while enjoying the aroma of his cigar mixed with the smell of chalk from his handmade cedar "striker call."

I remember the headlights bouncing through the trees and the low growl of an old Willys Jeep climbing

Turkey camp in the Ozarks sometimes included a Saturday afternoon bluegrass band.

1976 turkey season. Butch, Erbie, Ray, and Gary. One of the many enjoyable and fun parts of turkey season in the Ozarks is going to town to check in your turkey, read the info on who killed turkeys, visit with other hunters, and have breakfast in town.

up the narrow two-track road before daylight, as my uncle and I would drive to meet others for a morning of turkey hunting. After the morning hunt, the Willys filled with hunters, we drove to town to register our turkeys at the local check station.

This grocery, hardware, filling station, and turkey check-in station smelled of sawdust, gun oil, leather goods, fresh-cut wood, and gasoline. Turkey beards and deer "horns" graced the walls, and pictures of successful hunters as unfilled turkey tags adorned the main beams across the ceiling. Those were special times, filled with sights, sounds, and smells I recall as vividly as if it were yesterday. There was the aroma of dinner on a woodstove mixed with kerosene lamps. There was the smell of a big pile of cut firewood and the unique smell of the old general store, where I searched for a treasure to buy with the nickel Grandpa had given me.

There wasn't anyplace like the local barber shop on the main street in town, with its tall shiny chairs, and turkey beards attached to the light pull cords. The smells of talcum powder and assorted tonics filled the air, and hunting magazines were the only reading material to be found. Tall tales of super-intelligent, "unkillable" gobblers were usually the story of the day on Saturday mornings.

I remember back in grade school standing in front of my class, telling in great detail everything about my latest turkey hunting adventure. After graduating from high school, I returned after a morning hunt, carrying my gobbler into the school office for the coach, teachers, and school principal all to see and to tell them my story of the morning's hunt.

But there is no memory in this world as special as hunting with my dad when I was a little boy, sitting beside him against a huge tree just as daylight broke on the mountain, my small fingers wrapped around his Browning 12-gauge as together we listened to the first gobble of a new spring day. You see, there is so much more to turkey hunting for me than just killing a turkey. It's really all about the total experience, making and reliving all those won-

Grandpa's pocket watch and lantern.

derful memories, and spending real quality time with close friends and family.

Now let's return to yesteryear, back to those Ozark hills, for a special turkey hunt during my formative years, the time of my education at Johnson Mountain University. The lesson I learned then is one I still use today to kill gobblers all across America. The lesson called the "dance."

In the dim glow of my kerosene lantern, I finally reach the junction of the steep ridges at the head of Sawmill Holler, and pause once again to ease the pain in my burning legs and check the time on Grandpa's pocket watch, the same watch and lantern I carried up this mountain during my first turkey hunt back in 1962.

(The hunting season for turkeys was closed in 1937; Missouri's spring turkey season remained closed for the next long twenty-three years. But after an intensive turkey restoration program in the 1950s, Missouri's turkey season reopened in April 1960. During my state's first modern-day season, legal turkey hunting ran for only three days, and only in fourteen Ozarks counties. During that first season, only one out of eight hunters took gobblers, taking fewer than 300 turkeys across those fourteen counties.)

Pausing to catch my breath in the predawn darkness, I enjoyed a boisterous serenade from choruses of whip-poor-wills. It was Sunday morning at 4:30 AM, during the 1968 Missouri spring turkey season and as a fifteen-year-old boy I was more than delighted that Grandma allowed me to miss church service on this morning, to go turkey hunting. Continuing upward, I slowly worked my way straight up the steepest part of Hop Holler to the vertical main ridge, and then climbed onto the wide mountainside bench. Turning north, I headed toward the old Sutterfield sawmill holler.

"Hop Holler," at the junction at the head of sawmill holler.

Just maybe, I hoped, this would be the year I finally killed another spring gobbler.

First light streaks the eastern sky and the whip-poor-wills go silent.

Since taking my first gobbler in 1962, and a second in 1966, turkey season had been an absolute nightmare for me. I messed things up in every imaginable way: bumping birds, scaring the daylights out of turkeys, not shooting when I had an opportunity, and just plain missing gobblers too many times to count.

Finally I reached my predetermined destination, just below a long ridge; a gobbler should be roosted at the head of a holler somewhere down the ridge above me. Quietly, I sat down against a big tree, loaded the old hammer gun, blew out the flame in the old rusty lantern, and anxiously awaited first light, and the first booming gobble of an Ozarks Ghost.

As daylight streaked the eastern sky and the whip-poor-wills fell silent, a barred owl sang the "who cooks for you, who cooks for you all," from somewhere below, and in the direction of Pruitt Mountain, I heard the first gobble of my 1968 season. The gobbling increased as songbirds and cawing crows greeted a new day. The wild turkey love calls were now coming from every hill and ridge around the farm, including Dryfork Holler, behind the barn, above my great Uncle Mont's cabin and the "old lease."

With turkeys gobbling everywhere but here, I began to question my decision to hunt the Pruitt side of the farm, mumbling out loud that maybe I should go after one of the closest gobbling turkeys, but quickly changing my mind as two gobblers rattled from the long ridge above. Clutching Grandpa's old hammer double-barrel, I moved quietly toward the closer of the two gobblers. I set up and sanded my homemade corncob slate call, made my first yelps with my voice, and then followed hen yelps with clucks from my slate.

Only known photo showing Ray and his little brother Marty holding the gobbler from the 1968 "Dance."

Marty and Ray Eye with a pair of River Valley Ozarks gobblers from a double taken around 1980.

Both gobblers immediately responded, but to my regret they were moving steadily away, gobbling as they went. I began to panic, but then I remembered the advice grandpa gave me: "You're always in too big a hurry, boy," "Have patience, stop running turkey to turkey, scaring the daylight out of 'em," "Slow down, turkeys aren't going anywhere, they live there, they are on turkey time, not our time, so slow down, let things unfold, enjoy the woods, and the turkeys will come . . ."

I decided to stay put. Throwing out another series of calls, I slouched low against the tree while digging one of Grandma's homemade jelly

biscuits out of my faded jumper jacket pocket, hoping to quell my growing hunger pangs. As the morning sunlight warmed me, I was having a difficult time keeping my eyes open, and with gobbling subsiding considerably, and my chin on my chest, I slowly nodded off. I'm not sure how long I slept before I heard a sound; something was moving in the leaves behind me. Turning slowly, I saw an older, gray-haired man wearing a felt hat and bib overalls slowly coming my way. The old man was a bit on the skinny side, with a narrow, weathered, deep-lined, bearded face. He too carried an old double-barrel hammer gun, but the stock

There is nothing in this world as special as hunting with my dad when I was little, sitting next to him just as daylight breaks on the mountain, my small fingers wrapped around Dad's Browning 12-gauge as we listened to the first gobble of a new spring day. The family hunting tradition continues, as Daddy enjoys hunting with my son, David, just as he did with me.

I shot this gobbler in 1973, way before the camo revolution of today. It was the first time I wore full woodland camouflage and 'blacked' my face with burnt cork. I read about this strategy in one of the only, and at the time rare, turkey hunting articles I found back then. I was laughed at by many other hunters, but what really hurt was the heat I took at the local check-in station as "Wild Bill" called everyone outside to look at me and point and laugh.

had a small, sanded, chalked area for the cedar scratch call he was holding in his right hand.

The old turkey hunter eased closer, paused, then leaned against a tree close to me and spoke softly: "Boy, you ain't gonna kill that old warrior sitting here. This is his roost. He leaves here right after first light," he said. "Besides, you're on the wrong side. He flies up to the roost from that bench up there, same place he flies down to at daylight. So if you're gonna kill that old long-spurred turkey now, you gotta set up where he goes to do the dance."

"What's the dance?" I asked.

With a slight smile, he spoke again. "It's when the boss gobbler does the mating dance for the girls. He struts and displays as the morning sun reflects off his feathers at a place where he can be seen and heard, a place during first morning light where generations of gobblers have preformed the same dance. And if the habitat doesn't change, old gobblers will hold their dance there for years to come."

"Where is this place where they perform the dance?" I asked. The old man leaned in close.

"It's a magical place; sacred ground. It's in a clearing on a rock glade, a place where four types of habitat structure come together. It's the wild turkey gobblers' strutting ground. It's where a small

The old turkey hunter wearing a felt hat and bib overalls was slowly coming my way.

It's a magical place, a sacred ground, a wild turkey gobbler's strutting ground.

A spring-fed rock-strewn stream winds its way past an ancient Ozarks glade.

spring-fed stream winds its way past the ancient Ozarks glade strutting area, and then flows down a holler meandering through the middle of an ancient hand-cleared pasture, where the pasture's north slope greets the base of a steep ridge, and remnants of a split-rail fence run the length of the field.

Remnants of a split-rail fence.

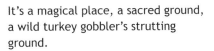

"Not far from that split rail, two hollers come together just above the crown of the pasture. There, on a small timbered bench, towers a gian, old oak tree, a majestic oak as old as the hills themselves. Rest your back against the huge base of that old oak in the springtime, face the open glade and the narrow corner of the wildflower-filled old pasture, and you're in one of the finest places in all of the Ozarks to kill an old, long-spurred gobbler.

"From here, go over toward the old lease, turn left at the corner of the old split-rail, stay low in that small holler, and go to the corner of the pasture. But stay in the woods. Crawl up to that huge oak next to the glade, and just off the corner of the old field, right where two hollers come together and the stream flows past the glade and on through the field, that's where your gobbler will go to greet the girls for the dance," he told me. "And boy, you really don't want to be late for the dance."

Suddenly, a squirrel chattered loudly, a crow screamed right above me, and I opened my eyes and realized I had fallen asleep. Quickly looking around, I saw there was no one there; all was quiet. It was all but a dream. I gathered myself, picked up the lantern and my gun, and turned to walk back down to the farm. But curiosity got the best of me, and so I changed direction as I walked toward the old lease.

I stayed low in the holler and found that huge old oak, just like in my dream. Crawling to its base, I set up, loaded the old gun, and scratched out a few yelps on my corncob slate; a booming gobble rifled back from just across the glade. Dropping my call as I raised my gun, I spotted a small brown hen walking up from my left, yelping as she came. Suddenly, just as I cut my eyes back toward the glade, I saw a huge gobbler with his head bobbing, running through the cedars, headed my way.

The huge tom crossed the split-rail fence, rocking from side to side with beard swinging as he came toward the glade. Waiting until he crossed the

glade and stepped into the corner of the field, I followed him with the barrel, aimed the old gun, and squeezed the trigger. That old, long-spurred warrior was now flopping in the middle of the wildflowers as the little brown hen cackled loudly and flew away. I jumped to my feet, ran out, grabbed that old gobbler by the legs and hurried down the holler toward the farmhouse.

Grandma greeted me at the springhouse and admired my bird, but told me how Grandpa was just about ready

Grandma and Grandpa in the living room of the old farm house during the 1950s.

Noah Eye.

to come looking for me. It was now after noontime and they'd just come back from church, worried because I wasn't anywhere to be found at the farmhouse.

I excitedly told how I fell asleep up on the big ridge and about the old man in my dream, and how he told me where to get this turkey. They both laughed out loud, then told me to hang the gobbler in the smokehouse and use the yard pump to clean up, because we were going over to my great-aunt Marie's house for Sunday dinner.

While sitting at a large oak table during Sunday dinner, a table that was covered with a ton of food, I just happened to look above the antique china cabinet where I saw big, heavy-framed picture. In that picture was an old man, skinny, with a weathered and lined face, and then I realized it was the old man from my dream.

"Who is that man in the picture?" I asked my great-aunt Marie.

"That's your great-great-grandpa, Noah Eye," she replied, "and he was quite the turkey hunter. He knew turkeys and the hills better than anyone. He was born back in 1857, and passed in 1935. Why do you ask?" she said.

I stammer, "Because that's the man I talked to on the mountain this morning. Because I think that's the man from my dream."

Everyone at the table laughed out loud, then Grandma, in a cackling voice, said, "Boy, you have such a wild, vivid imagination! Now clean up your plate. We're having blackberry cobbler for dessert."

3

The "Good Ole Days" of Turkey Hunting

I AM FORTUNATE IN HAVING THE OPPORTUNITY TO CHASE spring, to follow spring gobbler seasons from south to north, and from west to east. Chasing spring is without question a dream come true for any turkey hunting fanatic.

With my professional turkey hunting schedule, in just the past several years I've traveled to Florida, South Carolina, and Hawaii, and then continued my quest throughout the Midwest and north to Wisconsin and Minnesota, then northeast to New England, then finishing the first of June down in old Mexico, this past season including the Yucatan Peninsula, for ocellated turkeys.

It's an awesome experience having the opportunity to hunt so many states with such a wide diversity of habitat and a variety of subspecies of wild turkeys. Yet another bonus of turkey hunting across the American continent is that I have the opportunity to hunt with many wonderful old friends, as well as new friends met along the way. I share an abundance of fellowship in a wide assortment of turkey camps, and enjoy a wide variety of great food and some unique personalities.

However, during all these hunting adventures, it always seems as if something is missing, something I just cannot put my finger on. Maybe it has to do with turkey hunting tradition, or maybe because turkey hunting history is so diverse in other states? Is it possible I'm soul-searching? For I reflect on nothing more than those "good ole days" of turkey hunting.

Following a recent successful out-of-state turkey hunting expedition, after arriving home from another turkey road trip, I had a little rare downtime, so I decided to return to my Missouri Ozarks for a special, personal turkey hunt with my little hunting buddy, my dog Peanut. This was also a special hunt because it did not include a big camera crew or any outdoor writers to guide—just me and the turkeys. I planned to search my soul for whatever seemed to be missing from my turkey hunting today.

For me, there is no place anywhere quite like the Missouri Ozark Hills during springtime.

Just maybe I would find it—whatever "it" might be—and I was excited about returning to the place where my turkey hunting career began so many years before, the very same region I hunted as a boy with my dad in the national forest close to my grandpa's old farm.

After arrival, about an hour before daylight in the Missouri Ozarks at the base of the mountain, I was excited at what this special day might bring. After unloading my gear, I began my predawn journey up toward a favorite listening point on the highest part of the mountain. With the cool morning air on my face, and Peanut sitting next to me, I thought about how fast the years have passed, about my age and how hiking this route on foot during this early morning climb would take many hours of walking, with lots of heavy breathing. And that more than likely, I wouldn't make it to the top in time for sunrise.

Bouncing along the old logging road in the electric ATV, it also seemed somewhat strange to watch my progress on a GPS screen, looking at terrain features that used to exist only inside my head. I laughed out loud at how much had changed since my early days hunting on this mountain. Here I was, zooming up the mountainside on an all-electric four-wheel drive, while reading an electronic Garmin GPS unit.

Finally reaching my destination, I enjoyed this beautiful morning, cool and crisp and with an amaz-

Finally reaching my destination on the highest peak on the mountain, I pause to enjoy a beautiful, cool Ozarks morning.

The sun rises over the Ozarks.

ing sunrise developing to the east. I unloaded my personal video camera and tripod, and checked all my hunting gear. Inside my 500-pocket turkey vest, I had at least a dozen mouth calls, two slate calls, two box calls, a commercial owl hooter, a pair of gloves, a head net, and an electronic listening device.

In the large inside pocket I had food, Winchester turkey loads, and drinks. On my feet, Cabela's boots completed the wardrobe. My firearm was a Remington 1187 turkey gun fitted with an H. S. Strut Undertaker choke and glow-in-the-dark open sights.

After a short walk to my old oak tree, and just as the first early morning light was beginning to flood across the springtime ridgetop, I recalled a question I often heard from hundreds of turkey hunters and outdoor writers over the years: "How has turkey hunting changed since you began turkey hunting?"

Well, back in the mid-1960s and early 1970s, I hunted in old, faded bib overalls and a tattered blue-jean jumper jacket. Wearing dark-colored clothing while sitting still in the shadows was the name of the game, because there was no such thing as camouflage manufacturing companies producing custom clothing for turkey hunters. There was always a can of Copenhagen in my front pocket, and I called turkeys to the gun with my voice. Tennis shoes were the choice of footwear for walking and climbing all morning.

Turkey hunters were secretive back then, and few would share any information on how they succeeded in taking a gobbler. Hunting magazine articles on turkeys were few and far between, books like this one were rare, there weren't any how-to videos and DVDs, there were few hunting shows on TV, and turkey hunting seminars were never available in the Ozarks.

There weren't any factory-built, portable turkey blinds available either, so after locating a gobbling turkey by owl hooting with my voice, my setup was on the bend in a logging road or just under the crest of a ridge. The scheme was such that I could not see the approaching gobbler until I could kill him— the gobbler would have to come over a rise or around a bend to find the hen he was looking for.

The author in front of the Church with his Ozarks gobbler, after one of his return trips to where his turkey hunting career began many years before.

There was no such thing as turkey decoys—plastic, feathered, strutting, or otherwise—and I never met or knew of anyone who displayed a "stuffed turkey" in their home. Specialized turkey guns did not exist and were years away from production, as were custom choke tubes and turkey loads. Many times we hunted with low-brass shotshells left over from the fall small-game season.

My turkey gun was Grandpa's old Winchester '97 or my dad's faded Browning Humpback 5, and in my jacket pocket were three Remington-Peters green paper shells. If I killed a turkey, next year I would have two. Also deep in my coat was a jelly biscuit my grandma made, carefully wrapped in newspaper and secretly slipped into my jacket. The restoration of wild turkeys was still in its early stages. Many surrounding states, and even north Missouri didn't have turkey hunting yet. Hunters came from far and wide to hunt Missouri's public ground in the Ozarks that still held remnant flocks of the original wild turkey.

But overall turkey numbers back then were still low compared to today. You worked hard and walked a lot, and if you messed up on a setup, you prob-

ably would not have another opportunity that morning—it was always many miles to have even the possibility of finding another gobbling turkey. After just two national magazine stories came out with reference to this public hunting area, the pressure from other hunters interfering during your hunt was intense. It took just one gobbling turkey at daylight, and I really like this photo, at the gate to the family graveyard next to the old church.

there would be hunters from four or five directions closing quickly. It was not uncommon to be set up on a gobbling turkey and have another hunter just run past you, then set up out in front of your setup and begin calling.

It became difficult enough to hunt on your own with both local and out-of-state hunter interference, much less when guiding paid hunters. During the late 1970s early 1980s, I guided paying turkey hunters and in later years outdoor writers from my hunting camps, so the battle to get to a gobbling turkey first was intensified. Calling turkeys for paying hunters required unique, aggressive tactics, and I'm not just talking about hunting tactics. Sometimes it was necessary to park a decoy truck on the main road with three or four coffee cups set out on the hood, or even block a logging road that led to a roosted gobbler with a fake camp setup, complete with tents and a campfire.

My guides and I hunted the remotest areas, away from road access. We stayed away from main roads and entered public ground from private land, from the valley below the mountain. During the weekends, when hunting activity was at its highest and nonstop traffic on the logging roads was at its peak, we wouldn't begin hunting until around 10 AM, after many hunters had given up and left the woods.

During the first week, and especially on weekends, several of our favored areas with the best turkey hunting had huge out-of-state turkey camps partying late into the night. One such camp had more than twenty hunters driving four-wheel-drive trucks and stomping through the woods everywhere. They shut down turkeys for miles around.

These were the areas we waited to hunt until late in the season, after the turkeys had settled down and the many turkey hunting camps were long gone. Actually, during the year of the big camp, on the last day of the season, I called in a gobbler that my hunter killed right next to their stacked-rock campfire pit.

After two national magazine stories that referred to this particular public hunting area, the hunting pressure got really intense. This photo of me owl hooting was taken on public ground in the early 1980s. I'm wearing a borrowed camouflage coat and my first camo cap, and guiding a hunter I named "mask man," since he had that mask on at 4 AM when I picked him up for our hunt.

Another tactic we often used was to roost a gobbler early in the morning. Right before daylight and gobbling time, we'd simply walk under the roost and deliberately flush the turkey. At daylight, owl-hooting and yelping hunters would not hear a gobbler and would move on, and we would have the area and the turkeys to ourselves. Our next move was to set up in the area we know the gobblers used after fly-down (something we'd learned from scouting). Usually after a short time our gobbler settled down and returned to his normal routine, his strutting ground, or an area with hens, and we would be there waiting. Most of the time it really didn't take much calling to get him worked up and into the gun.

One great example of this was a three-bearded gobbler my buddy Pat had scouted and really wanted to kill. The only problem was that his turkey roosted at the head of a holler, above the river, at the junction of two main roads in a national forest. When Pat told me of this bird, he also asked me to help him kill it, so I asked Pat two very important questions: "Where does he go after he flies down?" and "Where do you hear him gobbling later in the morning?" Pat's preseason scouting was complete, and he knew the answers to both questions. But another factor was that he also witnessed other hunters the day before the season, on the gravel road, listening to our turkey gobbling on the roost.

But we had a plan. Early on opening morning, Pat and I arrived around 3:30 AM, parked his truck at the junction of both county roads, and then parked my Jeep on the road closest to the roost. We grabbed our gear and slipped in close to the roost, then lay down waiting for first light, as we listened to the soothing sounds of the river far below. It was still predawn darkness when we heard an owl hoot down the ridge, and the first songbird of the morning, and what we were waiting for—the sound of a gobbler in the dark, drumming on a limb. So I got up, and quietly and slowly slipped toward the sound of drumming, until the gobbler flushed from a tree above me and sailed down toward the river.

Pat joined me as we moved farther down the ridge and set up on a large, flat bench just above the river, in the area where Pat had listened to this turkey gobble after fly-down. At first light, gobblers in the distance began their morning love song ritual, but our gobbler remained quiet. However, trucks on the county road were numerous, with hunters often stopping, owl hooting, crow calling, and hen yelping. A half hour after daylight there was no response to my calling. But just a little later, right in the middle of my yelping, I heard

Specialized turkey guns did not exist back then and were years away from production, as well as custom choke tubes and turkey loads. Many times we hunted with low brass shotgun shells left over from the fall small game hunting season.

a gobble from somewhere down the ridge. I cut and yelped, more excited than before, but heard nothing in return. That is until we heard drumming just below the bench. It was really quiet now except for songbirds and the flowing of the river, and then the unmistakable sound of crunching in the leaves, growing ever louder.

I slowly moved my eyes toward the now very loud drumming and saw Pat shift his gun to his left. I heard a few more crunches, then Pat's gun roared, followed with wild flopping. By the time I got up and ran down the steep ridge to meet him, he and the gobbler were about forty yards farther down the hill, so I slid down the steep slope to join him, and he was giggling like a schoolkid, while holding up his three-bearded gobbler for me to see.

Today, with high-quality turkey hunting available all across the state, and with a dozen states in the Midwest around Missouri also offering quality turkey hunting, this same public ground is now virtually empty of hunters during turkey season, even on weekends. Today's turkey hunters have specialized turkey guns, turkey loads, high-quality calls, decoys, portable pop-up blinds, and specialized camouflage clothing and footwear. There is a wealth of great products too numerous to mention, all intended to enhance one's turkey hunting experience. Modern-day turkey hunters, unlike those in the early days, have a wealth of good how-to information available that not only enables them to be successful and quicker, but also helps them enjoy their success and pass on the thrill of turkey hunting to others.

Conservation efforts since the 1970s and numerous turkey restoration programs across America have brought wild turkeys back from the brink of extinction. The lion's share of these efforts was funded by millions of hunting dollars. The result is an unbelievably high number of wild turkeys flourishing today, an available and very accessible renewable resource for hunters all across America.

Peanut and me with our turkey, after zooming up the mountainside on an all-electric four-wheel drive with an electronic Garmin GPS unit.

With large numbers of wild turkeys, quality turkey hunting virtually everywhere, specialized turkey hunting products, and a nonstop turkey hunting information highway, things have certainly changed since those early days. I have a cool job—I hunt turkeys for a living. I feel so fortunate to be a spokesperson for hunting and humbled to be part of that information highway, presenting seminars and radio and television shows, and writing books like this one.

With Peanut by my side, I admire an Ozarks Ghost, a beautiful gobbler I just killed in my rugged Missouri Ozarks, at the very place my turkey hunting career began so many years ago. On the summit of this mountain, silently kneeling next to my turkey while taking in the view across the hills, I pause and reflect on my morning hunt and finally understand what I've been looking for, the one thing missing from turkey hunting today. On this beautiful spring morning, as my past overflows with these wonderful memories, I suddenly realize that turkey hunting just doesn't get any better than this, and that, without question, today is really the "good ole days" of turkey hunting.

As I had during past trips to the hills, I visited the family cemetery to show Grandpa and Grandma my gobbler and place wild flowers and dogwood blossoms from the mountain.

4

Secrets of a Professional Turkey Hunter

AFTER YEARS OF PROFESSIONAL TURKEY HUNTING, I HAVE condensed my calling and hunting tactics into the most important, the most utilized, and the most successful methods of calling, roosting, and setup. I've found these to be the keys to success with spring turkeys in order to kill gobblers consistently in all kinds of situations, during any turkey seasonality, in any kind of weather, or at any time of year.

I decided to share these secrets with America's hunting public just a couple of years ago, during my seminars. These tactics produce for leading outdoor writers, national magazines, and outdoor television shows. Every spring, these time-proven tactics produce twenty-five to thirty gobbler kills, regardless of weather, pressure, inadequate time, and an entourage of people along for the duration of my hunts. If these tactics work for me, they will help you, as a "casual" turkey hunter—well, at least compared to my hunting schedule. I am under constant pressure with limited time on a hunt, without any time to scout, and with way too many people in the field; but I have to produce a TV show and have to get results for outdoor writers.

I have to say that I was kind of surprised by the positive response from hunters attending my seminars after I quit teaching basic turkey hunting guidelines and switched to my professional tactics, all supported with video footage. I will say that for the first time ever, I did have a few nonbelievers get up and walk out of

Back in the 1970s, I refused to sit 200 yards from a gobbler and yelp softly three times and wait. I took it to the gobbler, yelping as I went, got tight just under a ridge, called hard, and killed the turkey basically in self defense. Am I doing it all wrong?

Jack and Lisa Thomas with an Ozarks gobbler taken with the tactics within this chapter. Under constant pressure, with limited time, without any time to scout, I have to produce for TV shows and get results for outdoor writers.

my programs. But the sheer number of those rushing to the front with questions, the many who seek me out on show floors, and especially from the hundreds of handwritten letters and e-mails I receive, I have little doubt that I made the right decision to share my tactics.

This chapter is important to set up the rest of my book, to ease you into the "call-shy" myth, to ease the pain of my radical roosting and turkey calling scouting sessions. I am a teacher of turkey hunting who believes that the best way to give you information, to help you with your turkey hunting success, is an age-old teaching approach. I tell you what I am going teach you, then I tell you, then I tell you what I told you—this is exactly how this book unfolds. My greatest challenge in teaching you is to break through the myths of turkey hunting, to disprove an imaginary turkey hunting rulebook that really does not exist. This "rulebook" claims that turkeys will not come downhill to a call, that calling to turkeys will make them "call-shy," and that guys like me call way too much.

This is also the rulebook that gives turkeys supernatural powers, and endows turkeys with human characteristics—what I call the "Walt Disney effect." You see, the biggest problem is that past generations of turkey hunters, right up to today's hunters, have all been told what *not* to do; that you can't do this, you can't do that. But no one ever tells turkey hunters what they can and should do. Well, I am willing to do just that with this book, and share with you my secrets, tactics that also include never giving up during a hunt. I am the first one in the woods, and the last one to come out. If it's turkey season I am in the woods, and if something is not working, I am willing to try something else.

For any turkey hunter, experience is the best teacher—time in the field, time out there, listening, watching, and learning from wild turkeys. But as a turkey hunter you will be around other turkey hunters, in the midst of your peers in hunting camps, in cafés and sporting goods stores, at sports shows and seminars, and at turkey calling contests. These are the many places you will hear about many different calling tactics, as well as tall tales and a wide variety of turkey hunting beliefs. Heated discussions go on late into the night, expressing many different opinions, many stories of super gobblers and of unkillable, world record, older-than-Moses turkeys complete with PhDs in outsmarting hunters. Throughout my life I have enjoyed many wonderful stories as part of our turkey hunting nostalgia. But wonderful or not, they really are nothing more than what I regard as the myths of turkey hunting.

So when it comes right down to hunting success, it's wiser to not believe every story you hear, to always keep an open mind, and to always utilize just a little common sense. You will always be a more successful turkey hunter if you concentrate on what really works for you. Learn from the turkeys, and they will tell you how to hunt them better than any hunting tactics dependent on turkey hunting myths.

So where is this mystical rulebook on turkey hunting all must follow and obey? Who makes the rules in turkey hunting and turkey calling? Not people, not hunters, not turkey pros, not outdoor TV stars, not outdoor writers. Nope, sorry. It is the turkeys. And when you do this for a living as I do, you have to produce for television shows and guide people like outdoor writers. I sometimes get dumped off at a place in the dark that I've never seen before and I have to produce. So I scout as I go, and learn the turkeys that morning—it's not

like I've been there before. But the turkeys will help you, tell you what they're doing. So it all comes back to the calling.

I remember the many things I've learned over the years from the turkeys, not from what someone told me. Of course even though I was killing the dog water out of turkeys, others told me I was doing it all wrong; I was calling too aggressively, too much, and too loudly. Since the 1960s, in regard to hunting and calling turkeys, I am scolded, told I'm doing it all wrong, preached that I am shutting turkeys down by the way I hunt. I'm breaking all the rules. Back in the 1970s, I refused to sit 200 yards from a gobbler and yelp softly

Challenge gobblers with the gobbler yelp, like the one I used to call in and kill this Wyoming Merriam's.

I use my call to locate gobblers during scouting, and to roost and call in gobblers during my hunt.

three times and wait. I took it to the gobbler, yelping as I went, got tight just under a ridge, called hard, and killed the turkey basically in self-defense. Yet I'm doing it all wrong?

Yes indeed, I have been told for years that I'm boogering turkeys, I'm making them call-shy, and that calling is really not that important. I just smile, work hard at my job, and consistently kill turkeys everywhere I go—the way I learned how to call, from the turkeys. So, are you going to listen to some self-proclaimed turkey expert who tells you you're doing it all wrong? Or are you going to listen to the wild turkeys?

I have hunted turkeys for forty-eight-plus years, in forty-three states and Mexico. Today, you can find experts and as much advice about calling turkeys as you can stand. There are calling experts just about everywhere these days, in sporting goods stores, at sports show seminars, and on outdoor televiion shows. At a recent hunting sports show, a local hunting hero pounded the podium like a tent revival preacher, on the sins of calling before hunting season, making turkeys call-shy, and tons of what you should not do, or face the consequences of your sins with shutting down the birds and never killing a turkey. It's no wonder today's hunters are confused.

I find it interesting that through my years of turkey hunting, in the outdoor media I'm considered some kind of an expert. Over the decades I've been really fortunate to have taken a lot of birds. But I've actually called in more turkeys for other people than for myself, and somehow that makes me an expert. I honestly just do not believe I am an expert. Every year I continue learning on the subject of hunting and calling turkeys. Experience and time in the turkey woods is what makes you a better turkey hunter and caller.

I'm also considered an expert because I've won numerous turkey calling contests, but quite honestly, turkey-calling contests do not make anyone an expert in turkey hunting. However, turkey calling contests will make you a much better caller. Those who compete practice more, call more, and sound much more like turkeys than the once-a-year, casual turkey hunter. I have been around professional contest callers for years, and all are phenomenal hunters and unbelievably consistent turkey killers.

Many of today's hunters just do not have the opportunity to hunt in other places, everywhere across America, usually hunting only in their home states, perhaps even the same farm, year after year. They just have not had the opportunity to experience turkey hunting everywhere, and can judge turkeys and turkey hunting only from their limited experience and from their limited time in a local area. Pro turkey hunters shooting TV shows in multiple states have experience from all kinds of situations with all subspecies of turkeys, and under all kinds of weather and pressure conditions.

It's as inevitable as the first gobble of spring; it will begin. The birds just aren't right. What's wrong with the turkeys? The answer, plain and simple: not a darn thing. They're just being turkeys. They're doing their own thing— eating, strutting, attracting mates, and doing all the things turkeys do. Turkeys are very social, and spend a large part of their lives in large flocks. But spring is different. Increasing daylight and warming temperatures trigger hormones in both hens and gobblers. Flocks break up, and the urge to breed takes over. Most state agencies attempt to schedule turkey season after the mating period—while most of the hens are sitting on the nest, incubating their eggs. This makes the gobblers much more susceptible to coming to the call.

This small window of opportunity is what all spring turkey hunting is judged by. If, for example, hunters experience an early season in which gobblers are running together and fighting, they are quick to say that something is wrong with the turkeys. It should be understood that the majority of the gob-

blers called in during spring seasons are two-year-old birds. These youngsters are trying to get in on some of the breeding action that is going on by responding to the excited calls of a lone hen, which in turn ends up being a hunter.

But when there is a drop in the bird population (bad hatches) like what's going on in many parts of the

In thick, wooded ridge country, use a more open choke and smaller shot size.

Learn the lay of the land and study turkey movement throughout the day.

nation, or the timing of the season is off, hunters get frustrated. Anything less than bluebird skies, nice sunny mornings, and fields full of gobbling two-year-old birds, and hunters groan that it's over. So what's a hunter to do? I'll give you my strategies and tell you what to do. But before you dive in, I'd like to cover a few basics with my "most-asked questions" and my top ten spring turkey hunting tips. I've presented these from most- to least-asked.

Most Frequently Asked Spring Turkey Hunting Questions

1. **Why are turkeys not gobbling?**

   It seems as if many turkey hunters judge "good" spring turkey hunting only from a small window of opportunity available at a time when most of an area's hens are on the nest, and an abundance of two-year-old gobblers are "singing their love songs" nonstop, running to anything that squeaks or even remotely sounds like a hen turkey. If anything outside this "perfect world" occurs during spring season, hunters grumble, "What is wrong with the turkeys?" So, if a gobbler does not run up to a hunter and he has to shoot the turkey off his leg, then something must be wrong with the turkeys. There is really nothing wrong with the turkeys—they are just being turkeys, and hunters have to learn more about turkeys' pecking order and be willing to change tactics with the times, keep an open mind, and use whatever works during the time they are hunting them.

2. **What type of calling device do you use?**

   I use a variety of turkey calls, including a good-sounding box call and a slate or glass call. But my overall favorite and my go-to call is the diaphragm mouth call. Hunting turkeys is a lot like fishing—a hunter has to experiment to find out what the turkeys in the area will respond to on that particular day, in current weather conditions, or the mood the birds are in at the time.

3. **What is the very first turkey sound you make in morning when set up on a roosted gobbler?**

   That depends on time of year, weather conditions, and type of terrain. Many years ago I would have recommended beginning the morning battle with a soft tree call, but not anymore. Today, I begin my day with aggressive calling, yelping, and cutting (not necessarily louder) because of hen competition. I want that gobbler's attention, and I want to hold his attention, call him to the gun, and kill him as quickly as possible before the hens get to him.

4. **How many times do you call, how often do you call, and when do you stop calling on a gobbler's approach?**

   This too depends a lot on time of year, weather conditions, and type of terrain. Turkeys do not count yelps or wear watches. Turkeys call how they feel, and you should as well. No two turkeys are alike, but all call with feeling and inflection. As a hunter you have to feel a bird out and find what he likes, call with feeling and emotion. Sometimes I call nonstop, sometimes I call less. This is a very difficult question, and the answer depends on the reaction from the gobbler, but usually I pour it on because I want a turkey worked up so I can kill him quickly. During most of my hunting situations during the heat of battle with a gobbler, I usually stop calling only after I pull the trigger.

5. **What is the difference between an alarm putt and a cluck?**

   I find it amazing that year after year I continue to hear this same question. I have a little saying I use when asked this question during my seminars: "If the putting sound is coming closer and closer, it's clucking." If the sound is steadily going away from you, it's an alarm putt." A turkey hunter should never worry about making an alarm putt; I personally have never, ever scared off turkeys by putting or cutting, but have killed a truckload of them putting. Turkeys putt, cut, and cluck aggressively. Always call just like the turkeys. Do what they do. I always utilize putting and clucking with great results and a lot of dead gobblers.

6. **How close do you set up on a turkey?**

   Of course, this all depends on terrain features, time of year, type of foliage, etc., but my experience is the closer you set up, the more successful the

Listen and watch turkeys in your hunting area prior to season. Turkeys will tell you how to call and hunt them.

calling session will be. I like to set up as close as the terrain will allow me without spooking the turkey. Fifty yards is good, forty is better. Today, with so many hens and other hunters in the woods, you have to get tight, get a gobbler in quickly, and close the deal.

7. **Okay, I have this farm with a creek, a ridge, and a field. How do I find turkeys and how do I hunt on my farm?**

(I am asked this same question over and over, no matter where in the country I'm presenting seminars.) I first ask where they see birds, and if they listen for gobbling. I explain how to scout and look for signs; find the food, you find the birds. Listen for gobbling, and watch the turkeys from a distance; the hottest track is the one with a foot stuck in it. Learn from the turkeys how to hunt them. Then listen for gobbling again, right before the season, and let the turkeys tell you how to hunt. Locate birds, and then stay out of the hunting area until it's time to hunt them.

8. **How many turkeys have you killed?**

I'm asked this question at all hunting shows and seminars. I honestly do not know how many turkeys I have killed personally or how many I am responsible for calling for others, nor do I really care. I'm not counting. I do not believe that turkey hunting or a turkey hunter should be judged on how big or how many turkeys he or she kills. The only counting should be how many others, especially kids, you introduce to the outdoors and turkey hunting by sharing your knowledge and experience with them.

Top Ten Spring Turkey Hunting Tips

1. **Turkey hunters need to change with the times.**

Wild turkey numbers today are at an all-time high. Hunters across America now have a great opportunity to enjoy this highly accessible, wonderful renewable resource. High turkey densities mean more hens to compete for gobblers. Turkey hunter numbers are also at all-time highs, meaning additional competition for gobblers. Turkey hunting has changed dramatically in the last twenty years. Hunters must change and adjust their hunting styles to keep up with the times. Wild turkeys change their habits according to the conditions in their environment, and what I call "hunter pressure."

2. Locating turkeys

Listening for gobblers prior to the season in your hunting area is essential for success. However, do not just listen from a distance. Stay awhile, follow turkeys in open country, watch the turkeys. Where do they go from the roost? Where are they gobbling later in the morning? Locate the areas gobblers use throughout the day. I use my turkey call to get gobbler counts in an area. Turkeys respond better to a turkey call than to an owl or crow locator-type call. When hunting a new area, learn the lay of the land as quickly as possible. Review a topographic map of the area. Watch, listen, and learn. Adjust your tactics according to what the turkeys are doing, and the cycle or seasonality they are in during the time of your hunt.

3. Roosting

For successful outdoor television and outdoor writer hunts, roosting is my greatest key to success and a finished television show. Locating numerous gobblers in your hunting area prior to the season is a must, but roosting the night before your hunt puts birds in the bag. I want to know what limb he is on and the direction of fly-up, and find my setup location the night before my hunt.

4. Pressure-shy

With both wild turkey and hunter numbers at all-time highs, higher turkey and hunter densities also represent more hens and hunters competing for gobblers, so today's hunters must change and adjust their hunting styles and tactics to

Roosting puts gobblers in the bag—like these two Ozarks gobblers.

bag today's "henned-up," pressured gobblers. Wild turkeys change their habits according to conditions in their environment, including hunting pressure. Turkeys that many would label "call-shy" I prefer to call "people-shy" or "pressure-shy." Calling (that is, a sound, a turkey vocalization) has absolutely no negative effect on turkeys. Wild turkeys do not like human activity. Heavy hunter traffic will shut down gobbling and cause toms to change their normal routines—not your calling. Minimize activity in the area you hunt before, during, and after the hunt. Scout and watch birds from a distance. If possible, let an area rest after hunting. And walk in to hunt, leaving trucks parked at the road.

5. **The hen factor**

Hens dictate toms' movements. Especially in areas with high turkey densities, find the food source, find the hens, and you will find the gobblers. With a gobbler on the roost with hens, get in early and set up tight—as close as possible. Be the first "hen" in the morning, and call aggressively like a dominant hen. Get that gobbler in and on the ground before all the hens are off the roost. When hunting later in the morning, don't call to the gobbler—call the hens, by challenging them with cutting and yelping, and the tom will follow.

6. **The final approach**

Your setup can spell the difference between just spending quality time in the outdoors and carrying a gobbler to your truck. Set up as close as the terrain will allow—the tighter the better. With today's higher turkey den-

sities, hunters have to contend with hen competition, and set up tight to compete with the hens. Use the terrain to your advantage. In timber, set up where you can't see the gobbler until he is in range, for example at the break of a ridge, or a turn in a logging road, and always set up to make it easier for the turkey to come to you. Always set up on a roosted gobbler

Practice your calling and learn to use a variety of calling devices.

on the same side he flew up from the night before. When hunting open country, watch where turkeys enter and leave fields. Adjust your setup to position yourself slightly inside those woods, between his roost and the field edge. Where you can shoot both woods and field, place decoys just inside the field edge.

7. Calling

A turkey call is my most important tool for success. I use my call for locating, roosting, and calling spring gobblers to the gun. Keep it simple—yelping and cutting is all that's necessary to call and kill spring turkeys anywhere in America. Practice calling prior to hunting season. Learn to use a variety of calling devices properly. Never be afraid to call—put feeling and inflection in your calling, and listen to and watch the turkeys—they will tell you how to hunt and how to call them. Practice with several types of calling devices: I use a diaphragm mouth call, a glass or slate call, and a good box call during each and every hunt.

8. Guns and loads

Today's turkey hunter has a multitude of choices in turkey guns, turkey chokes, ammunition, and shot sizes. It is imperative to match gun, choke tube, and shot size to the type of terrain you're hunting. In thick woods, or ridge country like the Ozarks, close encounters are the norm. Many shots taken are less than twenty yards, oftentimes just twenty feet. A standard full or modified choke is best, as well as smaller shot, such as #6, for close-range pattern density. Actually, in the old days, I killed many gobblers in

close-quarters, hand-to-hand combat with high-brass #7½ shot.

In semi-open country, such as wood lots mixed with open areas and small fields, a tighter choke like an H. S. Strut Undertaker and #5 shot is very efficient. Now in more open country, like north Missouri or the open spaces of Western states, a

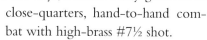

When hunting open country, go with a tighter choke and a heavy shot size.

much tighter choke (like an Indian Creek choke tube and #4 shot) is the ticket, providing a tighter pattern and greater shot energy at longer distance and with heavier shot.

All hunters should take the time, long before the season begins, to shoot numerous shot sizes, brands of ammo, and different choke tubes, to find what works best with their turkey gun. Always start patterning close, like ten yards on a big board. Shoot light loads to see where the gun is hitting, then go to turkey loads once you're tuned in. In addition, hunters typically handle turkey guns only once or twice a year. So to become familiar with your gun, shoot hand-thrown clay birds with light loads.

9. **The overthinking game**

Turkey hunting is a mind game. Never underestimate the power of your own mental state, be flexible, and get sufficient rest. Hunt aggressively and creatively, but do not overthink or over-evaluate any hunting situation. Too many hunters endow turkeys with human traits, all while turkeys are out there just being turkeys. If you're afraid to call or if you think you'll scare a gobbler with your calling, you probably will not call in many turkeys. Use the tactics that work best for you, but never be afraid to change tactics, try something different, and adjust to what the turkeys are doing at the time you're hunting them. Don't ever buy into any negative talk and/or lowered expectations expressed among hunters in your area. Positive thinking kills turkeys.

10. **Pecking order**

Every turkey, tom or hen, has its place in the social structure. For gobblers, I utilize the gobbler yelp. I challenge a gobbler's status within the pecking order, and I call in and kill more turkeys with gobbler yelping than with any other call. A challenged dominant gobbler will charge your position to run you off, to whip you—but he doesn't know you have a 12-gauge. It's just like a gobbler to bring spurs to a gunfight.

5

Pecking Order and
Seasonality of Wild Turkeys

FOR A TURKEY HUNTER, IT'S REALLY IMPORTANT TO understand wild turkeys and what goes on in the spring season. One time of the year—in the springtime—turkeys are different. Day length increases, triggering mating activity, and males gobble to attract the hens for mating.

During my frequent travels, I find that many of today's turkey hunters have little knowledge of wild turkey behavior outside of the spring mating season. Every season, hunters everywhere complain that the turkeys are different, of turkeys not cooperating with their calling, that something is wrong with the turkeys. They talk of strange-acting gobblers that run with other gobblers, ignore their hen calling, and just do not gobble.

Generations of turkey hunters are programmed with calling tactics that are useful only during the short span of the mating season, when everything is right, many hens are on their nests, and lovestruck two-year-old toms come running to the call. Years of turkey hunting lore have hunters believing only in a soft hen yelp, and calling very little within this short timeframe of the mating season.

Subsequently, spring turkey hunting quality and hunter success are measured only by this narrow window of opportunity. Anything outside this "perfect world" has hunters all across America grumbling that something

is wrong with the turkeys. So what's wrong with your turkeys? Not a thing—they're just being turkeys and going about their turkey business. But to understand why they're not gobbling and why they're not racing to your every call, it pays

Early-season hunting prior to mating or even during the heat of mating equals a ton of hen competition for gobblers, thus making life miserable for turkey hunters who rely only on the hen yelp to try to call in lonely, love-struck toms.

Generations of turkey hunters are programmed to
use calling tactics that work only during the short
span of the mating season, when everything is
right, many hens are on their nests, and two-year-
old toms come running in without caution.

to have a bit of an understanding about the wild
turkeys and their habits.

Take the pecking order, for instance. Every
turkey has a role in the social hierarchy of the
flock. When a dominant hen hears a new voice
(such as a hunter calling) she's either curious or
furious, and it is the dominant hen's business to
find out where this new voice fits in the peck-
ing order. So by calling to these dominant hens and playing to their natural
instincts, hunters make it so they can't help but come to investigate—possibly bringing their boyfriends in tow. So what call do you use to get this hen
interested?

State fish and game agencies everywhere attempt to set spring turkey seasons during this timeframe, when a majority of the mating is completed and
most hens are on the nest. But Mother Nature does not attend these meetings,
and more times than not this window of opportunity does not exist during a
hunter's only available time to hunt. Early season hunting—prior to mating or
even during the heat of mating—equals lots of hen competition for gobblers,
thus making life miserable for turkey hunters who rely only on the hen yelp
to call in responsive but lonely toms.

So to become a more complete and successful turkey hunter takes more
than just understanding the mating season. You really have to look at the overall picture of turkeys. The rest of the year, turkeys are just turkeys. Turkeys are
very social. They're in large flocks for most of the year and outside the mating
season, pecking order and seasonality of turkeys become very important to
you as a turkey hunter. In this chapter, I break down the four phases of spring
turkey hunting in regard to pecking order and seasonality. In later chapters—
where we cover early season, mating season, post-breeding, and late season—I
will explain my calling and hunting tactics for each of these phases. It's kind of
like which came first, the turkey or the egg? It is very difficult to explain my
calling tactics for each of these phases during hunting situations if we do not
cover the pecking order and seasonality first. Breakup, mating, and hens sitting

and tending nests don't necessarily happen at exactly the same time but can be overlapping. However, there are still four categories or phases of seasonality during the springtime cycle.

To become a more consistent and successful turkey hunter, it's important to understand wild turkeys and what goes on within the social hierarchy of a flock, but for you to totally understand the seasonality of turkeys, you really need to observe wild turkeys through the remainder of the calendar year, when they are in large flocks.

Hunters who experience a late spring, with gobblers running together or turkeys in the heat of mating, or during a time when the boys are covered up with hens, are often lost about what to do. They complain the season is off, something is wrong with the turkeys, and turkeys are acting different. But what these hunters are actually experiencing is normal behavior during other phases of turkey seasonality. There is only one time of the year turkeys are different, and that is during the mating season. Outside this very short timeframe, the narrow window of spring mating season, turkeys are just being turkeys, carrying on with life as normal.

However, it's important to note during this same period what hunters complain about—the season is off, early season, gobblers still in flocks—is also a time for those who know the pecking order and how to use it to have great success and consistently kill gobblers. Professional hunters and seasoned hunters with fall hunting experience will challenge turkeys' status with calling, and quite honestly, consistently kill gobblers during all situations and seasonality of turkeys.

The Four Phases of Spring Turkeys

Pre-breeding or early season

This is a time when gobblers break up from flocks and disperse into other areas depending on their place in the pecking order. Early in the season, gobblers remain in groups or flocks, but as day length increases, these groups of gobblers will disperse into other areas. Lesser toms are pushed out of the group, and as day length continues to increase, gobbler activity increases as well, with strutting and displaying and toms doing everything possible to attract the hens for mating. So, as days lengthen, toms begin to gobble with more intensity.

Also during this period, toms do a lot of gobbling to challenge other toms, as well as to gather hens. They push and shove, fighting to reestablish their status within the pecking order and social structure of all wild turkeys in their core area.

To become a more consistent and successful turkey hunter, it's important to understand wild turkeys and what goes on within the social hierarchy of a flock. To totally understand the seasonality of turkeys, you really need to observe wild turkeys when they are in social flocks for the remainder of the calendar year.

Breeding season

When the actual breeding time arrives, toms just don't gobble nearly as much because they're displaying and breeding the hens. It's a tough time for many hunters during the peak of breeding because birds become quiet during this phase. Toms really have no need to gobble—they've already called in hens and are busy with displaying and breeding.

Post-breeding

Conservation departments, fish and game departments, and wildlife biologists attempt to schedule turkey seasons all across the country during this time phase, when most of the hens are already bred and are on the nest, and when gobblers are much more susceptible to calling. Usually there is good to great gobbling during this phase, especially if there is an abundance of two-year-olds in your hunting area.

Late season

As time marches on and a majority of the breeding is completed there's usually a lull in gobbling, when things get really quiet. This seems to be the case quite often during the spring hunting seasons, and is yet another time when many hunters become discouraged, especially if it occurs on the only days a hunter has available to be in the woods.

After the mating season, as gobblers battle to reestablish the pecking order within the social structure of their area flock, gobblers will once again become very vocal as they return to their male bachelor groups.

It is possible that your spring turkey season could occur during any of these four phases, so you need to be aware and learn as much about the turkeys in your hunting area as possible, to know how to hunt and what tactics to apply during the phase that turkeys are in during the time you are hunting them.

6

Calling is Everything

IF I'VE LEARNED ANYTHING FROM ALL MY YEARS OF turkey hunting, it is that calling is everything. For me, it is the most important facet of turkey hunting, and realistic calling has more to do with my professional success than any other element of turkey hunting. After years of hunting all across the United States and Mexico, calling is what makes it happen for me year in and year out, and is why I stress that calling is everything.

To me it is ridiculous for anyone to state that calling is not a major factor in turkey hunting. Wild turkeys communicate year-round (see Chapter 5, Pecking Order and Seasonality of Wild Turkeys). As hunters, we communicate directly with turkeys and lure them into gun, bow, or camera, and calling is what makes turkey hunting what it is.

Hunters utilize calling for locating, scouting, roosting, and of course calling birds to the gun. The wild turkey's survival is dependent on calling, communication, pecking order, hens with poults, fall and winter flocks, mating season, and danger—so how could it be possible that calling is not important? I have many years of research invested toward my wild turkey

calling education—dedicated time, twelve months a year spent following turkeys with my video camera, documenting all phases and seasonality during winter, summer, fall, and spring. This has reinforced for me how valuable good, realistic calling skills are for consistent success in turkey hunting.

In today's turkey hunting world, other professionals and I hunt turkeys eighty-plus days each spring, from Florida to Hawaii to Mexico to Western states to New England and everywhere in between.

From this research, my approach to calling in the turkey woods is dependent on what the turkeys are doing at the time I'm hunting them, how they feel, and how they communicate with other turkeys during that particular time. I firmly believe that if more hunters would just pay closer attention to turkeys at the time they are hunting them—simply watch, listen, and learn—the turkeys will actually tell them how to call to and how to hunt them.

I feel fortunate, and could have a little bit of a calling edge, not because of my many, many years of calling experience, but because, unlike many of today's turkey hunters, I did not learn to call to turkeys from "experts," audiotapes, videos, seminars, or TV shows—I learned from the wild turkeys themselves, and my education is ongoing.

Statements that calling is overrated and it's not that important are something I've had to contend with for many years. Well, actually through all the years I've hunted, and even more so today. Yes, I continue to hear hunters everywhere I travel say that calling is not important. The interesting part is that not just everyday turkey hunters are saying this, but even seminar speakers, hunting guides, and outfitters. Even more astonishing is when outdoor companies, selling turkey hunting products, make such claims on their TV shows, during trade shows, in magazines, and in company advertising.

Oh, but the most amazing thing is turkey call manufacturing companies selling turkey calls while making claims that calling is not important! Go figure.

One spring season several years ago, up in a New England camp, on the last leg of a very long spring, which started in early March in Florida, the age-

old argument of "woodsmanship is 90 percent, calling is only 10 percent—and calling is not important" went on late into the night. The next morning, long

If there is just one thing I have learned from all my years of turkey hunting, it is that calling is everything. For me, it is the most important of all facets of turkey hunting. Realistic calling has more to do with my professional TV show success than any other element of turkey hunting.

before daylight, I was hunkered down against the back of a huge oak, and my late-night arguing partner was sitting at the front of the tree facing two roosted gobblers. At first light, they started gobbling like there was no tomorrow. I didn't make a sound, and I never made a call, even after both toms flew down and really started to blow it out. As the first gobbler turned to walk away, I still didn't make a sound.

My hunter finally turned toward me and whispered, "Why aren't you calling?"

"Because calling is not important. Calling is only about 10 percent of turkey hunting," I replied. Just as the second gobbler began marching away, gobbling as he went, I excitedly whispered in my hunter's ear: "You'd better hurry up and put some of that woodsmanship on 'em—they're fixin' to leave!"

Even way back in the day, during the 1960s and early 1970s, in the Ozarks calling was a major factor of turkey hunting success. Turkey calling skills were considered a high art form, and hunters with superior calling skills not only killed more turkeys than others, they were treated like kings at the local barber shops and country stores. Those were the kinds of places where, when hunters gathered, you'd hear things like: "That ole boy from over Iron County, yelping with his natural mouth, makes an ole hen ashamed of herself," or "Old Jimmy could call a hen right off her nest," and my all-time favorite, "Billy Dale is so good with that caller, he could call an ole gobbler right off a hen's butt."

There was a downside to all of this back then, in that very few if any Ozark turkey hunters would share any information about calling turkeys. In fact, there was little other information available to help new turkey hunters learn about successfully hunting and calling turkeys. In today's turkey hunting world, other professionals and I hunt turkeys eighty-plus days per spring, from Florida, to Hawaii, Mexico, the Western states, New England, and everywhere in between. With limited time per hunt, regardless of the weather or seasonality of turkeys, we have to produce—no excuses. Pros must produce results for TV shows, websites, national magazines, and outdoor writers. We have to make it happen, and our livelihood depends on it.

There is a huge difference between someone turkey hunting only a couple of times a year and what professionals have to accomplish. It is common for a new hunter to think turkey hunting is easy when hunting alone on a perfect morning, when weather is good, gobbling at its peak, most hens are on the nest, and two-year-old gobblers are running wild. Yes, days like this can make anyone look like a pro. But this is only a very narrow window of opportu-

I have invested years of research in my turkey calling education, and dedicated time behind a video camera documenting all phases and seasonality during winter, summer, fall, and spring.

nity, one's turkey season does not always fall into place during this phase, and this is what separates part-time turkey hunters from the pros.

For pros and part-time turkey hunters alike, it is important to achieve the same reaction from turkeys with your calling that turkeys react to when calling each other, and that will only happen when hunters sound like a turkey. Neither I nor other pros are trying to say anyone's calling is wrong—if you have success with how you're calling, that's great. But I assure you that if you learn to call with more realism, and you are not afraid to call, and are willing to learn from the turkeys, you will consistently call and kill more turkeys, regardless of turkey phases, weather conditions, or where you are in the country. Calling is everything.

After years of hunting turkeys all across America, including Hawaii and Mexico, I know that calling is what makes it happen for me year in and year out. That's why I stress that calling is everything.

7

Myth of the Call-Shy Turkey

OF ALL THE SUBJECTS THAT TURKEY HUNTERS ARGUE about, nothing increases blood pressure like a debate over how much one should call and that calling somehow "creates" call-shy turkeys. Before we get into the subject of call-shy, I feel it important to tell you that this is not just a rant on my part. I'm not just crying in my milk or whining about how I'm mistreated in hunting camps.

Much of the call-shy information in this chapter will affect you as a turkey hunter. Every year across America, millions of working-man turkey hunters with limited hunting time will not kill a turkey simply because of this call-shy belief. As a professional cameraman, field producer, and guide for outdoor media, I'm faced with the call-shy myth pretty much everywhere I travel to hunt. After a late-night flight into a new state (always after a rough several hours' drive to camp), I'm up early the next morning, with little sleep, then transported to an area in complete darkness, and always someplace I've never seen in daylight before. It would seem I have enough of a challenge to kill a turkey on camera without this call-shy thing, but more times than not, the local guide warns me not to call to his turkeys because they are call-shy.

So, I share with you calling and hunting tactics that work for me that will in fact help you kill turkeys. I have learned them from years of battling this call-shy nonsense, against stubborn guides, outfitters, and local hunters who scorn my calling. Yet we have continued to kill turkeys consistently, regardless of call-shy beliefs. If you are a firm believer in call-shy, all I ask is that you read this chapter with an open mind, think about some of your past hunts, and consider that maybe if you'd used some of this information, it might have worked, especially on a hunt when you did not kill a turkey mainly because you did not call, held back your calling, or called very little.

So, it's time—let's dive in. Some of this might be painful to call-shy believers, but I assure you, it works for me. And for those of you who are new turkeys hunters without strong opinions already in place and who are

As a professional cameraman, field producer, and guide for outdoor media, I'm faced with the call-shy myth almost everywhere I travel to hunt.

open to learning from my experience, this information will turn you into a turkey killing machine.

All across the wild turkey's range, there are hunters who subscribe to the notion that you should call just barely enough to let the birds hear you— maybe once, maybe twice, perhaps three yelps every thirty minutes—and then sit back and allow that wily tom's patience to run out, at which point he might show up at the original source of the appropriately subdued calling.

To call more than that, the theory holds, is to poison the air with turkey noise pollution certain to ruin not only that day's hunt, but the prospects of other hunters unfortunate enough to enter that same territory for the rest of the season. "That fancy contest calling crap" is believed to create a negative reaction among turkeys that somehow become conditioned to avoid the sounds of their own kind. The turkeys are call–shy. As soon as you start calling, they run the other way.

But in reality, turkeys just do not turn into call–shy phantoms. If anything, they become people-shy. It is excessive human activity that shuts down gobblers, not calling, and this is something I learned many, many years ago. It amazes me that any hunter could actually believe wild turkeys can, in the span

of a few weeks, or even a few years, learn to "know" it's a hunter making the sounds. They don't know we imitate them. They can't know this. They have no capacity to know this. Sorry, but turkeys do not know we humans are calling to them and are merely duplicating their language.

Depending on who you talk to, the case is made that aversion to excited

Outdoor media camp hunters with their "call shy" turkeys.

calling gets passed on to turkey eggs before they hatch. What is the bottom line on calling? Is it possible for humans to "educate" wild turkeys, to cause them to stop gobbling, leave the area (or both), by calling excitedly on a box call? If you really believe this, think about what you're saying.

It just does not seem possible that a wild turkey vocalization, a hen yelp, something that is so very important to turkeys, could somehow create a call-shy turkey. But because of this call-shy myth, many turkey hunters are pro-grammed to hold back, or call softly. Many are afraid to call when in fact, if they would call, they could actually kill a turkey. It totally amazes me that hunters really believe that a sound, a vocalization from a distance, would scare a turkey, shut turkeys down.

But quite honestly, I think it's absurd to presume that wild turkeys could evolve—even learn by association—to shy away from the calling of their own kind, a vocalization, a sound, especially when it is essential to the perpetuation of the species to respond to it, and their survival depends on it. Call-shy, or "caller-shy" as it was labeled many years ago, is nothing new and is something I have had to deal with my entire turkey hunting life. It wasn't as bad back in the old days—I just did what I had to do to call turkeys and took the heat from superstitious, call-shy-fearing local hunters.

So, now let's travel back in time and review a little call-shy history from days gone by, because believe it or not, call-shy is not just a modern-day myth. I know, here I go again, okay, I'm old, but back in my early Ozarks days, tur-key hunters gathered at local check stations and restaurants, filling the air with both calling and hunting stories—talk of smart, elusive gobblers, tales cloaked in myth, tall tales of super-intelligent, mystical birds. For me, these stories are all part of the allure and mystery of my early turkey hunting experiences. I remember a story told many times around our Ozarks campfire. At the old trapper's cabin on Buford Mountain, if someone were foolish enough to light a cabin lantern just before daylight, that "ole bronzeback" wouldn't gobble for a month.

Here's one told many times at the local turkey check-in station: "There is no man alive, near or far, that has a chance against the caller-shy 'Ghost Gob-bler' of Clinton Ridge. One soft cluck from any hunter at daylight, and it's over; that mountain ghost will not gobble the rest of the season."

What about "ole long spur" of Dryfork Holler—now there's a challenge. That old gobbler outsmarted every man who ever toted a box call and chalk, and all it took was just one owl hoot at daylight, and he'd go silent the rest of the season. Heaven forbid if anyone ever tried to call in "ole broken toe," the King of Bell Mountain; one soft cluck and he'd be headed off into the next county.

This is one true call-shy story from the 1970s, down in the Ozark hills in the area called Dryfork Holler. After hunting there several days, I noticed turkey gobbling decreasing with every passing day. As the season progressed, especially on weekends when scores of hunters entered the same public-ground holler, gobblers would go silent. So I would pack it in and go somewhere else to find gobbling turkeys. Numerous hunters from the area blamed me for nongobbling turkeys in Dryfork Holler. It was said the turkeys were call-shy, that I and others called too much, too loud, and shut them all down. So I asked my dad if this was in any way possible.

My dad just laughed out loud and said, "Call-shy is just a turkey hunter's excuse. If a turkey doesn't come to his call, it's not the calling you or anyone else did to scare those turkeys into silence or move them away from that area for awhile; it is all of the noise and movement, it's the intense hunter activity in there every day.

"It has nothing to do with calling. It's all those people walking everywhere, running to a gobbling turkey, driving Jeeps everywhere, bumping turkeys, hunters skylighted, and all the head bobbing on a turkey's approach. Wait a couple days after all the city hunters leave the mountain and things settle down, then go back to Dryfork Holler and kill your gobbler."

A few years later, around 1973, I made my turkey camp on the main road through national forest land, with a friend who at the time was fairly new at turkey hunting. He usually hunted with a group of hunters west of Potosi, Missouri. This group and others they hunted with as well as others in the area all firmly believed every turkey hunting myth ever told. I invited another friend, an older, seasoned hunter from southern Iron County to join us for a morning of turkey hunting. After his early afternoon arrival in camp and a quick tour of our national forest hunting area, we settled in for a quiet campfire dinner. Not long after dinner, my friend asked if turkeys roosted anywhere close by, especially in the deep holler behind the camp. As I had not heard any turkeys while in camp, and not around camp at daylight, but miles away in a more remote, prescouted area, I really didn't know.

Tom grabbed his old, weather-worn box call and said, "Well, let's find out," as he walked away from our campfire and let her rip with deep, loud, raspy yelps. But before the echo of his call faded away in the distance, and before we had even had time to listen, my other guy in camp went crazy.

"What in the hell you think you're doing?" he yelled at Tom. "I have to hunt around here. What are you trying to do, shut all the turkeys down? Stop calling now!"

I couldn't believe a new hunter had the nerve to yell at a seasoned turkey hunter, someone who probably had killed more turkeys than this new guy had ever actually seen in the woods, someone known for his many years of killing turkeys consistently, not just for himself, but for many others as well. Tom, with a puzzled look on his face at first, shook his head with a big smile as he slowly slid his old call back inside his front pocket. He walked back to camp, loaded his bedroll and gear in his truck, and told me he was sorry, but he had to go—he would go somewhere else where his calling was not judged, and we would have to hunt together another time.

Today, as a hunting professional traveling across America, I find that the call-shy "movement" has grown to huge proportions, to the point of becoming a major roadblock for my many on-the-road turkey hunting adventures. My greatest call-shy challenge is always in Florida. Somehow the Osceola turkey is thought to be the king of call-shy, and Florida seems to be the call-shy capital and the national call-shy headquarters.

"Our turkeys are different," some Osceola hunters and guides tell me. "You might get away with that aggressive calling where you come from. But it won't work here. Our turkeys don't like calling. But if you must, just a soft cluck. The only way to hunt our turkeys is to set up and wait for one to walk by going to or coming from the orange groves. Roosting doesn't work with our turkeys." My all-time favorite, though, is local guides sizing up any of us pros when we come to town, just like a Western gunfighter.

The first time I called turkeys in the Florida swamps was back in 1982; I have hunted in Florida many, many times since then, for outdoor media hunts, shooting outdoor TV shows, or just hunting with good friends. Now don't take this the wrong way—I love Florida, I love the people, all the many friends and family I have from all my many years of hunting, and of working seminars and trade shows in Florida. And I have experienced some great hunts without the interference of the call-shy myth, but they have been few and far between.

Here are just a few examples: guides will take my camera crew and me to the very setup where they (for whatever reason) didn't or couldn't call in a turkey (are you ready for this?), just to see if I can call the turkey, regardless of the real reasons why they didn't call him in. Many times after the first morning's hunt, because of my calling an outfitter has assigned me an area (which I call the "penalty box") with the least chance of me to "booger" their turkeys with my calling. More than once, outfitters have sent me into an area where "no one has killed a turkey in years," just to see if we can. I really do not have time for any of this—I have to get a TV show done, and I usually just pack up and leave.

But I have not always packed up on my own. I have been asked to leave ranches several times because of my hunting and calling style, even though we had completed a TV show with multiple on-camera kills. Now, I have to admit that sometimes it's my own fault. On a ranch with a huge outdoor media hunt, we were told the turkeys were call-shy and did not like calling. The game plan was to sit and wait for turkeys to walk by. Well, I did the first morning, but in so doing, I listened to turkeys on a roost in the distance. That afternoon I asked a ranch hand about that area. Given the okay to go in there, I roosted turkeys that evening.

The next morning, I set up tight on the edge of a field, where four of us witnessed unbelievable roost calling, an in-your-face fly-down, fighting, strutting, and an awesome kill for the show. All this involved two of us calling nonstop, to make it happen. Back at the lodge, tired with travel and the call-shy battle, as I was reviewing some of my footage for the outdoor writers, the outfitter just happened to walk into the room.

Just as soon as he saw the footage and heard our calling on the big screen, he said: "Boy, what in the world are you doing to my turkeys?"

And I said, "That would be killin' 'em, sir." Yep, that's when I was asked to leave.

My greatest challenge in completing a media hunt or outdoor TV show is not always the weather, time of year, or even the turkeys, oddly enough. It's usually the people I have to deal with. There is always some outfitter, guide, or even local hunter who becomes a stumbling block to complete my hunt because of a call-shy mentality. But more often than not, just after my arrival in a new place, immediately a

Several years ago, on my arrival in New England I was greeted with "it's over; the turkeys are all call shy." But I really do not have time for this. I have to guide outdoor writers and complete TV shows, so I hunt like I always do and never hold back on my calling.

call-shy warning is delivered by an "expert" guide with about three years of turkey hunting experience, who has never hunted outside his own county much less away from his home state. It's always the same about calling to "their" turkeys, "their turkeys are different," and "because it won't work here."

"You might be able to call like that where you come from," they say. "But if you call like that around here they won't gobble for a month." Hmm, how do they know that? Do they follow the turkey around for a month just to see if he gobbles?

On many tightly scheduled hunts, I only have three mornings to make it happen, and I am more than willing to listen to the outfitter or guide about his turkeys. They usually know where they roost, where they strut, and where they gobble, which is all very important information, and quite honestly, no one knows the turkeys on their place any better than they do.

Once in the field, as soon as the call-shy thing comes up, I put my plan in place. First morning, I do whatever is asked with how they want me to hunt their place, all the while learning the turkeys' habits in that area. It is on the second day that I start my plan of attack. The last two days, I hunt, scout, roost, and call my way, and we have completed many more shows my way than their way and with a very high success rate, calling so-called "call-shy" turkeys, especially on the last day.

I also find it interesting because it's always that third day when the locals get upset, because they continue to believe my calling is scaring their turkeys. Even after we kill them. (The turkeys, that is.)

Now, I'm not claiming everywhere or everyone I hunt with is into this call-shy phenomenon. I've hunted with some really good outfitters who just tell me to have at it, and I have hunted with guides who turn me loose, and tell me to just do my thing.

But I also have to tell you that after thirty-some years of hunting in Western states, call-shy has never been something I had to deal with during any Western hunt. This includes Rios in Texas, Oklahoma, and Kansas, Merriam's in New Mexico, California, South Dakota, and Wyoming, and everywhere in between. Of all the hundreds of Western hunters, guides, and outfitters I've hunted with over the years, not one of them has ever heard the term call-shy. They don't even know what it is. So is it possible, just maybe, that this call-shy thing only affects the Eastern turkey and the Florida Osceola turkey?

The truth is that it's the hunter's mind that creates more problems with killing turkeys than the turkeys actually do. Turkey hunters everywhere need to realize what a huge mind game turkey hunting really is. Something I talk about in my seminars is how during the heat of battle with a gobbler, the hunter is thinking the gobbler is outsmarting him. Hunters think the turkey has a PhD; they give turkeys human characteristics, and all the while the gobbler is out there just being a turkey.

If a hunter thinks a turkey is call-shy, he does not call as he should to kill the turkey. If, before a hunter begins to call, he thinks a turkey will not come to his call, the turkey will more than likely not come to his call. The mind games that so many hunters play actually prevent them from killing turkeys in many situations. A positive approach, confidence, determination, clear thinking, and a never-give-up attitude kills turkeys.

A great example of the turkey hunter mind game came during one of my media hunts in the late 1990s, in the second week of Missouri's spring gobbler season. With two-year-old gobbler numbers down, older gobblers were covered up with hens. There was plenty of breeding and strutting, but little gobbling. Hunters were frustrated with little response from the gobblers, and during this phase, many times when a hunter did get a tom to gobble to his call, hens would lead the gobbler away. With the first week's statewide kill total way down, hunters were preaching the gospel of call-shy. The season was off, something was wrong with the turkeys—this message was spreading like wildfire throughout Northern Missouri.

My media hunt was scheduled to start in the middle of the second week and run through the weekend. With outdoor writers flying in from all across the country and my professional guides from Arkansas arriving in a few hours, I really needed to find an area for them to hunt without a lot of pressure on the turkeys. A good friend who lives in the area located a 3,000-acre tract of rolling timber with a network of small fields, an awesome timbered river bottom, and an assortment of old crop fields.

Idaho gobbler taken by NWTF public relations director Brent Lawrence during a Western media hunt. "Call shy" with Western Guides and Outfitters has never been much of a problem.
PHOTO BY JOHN HAFNER

My professional guides driving from Arkansas were to meet one of my local guides in town as soon as they arrived and come straight to the new property to meet me, as we had little time with our media hunters arriving the next day. The good thing was that my Arkansas guides had already hunted four states and were seasoned guides and great turkey hunters—a very important element in having a successful hunt for my outdoor writers.

My friend, the ranch manager, and I drove around the property to scout and to learn the lay of the land, to see property boundary lines, and where he had seen gobblers strutting and heard gobbling. As I have done for many years, at each stop I cut and yelped to get an idea of turkey numbers and gobbler locations at around 10 AM. However, the ranch manager was shaking his head in regard to my calling because these turkeys were so "call-shy," he said. Family members on the ranch had little success the first week of season with the call-shy turkeys and it was the worst season ever on this property.

But, as we stopped on an old dirt road on a big long ridge with multiple spur ridges and deep hollers, from what I'd seen I was excited about the chances of a great hunt. These beautiful rolling ridges are just not the usual type of terrain found in northeast Missouri. As I was walking to the back of the truck while digging out my calls, the manager warned me again about calling, and asked if was I sure I wanted to do this "calling thing" before my hunters arrived. During my very first series of cutting and yelping, two gobblers rifled back a reply, just as my guides pulled up to our truck. I asked the manager not to say anything about "call-shy," and after quick introductions, I told my Southern guides that maybe they should kill a turkey before the writers arrived, and get it out of their systems. Of course they were in disbelief that I would allow any hunting before the writers arrived, but I assured them it was okay. I cut again, and both gobblers down in the holler on a bench, and others somewhat closer, rattled again.

"So guys, why are you standing here?" I asked. "Don't you think you should kill those gobblers?" With wide eyes and in a mad rush to pull their guns from the truck, they were falling all over each other. Down the hill they scrambled, stopping only to call quickly, then keep moving. We heard them close the distance, then set up and cut again. Both turkeys were gobbling non-stop, and now sounded like they were in my guys' laps.

After two quick gunshots echoed down the valley, we heard a little flopping and cheering, then all was quiet. Let's see—this entire deal took around five minutes from start to finish. The ranch manager seemed to be in shock or in disbelief as my guys topped the ridge, each carrying a big gobbler, and placed both birds in the back of the truck, as they thanked me over and over.

This is when I ask my guys: "What do they think you're doing? Why would you call like that to these turkeys? The season is off, something is wrong with the turkeys. Don't you know all these turkeys are call-shy? That actually the turkeys are call-shy all across north Missouri this season?"

"NO body told us they were call-shy!" they both replied excitedly.

The moral of the story is that after a twelve-hour drive to get there, no time to talk to anyone, without a clue the season is supposed to be off or that turkeys throughout the area were supposedly call-shy, my guys didn't hold back with calling. They called just as they always do, and with great results.

If hunters believe turkeys are call-shy, they are very hesitant to call, and receive little response to very little soft calling—or no calling—when in fact they actually should be calling. This is the when talk of call-shy spreads like the plague. What it all comes down to is that "call-shy" is just part of the human mind game. It's not the turkeys themselves, but the state of mind of the hunters.

On the lighter side, I've had fun with this call-shy thing many times over the years. Back in the 1990s, while working a turkey media camp in southern Missouri along the Meramec River with some National Rifle Association leaders, talk of the turkeys being call-shy began shortly after my arrival. During the first evening, while our NRA hunters remained at the main lodge relaxing and consuming adult beverages, several of the local guides and I departed for a late evening of roosting. After separating to cover a larger area, the guides and I met right at dark on an old road overlooking a beautiful river bottom. As I walked up, they shushed me, and told to be very quiet because several gobblers had roosted a couple of hundred yards down the main ridge.

I hadn't heard them yet, so I told them I was going to owl hoot. That's when one of the guides grabbed me by the shirt and said: "Listen now, don't you hoot unless you sound just like an owl, or they'll know we're here!"

"So," I asked them, "who are 'they'?"

"The turkeys—they'll know we're here," one of the guides replied.

Shaking my head in disbelief, I said, "Okay, I'll do my best so they won't know we're here."

Several hoots later, and after only a couple of weak gobbles in return, and thinking out loud as I pulled out my mouth call, I said, "Let's warm 'em up a little with some cutting, and a fly-up cackle, and see if there are some other gobblers in this area, too."

This is when one of the guides grabbed me in a bear hug, while frantically reaching for my call case. "What in the world do you think you're doing? If you call, we'll never kill any of our turkeys. Not just tomorrow—but the rest of the week!"

"Okay, Okay, I won't call. After all, we don't want them to know we're here," I said. "I'll call when I roost by myself. Sorry, but it works it's something I've done for thirty years. I get a better reaction with a turkey call than with hooting."

As they started walking back to their truck, shaking their heads in disbelief and disagreement, I quickly ran back to the edge of the road and blew out a pig squeal, a mooing cow, and a chicken. Suddenly both turkeys sounded off in multiple gobbles, and three others farther down the ridge joined in. Grinning, I said, "You see, I didn't turkey call to them . . . so we should be all right in the morning."

Can you believe that they actually spewed rocks against my rental car with their truck tires as they sped off in a huff?

During the next morning's hunt, with a different local guide and my two NRA hunters in tow, the call-shy deal came up once again. After our daylight hunt was busted by a trespasser from state land, we moved to a new area and I really got on my call. Even after a turkey in the bottom gobbled right back at me, my new guide said, "Should you really be calling like that?"

"I really do not have time for this," I grumbled as we quickly moved in for a setup.

As we set up in a low corner of an old field next to the river, our turkey was gobbling just over a hump in the field. As soon as I hit my call again, this turkey was on his way—the only problem was a hunter with a box call on state land, closing fast, yelping as he came. I got back on my call just as I saw not one, but two fans come up over the hump. After witnessing a beautiful double gobble from twin toms, I told my hunters to get their guns up and stay ready. We needed only another fifty yards or so, and it would be showtime.

The box-calling hunter was now at the river's edge, and really close to our fence. He called and both turkeys gobbled, but then they kind of slicked down from strut to half-strut, took on an alert posture, and began to moving to our left. One of my hunters and the guide both asked what was going on. As I repositioned both shooters to our left, I calmly explained our current situation.

"Okay guys, here's the deal. We were doing fine once we closed the distance and called from here. The gobblers thought the hen was coming to them. But when the guy on state ground called, it kind of confused them at first. But because of how I can read turkey body language, and since I have done this for so long, I can almost tell you what those gobblers are thinking.

"Once the other hunter reached the river's edge and called much closer, those turkeys knew he was a hunter—especially the lead bird, which promptly told the other turkey; 'We need to move away from here, that is a hunter, not a hen, and what we think is a pretty girl is really a human with a lynch box call with a rubber band and white chalk.'"

My next aggressive set of calls immediately received two very loud, close gobbles, to our extreme left along the field edge, so I quickly moved my shooters several yards up the field edge and slightly farther to our left. Just as my hunters raised their guns, both gobblers appeared at twenty yards, just as they topped a slight rise in the field.

"Kill 'em," I instructed. Both guns roared, and as cool a double kill as you will ever see concluded our morning hunt.

Of course I did not tell them until after the hunt that turkeys do not know we are calling or hunting them, and that it was our box-calling hunter's movements down at the river's edge that had caught the lead turkey's attention as the hunter was trying to find a way across the river to trespass and get to the gobbling turkeys.

Origins of the Call-Shy Argument

Let's analyze the logic behind the notion that calling can wise up turkeys and make it harder for everybody to score. The flawed assumption by many hunters is that, if they call, and the turkeys don't come, the turkeys aren't coming for other hunters either. They aren't even coming to each other. The mating season has been artificially ended by hunters calling their heads off out there. This is where the belief comes from that those other hunters calling "too aggressively" spoil it for everybody, because they are just adding layers of call-shyness to already educated birds.

My great friend and hunting buddy Frank Imo holding a late morning Illinois "call-shy" gobbler, called in this turkey with a box call.

For starters, think about the natural progression of spring mating season. Boy turkeys are in the mood and fired up about mating season before girl turkeys are. The system works well, in the sense of producing more baby turkeys, because it ensures that girl turkeys won't be ready first, which would create a problem. It makes sense then that the toms take up positions on the dance floor, fight each other over the best spots, and start the dance by themselves so the hens will really be impressed, once they also get good and ready.

On some hunting days, the natural order of things matches pumped-up gobblers against a lot of not-yet-receptive hens, and lucky hunters just happen to be sitting at the base of a tree, right between them. Talk about being in the right place at the right time! When these fortuitous stars align, when you're crossing a fence, if you just squeak the rusty barbed wire up and down with something that approximates a turkey rhythm, you might not have enough time to get your gun off the ground and reloaded before a lovestruck strutter shows up and begins humping your leg.

On such days (and occasionally at other times), hunters who never practice calling can bring big fat gobblers right into their laps, by squeaking out a few noises on their calls of choice. This confirms, in the minds of those hunters, that calling is not an important aspect of spring turkey hunting—you don't have to be a good caller to kill a turkey. As proof, photos of big toms, tails all fanned out, are submitted as Exhibit A. As long as nobody calls too much, the fragile conditions that allow such hunts to play out remain in full force, according to those who subscribe to these beliefs. But if even one person so much as strings together a little bit of that fancy contest-calling crap, it ruins it for everybody. It shuts up the turkeys. It moves them into tunnels they have dug for such emergencies.

Next let's consider the possibility that, when calling does not produce results, it could be that the calling was not realistic enough to get the hoped-for reaction from the birds. When the stars are not perfectly aligned, as above, a lot of hunters set up, call sparingly, and then nothing happens. They might hear a decent amount of gobbling on the roost and get answers to their tree calls, but the turkeys fly down, shut up, and go the other way. Flawed deduction: it was the calling that shut them up and caused them to go the other way.

What if the calling, on the other hand, had struck a chord with those turkeys? What if, even when toms are not likely to break from the harem and come, the caller had engaged the hens? What if the calling got the birds yacking and excited, and the whole works came marching to the source of the sounds, hens ready to see who the heck is picking at them, rounded tail fans trailing along? Would you believe in the value of calling then?

Many hunters have better luck when they call sparingly than when they give in to an experimental mood and call more aggressively. Think about this. If you cannot produce realistic—truly realistic—turkey sounds, would you expect that making those sounds louder and more often would cause turkeys to just come running? However, this is the foundation of the many arguments that "overcalling" screws it up for everybody. The call-shy thing gets repeated all the time, even by call manufacturers, so it's not surprising that a lot of hunters buy into it. In the enthusiastic marketing of the latest super-secret call, the sell message has been known to include the notion that this new sound will call up wizened gobblers that have become conditioned to more traditional calls.

Wild turkeys know authentic turkey sounds when they hear them. They live with other wild turkeys every day of their lives. They call to each other constantly. They come to each other a lot, but not every time. And they don't run or fly away at the first hint of a real yelp. The call-shy case crumbles in the face of reality if you think about how silly it is to presume that wild turkeys can somehow become conditioned to avoid the voices of other wild turkeys.

Believe what you will, but if you knew how many turkeys good callers can bring right to their boot tops, consistently and regardless of the phase of the breeding season and other mitigating factors, you would sit up straight and start practicing immediately. The mating urge doesn't control gobblers all spring long. From minute to minute, what it takes to call up turkeys changes, and the lifetime study of these variables is an important aspect of spring turkey hunting that many hunters are not aware of.

For example, spring weather that turns cold and stormy (it can snow in the Black Hills in May, and tornadoes and big rains come often enough) can call a sudden halt to the mating urge. Head into the woods in the aftermath of these conditions, call subtly like a sweet hen, and you might as well have pulled your sleeping bag over your eyes back in camp. You are not going to call up a turkey. But go forth under those same conditions, and sound like a strange gobbler who's yelping and cutting and poking his index finger into the chest of every other gobbler in the area, and things can be very different. I challenge toms with gobbler yelps, and many springs I call up and kill many more toms using gobbler yelps than hen yelps. It all depends on the situation.

Even under favorable conditions, being able to size things up and adapt can work wonders. If you get a soft gobble in response to excited calling, consider that it's a subordinate tom that wants you to hear him but not any other nearby gobblers. Slide up a little closer to the soft gobble, give him some excited invitations, and get your gun up.

Do everything you can to engage every hen you hear. Try to call up every one, because you don't know when you'll get a bonus silent strutter hanging onto the tow rope. If you engage hens but the source of the hen calling moves away, take a tip from Hawaii turkey guru Jon Sabati. Reposition, and try to sound like a lost hen that wants nothing more than to join the group, and see if they don't come to gather you up.

This is what it comes down to. Your calling has to sound realistic, and to rationalize away the reaction of turkeys to unrealistic sounds is to blame the turkeys and fellow hunters for your own unwillingness to practice enough so you can make those realistic-sounding calls. This gets to the heart of the matter, to the essence of putting the odds in your favor: You should not even bring calls into the woods that you are not proficient with. It isn't macho to use a mouth call if you cannot make realistic turkey sounds with it, and it actually hinders your chances of calling up birds.

Counter to the call-shy culture that permeates turkey hunting camps and message boards, there is no question that your chances of getting close to any given turkey are better if you sound excited to get together with them or are challenging their standing in the social order. Let's consider the possibility that other forces—some natural, some manmade—can quiet turkeys down and even move them to other locations. People pressure is huge. So is the natural order of mating season. When dominance is (sorta) settled, and kingpin gobblers sleep tight with harems of hens, you don't hear nearly as much gobbling as you do at other times, and it's harder for anybody, even real hens, to call up a tom.

The true variable when it comes to calling is that wild turkeys are fickle. It does no good to try to read things into it when you make realistic calls and they still don't come. All turkeys do not come to all turkeys calling to them. Don't worry about why the first one didn't come. Just call to the next one and see if he will. And if nothing seems to be working, practice more—both as a woodsman and as a caller.

One last thing—this is not a plea to fill the air with your calling. Everyone should hunt the way they like best. But, please, can we stop blaming excited and realistic calling when things don't go well out there for all those who are just too scared to call because they somehow believe their calling will make turkeys "call-shy"?

8

Tools of the Trade

OF ALL THE WIDE VARIETY OF HUNTING EQUIPMENT AVAIL-
able for the turkey hunter today, a turkey call is going to be a hunter's most
important tool when it comes right down to killing spring gobblers.

Since my career in the hunting industry began forty-plus years ago, I've
witnessed unbelievable growth and change in the outdoor industry. Turkey
hunting paraphernalia, turkey toys, and accessories are a major part of that
growth. Today there is a wide variety of turkey hunting equipment easily
accessible for every conceivable facet of turkey hunting, especially turkey
calls. One might just begin to wonder how in the world anyone ever killed
a turkey without all the gadgets and bells and whistles now available.

The good news is there are many good products available that will help
hunters on the road to success, but there are also some marginal products
and a few others that are nothing more than gimmicks and a total waste
of your time. I remember a time when there were very few turkey hunting products available, just as how-to information was not obtainable for

turkey hunters. But today's turkey hunter has
easy access to a ton of products and a wealth of
information, including DVDs, books, seminars,
hundreds of magazine articles, and the unlimited
how-to information now available on the Inter-
net, which can all help hunters enjoy a successful
hunt.

However, there is a downside, in that modern-day hunters can become confused from a
constant bombardment of mass marketing and
high-dollar advertising, sometimes for nonfunc-
tional or nonessential products, marketed only
with a "let's-see-how-many-we-can-sell" attitude from some manufacturers. A great example

**The different ways to hold a call determine the
kinds of sounds you can produce.**

Practice your calling skills and learn to use a variety of calling devices to sound like multipliable sounding turkeys.

is a bottled "turkey scent" lure that is supposed to affect the sensory glands in the turkey's beak, with the promise to bring ole tom a-running— hey, just ask "Doctor Tom," the guy wearing a doctor's white coat—he guarantees it works. Or how about those awesome space-age turkey decoys you pull over your feet, then lie down in a thicket and wiggle your feet for realism?

I work in the hunting industry, and I realize I'm very fortunate to be someone teaching and helping others. But just how many gadgets and accessories does one need to shoot a turkey? Just how much more "stuff" is one expected to carry into the woods? Think of it this way: If you load your turkey vest and jacket and pants pockets with everything the pros, seminar speakers, magazine ads, and outdoor television shows tell you must have to kill a turkey, you could not walk, and would more than likely fall over from the sheer weight alone.

Another factor is that too many of today's turkey hunters have become way too dependent on equipment and the latest "magic potion," more so than just relying on traditional, old-fashioned hunting and calling skills. Another reason for this is because we live in a "have-to-have-it-now" world today, a society where everything is right now: fast food, fast service, fast gratification.

And many hunters expect results the same way—they not only expect but demand immediate results, and they also have a "right now" attitude, even when it comes to turkey hunting.

During a recent turkey camp conversation, discussing today's turkey hunting gadgets and turkey toys with my lifelong buddy Ralph Duren, and

Of the wide variety of hunting equipment available today, a turkey call is the most important.

how turkey hunting has changed since we began hunting turkeys back in what we now call the "old days," Ole Ralph kind of went off on a rant about some of the "I-have-to-have-it-now" turkey hunting crowd of today. And I quote: "When hunting public land, way too many guys sound like a chuck wagon coming through the woods, with pockets rattling on their forty-pound turkey vest, and they couldn't climb an Ozark mountain if they had to. So they buy a noisy ATV and trailer to haul it all around, and then drive it right into the turkey woods where the turkeys live, rattling trailer, and all.

"And they usually show up about the time my gobbler is getting into shot-gun range and scare my turkey and everyone else's off. They arrive too late, right after daylight, run the turkeys out of the field, then set up a blind, unload everything, hide the ATV, then set in the blind for thirty minutes tops, then load up and go somewhere else, and wonder why they can't kill a turkey since they bought every gadget known to the free world.

"They have *no* patience and *no* hunting skills whatsoever. They think it should only take twenty-five minutes, just like they watch hunting shows on Outdoor Channel. What I can't understand is how they find me so often! It always happens when nothing is gobbling until I get turkeys going and have them almost in range. You can quote me on that!"

When I'm presenting turkey hunting seminars across the country, I always advise my audiences that turkey call choice will vary from person to person. I preach endlessly about always using what works best for you, what you have confidence in, and remembering to utilize a big helping of common sense. Let's take a look at turkey calls. Many types of turkey call designs can seem very functional at a sports show, sporting goods store, or seminar. But the real test is in the woods, on a turkey hunt, which is when you separate the good from the bad and the downright ugly.

Mouth Diaphragm Calls

The diaphragm turkey call is without question the most popular of all tur-key calls today, and there is a very wide variety of choices as to the number of reeds, type of sound, and colors, as well as some bizarre names. The diaphragm call has come a long way in quality and manufacturing materials, so let's discuss my history of these "mouth yelpers." Way back in the early days, my first choice for calling turkeys was always my voice. The reason I voice-called almost exclusively was because it worked on turkeys and sounded much more like a real turkey than the diaphragm mouth calls of that era.

Quite honestly, I just did not like the sound of the Propolastic, thin, single-reed, diaphragm mouth calls. To me, they did not sound anything like a real turkey. I honestly could not believe turkeys would actually respond and come in to this call, but many did, especially lonely two-year-olds when 90 percent of hens were on the nest.

Fall-calling turkeys was a great deal tougher. A few jakes would respond to this call, but the best success came with peepers scattered from their mommas, with not much success calling older birds, especially fall gobblers. So I continually worked with hand-building mouth calls, to try and find that just-right realistic sound of a real turkey, not just for hunting, but for calling contests as well.

I built my first handmade mouth call to hold the single thin rubber in place without any adhesive tape. I used soft plumber's lead for the frame. I used a condom—Trojan was the best for a single, thin reed. My wife Janet claims that using bare lead-frame calls during all those early years is, without question, why I am so dysfunctional in many ways and what's pretty much wrong with me today.

I fared pretty well in Missouri turkey calling contests in 1975 and 1976 by using this call in combination with my voice. But a whole new chapter with mouth calls opened for me in February 1977, after traveling to Hershey, Pennsylvania, for my first National Wild Turkey Federation (NWTF) conven-

tion. This was also the first time I had the opportunity to visit with turkey hunters from all over the country, not just from my area in the Missouri Ozarks. It was during this first Grand National calling contest that I heard my first double-reed call, and it was pretty obvious that Eastern hunters were way ahead of the game with turkey call building knowledge and with turkey calling skills.

This NWTF conference was also where I first met Jim Clay, Harold Knight, David Hale, and Rob Keck. It was also pretty special because I met Terry Rohm, his brother Robbie, and their dad, Dale Rohm, and all three helped expand my diaphragm calling skills. After that convention, I was ecstatic

The mouth diaphragm call is preferred for aggressive cutting and yelping.

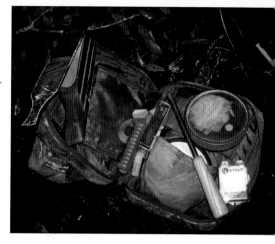

Tools of the trade. My workbench during a turkey hunting setup.

upon my return to Missouri with a pocketful of double reeds, and I honestly believe I was one of the first (if not the first) Midwest hunter to have and to use a double-reed mouth call.

I hand-built my first double reed right after my return, but I was still forced to use condoms, as it was impossible to locate the new rage at the time in mouth calls from the East: surgical latex rubber for the diaphragm reeds. During the spring of 1977, calling with my new double-reed call, I won first place in every contest I entered but one, and placed second in that one. In 1978, the NWTF national convention came to Kansas City, Missouri, and this was where I first met Ben Rodgers Lee, Lewis Stowe, Carl Brown, and Kelly Cooper, just to mention a few.

I also reunited with friends I'd met the year before at the Hershey convention, friends who brought me the new latex for my personal call building. During the spring of 1978, I swept calling contests all across the state and the Midwest, winning almost every contest I entered with my new latex double-reed calls. Winning many calling contests, and consistently killing turkeys, especially for others, created a demand for my turkey calls. Turkey hunters wanted my calls, so Ozark Mountain Calls was born. After I was selling calls to hunters at calling contests, archery shops, sporting goods stores, and even the local Wal-Mart, all who ordered my line requested that I teach their store's customers how to use my turkey calls. These were my first in-store promotions.

At that time, Ozark Mountain Calls offered corncob slate and double-reed calls, sales were good, and we just couldn't build them fast enough, so I had to build mouth calls with the condoms instead, as latex at that time was still impossible for me to purchase in bulk. For call building, I purchased expired dated Trojans by the gross from a good friend at the local drugstore, the same place I'd bought them for my personal call building for many years. After several large call orders came in, I called the drugstore requesting the purchase of all they had in stock, expired or not. The bad thing was that my friend George

During the spring of 1977, with my new double reed call, I won first place in every contest I entered but one, and in that I placed second.

would not be at work that day, but he would have my order with my name on it under the counter for pickup.

In the store at the prescription counter, there is no way to put into words the expression on the face of the substitute pharmacist (who was not a turkey hunter) when I told him why I was there. After he located my multiple boxes and many grosses of Trojans, as he took my money, he leaned over and whispered to me, "Either you are the most popular guy in the county, or you are one really sick puppy."

It got worse on my return home. In those days, my kitchen table was my call-building shop, and a young lady I hadn't seen in some time arrived at my house while I was in town. When I walked into my kitchen, she was on the old dial wall telephone with her sister when I threw my call-building necessities on the table, including several handfuls of the little square deals. Her eyes got very wide, and she excitedly told her sister that she really had to go. She hung up the phone, but I immediately sat down and started building calls, not really sure just when she left my house. Oh, well.

The 1979 NWTF national convention was held in Birmingham, Alabama. Kenny Mounce and I loaded up our old cars and drove to Alabama, and this is where I first met Dick Kirby, Tom Stuckey, and the newest rage in diaphragm calls, the triple-reed mouth call. I also placed second in the first-ever Grand National Owl Hooting contest, which my friend Terry Rohm won by edging me out by one point. (I then won the owl hooting the next year in Niagara Falls, New York, where I first met Paul Butski.)

On our return to Missouri, Kenny and I went to work building triple-reed calls, now with aluminum frames, but still no tape, and other triple reeds with newly acquired surgical latex, and a few with condoms for soft work, as well as tree calls, and the "kee-kee" type calls. Kenny and I were neck and neck in contests everywhere that spring, and we won just about everything we entered.

During Missouri turkey season, in the spring of 1979, Mike Held and I were on a ridgetop on Johnson Mountain, and the reeds in my older call were really stuck together from overuse. This gobbler just down the ridgetop was blowing it out nonstop, and I was in hurry to get my call going, so I pulled really hard on the top reed, and it tore, a chunk in the corner came out, and so I threw the call on the ground and grabbed my last and only call. I pulled on the reeds, and it tore as well. I finally just gave up and threw it in my mouth and blew the call anyway, not sure who was more surprised at the sound: me, Mike, or the turkey, who was now running at me like a racehorse, gobbling every step of the way. I killed the turkey, but did not even go over to the flopping bird, because as Mike was tearing the crap out of his calls, I was too busy looking for the other call I'd just thrown away. Quite by accident I finally found the sound I was searching for in a mouth call, and that fall, several gobblers paid the price. Mike and I swore each other to secrecy, and I did not build this call for anyone or for sale until many years later.

Up in New York in 1980, and in 1981 in Virginia at NWTF conventions, I found I was not the only one with this type of call. My good friend and turkey hunting brother Paul Butski had designed a call, which later became known as a "cutter call," but he cut out a smaller chunk than I had. The other call design was from Lewis Stowe from South Carolina, but he tore out half the top reed. My own call tear size was between Paul's and Lewis's designs. Lewis's call was known as the original two-and-a-half reeds, subsequently the name shortened to the 2.5, and the rest is history.

Later, in 1985 the Ozark Mountain Calls line became part of Hunter's Specialties new H. S. Strut line, and Tom Stuckey and I went to work full time for H. S. Strut. Also, as a call manufacturer, I built mouth calls for H. S., and they wanted a 2.5 for their line, because of the Lewis Stowe design. (I still kept my personal design a secret, showing it to no one.) H. S. Strut requested a much smaller cut in the top reed, however; they still named the call the Cutt'en 2.5, which became the very first mass-marketed cutter call.

Later on I offered one of my newer cutter designs to H. S., which was in their mouth call line for a while, but H. S., the public, or both just did not understand this call or realize what a killer it really was. The name probably did not help—H. S. named the call the Gobbler Yelper. As hunters related spring turkey hunting only to hen calls, and few called to turkeys in the fall, with the resulting slumping sales, H. S. discontinued this call in a year. This is the very same call with which I'd won the 1984 Levi Garret Calling Championships in Crossville, Tennessee, and the 1984 and 1985 National Championships in Arkansas, and you also can hear this call on my 1986 *Eye on the Wild Turkey* video series. My second designed cutter call, back in 1984, was way ahead of its time, and today I continue killing turkeys with that very same call design.

Since that time I have designed several other varieties of this call—double-reed cutter, thicker latex, thinner latex, and set-back reeds. While many competition turkey callers and turkey hunters have discontinued use of the cutter-type calls for their newer designs, I continue using cutters on my DVD productions and while hunting, including in the 2011 Outdoor Life Chasing Spring™ tour.

The cool thing about realism with a call is that things happen that a hunter doesn't see with basic calling sounds, or from calling very soft and very little. When using this call to locate turkeys from a road ditch, we have had hens fly in, land in a tree, and walk on a limb right above my truck, cutting and yelping, an event witnessed by many, including my friend Rick Story. I built Rick this call, and he kept his word by not showing my design to anyone. Another time when I was using this call during an H. S. video shoot, a hen flew in from a ridge above us and hit the ground calling, then tried to climb into the blind with me and the cameraman.

Another interesting note: I ask hunters in turkey camps everywhere what they think about the call and if they like the sound, and they usually say no. I was in a New England camp one time with a group of writers and industry people. We were sitting in the yard barbecuing in the afternoon, and I asked them all to listen to several of my calls. I blew two different calls, and they all really liked both of them. But the third call no one liked, and they suggested I use the other two and not this call. But the third one is the call turkeys really respond to best, and I've killed turkeys from Florida to New England using this same call, during times when no one else was killing turkeys.

The last couple of years I've been using my favorite mouth call for spring hunting, and it is death in the spring, a real "cutting machine." The sound has more of a "chop-yelp" to it, more snappy, like a pissed-off hen, and it really tears up spring gobblers. I also made this call for H. S., and it was also in the line for a while and lots of hunters really liked it. It is a 1.5, a double-reed cutter made with the same cuts as my triple-reed.

The old-time "scratch call" was a type of friction call very popular in the Ozarks back in the day.

Find a mouth call that works best for you, one you have confidence in. Do not rely on what your friends or other hunters tell you—go with what the turkeys tell you. If your calling consistently has the hens responding, yelping, and cutting to your calling, you are in the game no matter what anyone else thinks of your calling.

Box Calls

Those who hunt with me know how much I depend on a well-tuned "real-hen-sounding" box call. A good piece of advice for all turkey hunters—if you really would like to sound like a real hen, as you should to kill any gobblers—find a good box call and keep it with you on every hunt. The old-time "scratch call" was yet another type of small box-type friction call that was very popular in the Ozarks back in the old days. Many hunters, including my Grandpa, sanded and chalked their gunstocks to call with ease with their guns up in place.

I love the sound of old-time box calls. Those handmade works of art produced real turkey sounds, with a pretty double high-low yelp. You will have to go through a lot of box calls in stores and at shows to find a really good one.

Box calls are also very easy to use: simply pull the lid (without picking it up) across the calling edge, and learn to call with turkey rhythm. One of the things I do, which is different from the way some hunters use a box call, is to use the bottom of the call to strike against the lid of the call rather than using the lid of the call to strike the sides of the box. I do this by holding the

Box calls are easy to use.

To sound like a real hen, carry a
good box call on every hunt.

lid in my left hand straight up, and then holding the
box in my right hand and hitting the box against the
lid, to cut and give loud, excited yelps.

One of the things to remember about a box call
is that the different ways you hold a call determine
the kinds and variety of sounds you can produce.
Many times, just changing your hand position in
the way you hold the call will actually change the
sounds that the box call produces.

To produce yet another sound, I hold the box in
my left hand, with the paddle handle up, two fingers holding the page end, and stroke the lid across
the edge for yelping. But this is also the best way
to cut on a box call, with using rapid short strokes
against the edge. My box call is loud when needed, in open country or windy
weather, but also soft when needed, for close-in realism on a calm day. I use
my box call for locating turkeys at long distances during a hunt, but also for
roosting turkeys. They respond right at dark better to a turkey sound than to
any locater-type call.

For new hunters asking what call they should choose, I recommend a
good-sounding box call, for ease of use, but also because in the hands of a nov-
ice, a good box sounds more like a real turkey than any other turkey call. The
box call is a very effective turkey call, but after hard use, temperature changes,
and simple handling, many boxes need to be retuned and rejuvenated.

I have tuned thousands of box calls
in the manufacturing processes, at sports

Calling turkeys is a skill, but one worth
learning well. A good box call is one of my
favorites. To acquire a different sound,
I hold the box in my left hand with the
paddles handle up, and with my two
fingers holding the page end, I stroke the
lid across the edge for yelping. This is also
the best way to cut on a box call, with
using rapid short strokes against
the edge.

I love the sound of old-time box calls; those handmade works of art produce real turkey sounds, with a pretty durable high-low yelp. You have to go through a lot of box calls in stores and at shows to find a modern one that compares to them.

shows and seminars, and for hunters in camp. But there's a fine line between tuning and ruining a call, and the last thing a call manufacturer wants is someone haphazardly messing with their box calls, then sending them back, saying they are defective. Most quality box calls are relatively easy to tune. However, there are some of today's mass-marketed calls (made with plastic parts) that are far more difficult to tune.

Several factors cause the loss of quality sound. With regular use, for example, the lid screws back out slightly, deadening sweet yelps. More often, calling edges will wear down, or oil, dirt, and grime will collect on the edges, causing a loss in tone. The best place to begin is to clean the edges and the paddle surface with very fine steel wool or very fine sandpaper. Use just enough pressure to clean but not sand the wood. Now chalk your call lengthwise, being sure to go *with* the grain of the wood.

Now listen to the call, to adjust to how you want the call to sound. If your call sounds a little off or just doesn't sound the way it used to, a screw adjustment may be necessary. Start by marking the screw position with a black

Winter is the perfect time to clean and tune your box call.

Always clean one direction, with the grain of the wood.

Lightly clean calling edges with a fine steel wool or sanding pad.

Box call screw will back out slightly with use.

marker, using this as a reference point. Because it is most likely that the screw has loosened from repeated use, tighten it just a touch by turning it clockwise. Now try the call. If there is a worn spot in the lid or side rail, or the screw turned just from use, you should now be good. Try the call again. Repeat the process until you hear the right sound.

Typically, the calling rails on the bottom portion of the box are curved. There are two reverse radiuses where the lid or paddle meets the bottom edge. Move the paddle to the middle of the bottom edge's radius, placing the exact center of the lid's radius to the centermost part of the call-bottom radius. If the call is properly tuned, the paddle should sit in the center of both radiuses. These steps always bring life back into my favored box calls, and should work well for you, too.

Mark screw and lid for reference point to return to if needed.

Adjust the screw clockwise slightly and try the call, then repeat as necessary to achieve a good sound.

A quick story about tuning a box call: Several seasons ago, Joel Shipman and I were hunting in northeast Missouri all morning, with little success. Some of our problem was self-inflicted, with us bumping a few birds, but we also encountered hens that took our gobbler away from our calling to their happy place. This particular season was a tough one: open woods, little gobbling at daylight, and overall kill numbers were way down all across the state. Feeling defeated, by late morning we returned to Joel's house, arriving about a half hour prior to the 1 PM closing time for the day. While we were unloading our gear in his driveway, Joel asked if I would check and tune his box call. Pulling the lid across the edge several times, I agreed his box could use a little tune-up. I continued stroking the lid as I adjusted the lid screw.

Then, just as I said, "There it is, that's how it's supposed to sound," a turkey gobbled behind Joel's house to his newly tuned call. After laughing out loud because I'd said the call was right and a turkey gobbled, and realizing we had little time left for the day's hunt, we grabbed our guns and video camera and cut across his backyard toward the gobbling turkey. (Joel has permission on land behind his home, but had had little success there earlier in the season.) We moved past the clothesline, around the swing set, and past his deer archery targets, stroking the box call as we went. About seventy-five yards behind his house, inside the woods and at the edge of a beanfield, two very loud gob-

bles went off right in front of us. With no time to sit down, I turned on my camera and loaded my gun. Joel stepped to my left, standing as he raised his gun.

I saw both gobblers at about fifty yards, in full strut. They folded and dropped into a low area while coming right at us. I cut on my mouth call, we heard one really loud, close gobble, and they stepped up in front of us at about ten yards. Two quick shots and we had a double kill on the ground, with one minute remaining in the day's hunt. Now, earlier, we couldn't buy a turkey, and now we had a double that all started with a little box call tuning in the driveway. Oh well, so it goes with turkey hunting.

Two quick shots and we have a double kill on the ground.

Slate and Glass Calls

From my very first corncob and cedar-striker slate call, to later years using corncob with acrylic striker, and then on to pan-type calls, I have always liked these types of friction calls and had great results for years calling and killing turkeys with them. In more recent years, new styles of glass calls offer additional opportunities for realism with friction calls. Today, I really enjoy using a glass or a slate call like the H. S. Strut Glass Witch Call anytime I'm hunting.

Remember that each individual hen has a distinct voice, and I believe that by using various calls you may sound like a particular hen that the gobbler knows. You will know when you strike the right chord, when you hit that hen sound the gobbler has been responding to all spring, a real hen in his area. Therefore, I use several different calls every time I go hunting in order to find just the right call that will speak to and elicit an answer from any gobbler I'm hunting.

I hunt turkeys the way I fish for bass. Let me give you an example. When you go bass fishing, you're constantly changing lures until you decide on a lure that the bass will take whenever you cast it. Turkey hunting is the same way. You should use many types of calls until you find the one the gobbler will answer and come to. Generally, I'll use different calls to sound like three or four hens, to bring a gobbler into gun range.

One of my favorite times to use the H. S. Strut Wood Witch Call is early in the morning. I like to do a tree call on the Wood Witch because I can

Another of my favorite friction calls and one I always have with me when turkey hunting is the Ring Zone Starfire.

call softly and produce soft clucks and purrs that sound just like a hen on a limb. Other times I prefer to use the Wood Witch would be after I've called a gobbler in close with a box or a diaphragm call, and I can hear the turkey strutting and drumming, but can't see him. That's when I pull out the Wood Witch, and give him some putts, purrs, and beautiful "clear rasp" yelps to close the deal.

I fell in love with the Glass Witch when the friction call first came out. It's a glass call in which I have a lot of

You struck the right chord when you hit that hen sound the gobbler has been responding to all spring—a real hen in his area.

confidence. For late morning or mid-day locating, I like to use the H. S. Strut Ring Zone Ceramic Call. This call rocks with unbelievably loud, sharp cutting and yelping. And another of my favorites that I always carry is the Ring Zone Starfire. Hunter's Specialties has a wide variety of friction calls, and they are all good. So pick the one that suits you best.

Calling Information

Now let's cover some basic calling information. When I locate a turkey, I start trying to call him in with two calls—a box call and a mouth diaphragm call. I like to use more than one call so that I sound like a flock of hens rather than one individual hen. I believe that sounding like a flock of hens will pull more gobblers in quicker than sounding like only one hen. So whenever I locate a gobbler, I will begin to call to him with both the box and mouth diaphragm calls.

I like the mouth diaphragm call for my aggressive cutting and yelping. The squeaky wheel gets the grease, I learned many years ago, and the aggressive and vocal, dominant "real" hen gets the gobbler.

Every situation is different, but I usually use my box call to speak to the turkey the first or second time. Once I have the turkey gobbling and coming, I'll change to the mouth diaphragm to continue to call to him, especially if the situation is long-range. Although I use a wide variety of diaphragm calls, I prefer the 2.5 cutter-type diaphragm calls. I believe that hunters really need to learn to use and carry four or five different diaphragm calls.

Although the 2.5 is my favorite, on some mornings during the spring, when the turkeys won't answer that call, I'll change to a different diaphragm call, like a double-reed cutter, and be able to work a bird. You never see a fisherman go out on a lake with only one or two lures, and a turkey hunter shouldn't ever go into the woods with only one or two calls.

Once I locate a gobbler, I use six or seven different calls to try to bring in that turkey. I'll usually use a box call and a diaphragm call to start the turkey coming to me. Then I'll change and use two or three different diaphragm calls to try to just keep the turkey coming. As the turkey gets close, I'll use a different diaphragm call and the Wood Witch to bring the gobbler into gun range.

Also remember that not all turkeys will gobble to all calls every day. I've hunted on one farm where the only call the turkeys will gobble to is a diaphragm call. So I just talk to the turkeys with the diaphragm. The next morning, I'll go to another farm a quarter to a half-mile away, and not get a single turkey to respond to a diaphragm. But they may light up the woods with their gobbling when I use a box call. Always carry a variety of calls. Many times, just changing the type of call you're using will make a turkey gobble.

So choose a call that fits your needs, practice religiously with that call to gain confidence, then move on to other types of calls and learn to use them all as well. This will make you a very good turkey hunter who will consistently call turkeys to your gun, every season.

From my first corn cob and slate call up to the new pan type calls, like the HS Wood Witch, I have always had great results calling and killing turkeys with slate and glass calls.

9

What is Aggressive Calling?

OKAY, I ADMIT IT, I AM A "YELPALCOHOLIC." YES, AND I HAVE a problem, but I'm getting help from everywhere across America, I'm getting better with my therapy sessions spent killing turkeys for ninety-plus days each spring. Yes indeed, in many turkey hunting circles, I'm considered a way too aggressive caller, one who does nothing but make turkeys call-shy.

In addition, I've heard through the grapevine, I call nonstop only to hear myself call. That entire fancy stage calling stuff just doesn't belong in the woods. Well, sorry, but all of the above is totally ridiculous, especially when my calling is nothing more than a duplication of turkeys, just like I've heard real turkeys call everywhere I've ever hunted. It's very apparent to me that those who make such accusations, who point fingers, have little experience or knowledge of wild turkeys, and more than likely only repeat what others say. However, I guess there are some who continue to believe this crap that I call too much, I call too loudly, I'm too aggressive, and I make turkeys call-shy.

But maybe one should reconsider; maybe there is a sliver of truth to these accusations, which might be true if only we didn't consistently leave behind piles of feathers everywhere we hunt in the U.S. and Mexico. How do you argue with years and years of success? Each and every year while chasing spring, my too-loud, too-aggressive calling is directly responsible on average for thirty-plus kills from Florida to New York. And this number is much higher if you include every hunter I call for during my outdoor media hunts.

Professional turkey hunters have to consistently kill turkeys, from the South to the Northeast, documenting as many as thirty to forty kills every spring for TV cameras and outdoor writers. Usually this takes place with no fewer than five people with us at all times, in the rain, in the snow, in the wind, and in places one has never seen before daylight. Without aggressive, realistic, hardcore calling, this success would just not be possible.

Late morning New England hunt. I had to really get on the turkey call to make this on-camera double happen.

I'm not sure who wrote that imaginary rulebook on calling that describes aggressive calling as bad, and says that calling too much and calling too loudly is a sin. It's the same book that outlines all the rules of engagement, the rules I break and continue to break time and time again during all my hunts everywhere.

But how or what is considered "aggressive" calling? Just who determines what aggressive calling might be? With old-time turkey hunters, any sound made after three yelps and one cluck during the entire morning would be considered aggressive. Many hunters in the Southern states would consider any calling that is not "soft calling" to be aggressive.

I would think it is all just a matter of opinion. One's personal style or method of calling may or may not be considered aggressive depending on when and where it's done, the time of year, and what the birds may be doing at that time. I do know from my experience that the term "aggressive calling" varies from hunter to hunter and also depends on where in the country you hunt. Any sound I make in the South is considered aggressive, but in Pennsylvania, New York, or Massachusetts, my calling never raises an eyebrow—with the exception of nonstop cutting on a mouth call while beating a box call to death, gobbling, then flopping my hat while fighting, purring to simulate a fight—OK, maybe just a little bit of overkill.

To add to all this, there is something my lifelong friend and turkey hunting brother Ralph Duren said once at a major sports show seminar, something I find quite fascinating. As Ralph was pre-

These days, to be able to cover a lot of ground, most professional hunters haul a video crew and all related equipment in an electric ATV when they're out in the field.

paring to take the stage during a program all about calling, the speaker on stage just before him—a self-proclaimed turkey hero—went into digression and spoke in great detail about how calling is overrated, hunters call too much, contest calling does not belong in the woods, and too many of today's pros overcall, shutting turkeys down and making turkeys call-shy.

After Ralph calmly took the stage and thanked everyone for coming, with a huge smile he leaned into the microphone and said, "It always amazes me how a seminar speaker with such little calling skill can make such outrageous claims about calling, when in fact it's always someone who can't call, calls terribly, has little calling ability, and quite honestly has no idea how turkeys really respond to calling.

"Those who make these outrageous claims usually have little self-esteem and call very little, because they believe such nonsense that a turkey sound will make turkeys call-shy. Just because they have little success calling turkeys and sound nothing like a turkey, it is astonishing they will condemn others' success, instead of learning from them. Unbelievable."

As you probably know, the old school of turkey calling was to yelp softly three times, every half hour by your watch. If a turkey responded, you'd just shut up and let the gobbler look for you. This soft three-yelp method will still work at times—if everything is right, hens are on the nest, there's little hunting pressure on turkeys, and the weather is perfect—and only during the brief time span of the mating season.

Sorry, but times have changed. With the success of restoration programs and the huge numbers of wild turkeys, there is more hen competition for hunters to deal with than ever before in the history of turkey hunting. Three soft yelps rarely close the deal anymore. Aggressive calling is the only way for hunters today to compete with

Hawaiian guide Jon Sabati, Ray Eye, Jay Cassell, and Jay Norman at the Hulett motel in Wyoming. Jay took this Merriam's during early season when aggressive calling to draw in the hens was the only way to kill a gobbler.

Bill Hoefgen, Ray Eye, and Rob Keck with Ray's late afternoon Kansas "limb hanger" after non-stop Ray and Rob team-calling to hens that this gobbler was following. Bill stated he had never in his life heard so much aggressive calling in one place and at one time.

real hens. I always call aggressively—whatever the term "aggressive" might be—to work turkeys up into a frenzy; only because I can kill more of them by doing just that.

In reality, all hunters should always keep an open mind. Be willing to try something else if what you're doing is not working. But more importantly, call depending on how turkeys are reacting at the time you are hunting them. How I call or when I call all depends on the turkeys, but I always call with inflection and feeling—not necessarily louder, but more excited.

Take the time when I was cutting and yelping nonstop in a very high Texas wind, and three Rios came running, then flew across an eight-foot-high fence, crossed a creek, and circled behind us, as it was difficult for them to follow the sound of my calling in the high wind. I quickly turned around and repositioned my hunter, an editor of a national magazine. He shot the lead turkey running right at us, but then he jumped up and marched back at me screaming, and I quote, "I cannot believe you called like that! I would never call to a turkey like that!"

To which I calmly replied, "See that dead turkey over there? Go over and tell that to him."

On the positive side are the hundreds I've hunted with over the years who never complained about my calling. Since hunting with me, many have grown into awesome turkey killers, especially the gals and youngsters, who didn't have an opinion on calling, and still use my tactics and calling style today. So I guess I leave a lasting impression on many people—some good, some not so good, and some bad. One impression I didn't even realize was with good friend and outdoor writer, Doug Howlett. I just happened to read one of his turkey hunting articles. The interesting thing was that this article was not about me, but rather a hunt he did with someone else. In his article, Doug was talking about a hen marching in that was worked up from his calling, and

I quote, "That hen turkey was yelping more than Ray Eye on a pot of coffee and a can of Red Bull." Yes, I'm really proud of that statement.

Who's to say what is aggressive, or what is right or wrong? All hunters should always use what works best for them. I believe hunters' calling styles are dependent on their experience, whether it's limited experience or hunting for many years. I find that most call the way someone told them to call, maybe from what they have read somewhere, or something they heard at a seminar.

I call and have always called depending on what the turkeys are doing, and how they are calling at the time and place of my hunt. One thing I have always said in regard to what many say is aggressive calling, is that I always call like turkeys. And I listen and learn from real hens, not from other people.

After some forty-plus years of hunting turkeys, I have never heard

It took hard calling to kill this New England gobbler. Three soft yelps rarely close the deal anymore. Aggressive calling is the only way for hunters to compete with real hens today.

a wild hen, or any wild turkey for that matter, that really wanted to go to another turkey, locate another turkey, or was trying to mate during the mating season, that soft-yelps three times and then waits. Calling very little and very softly is not how turkeys call when they are excited or attempting to locate other turkeys. From my experience it is the "aggressively" calling hen that usually gets the gobbler.

All I can say is that I only hunt and call as the turkeys tell me, and that the way I call is how I hear turkeys calling. I keep an open mind, making changes as necessary. I adjust my calling dependent on the situation, time of year, weather, and as the turkeys and the terrain dictate—and if I am labeled an aggressive caller as a result of that, so be it.

10

Turkeys are Just Turkeys

I WOULD LIKE TO SHARE SOMETHING WITH YOU: TURKEYS are turkeys, wherever in America you may live, and anywhere you hunt.

Yet I continue to hear: "Oh, but our turkeys are different." Everywhere I travel, it's always the same: "You might get away with calling like that where you're from, but our turkeys are different, and that kind of calling will not work here."

Well, I'm sorry, but from my years of experience hunting all subspecies of turkeys, I have to tell you, turkeys are just turkeys wherever I hunt. I've been really fortunate, actually blessed, to have hunted turkeys all over the United States and Mexico. I've hunted in Florida, Alabama, Mississippi, Georgia, the Northeast, the Midwest, the West, and Hawaii. I've also hunted turkeys in the wilds of Old Mexico and the ocellated turkey of the Yucatan Peninsula.

Take the Gould's for instance, a turkey that is supposed to be different from turkeys in the U.S. The Gould's turkey lives in a land of few fences, with flocks of them moving freely, seeming always to have somewhere else to go, and flashing us glimpses in the wiry underbrush. Both tall and large, Gould's turkeys look bigger than our turkeys, yet they're still much the same. But just like turkeys everywhere, they respond very well to calling.

Hens go to toms and toms to hens, just like anyplace else, and toms fight each other for the right to court hens, and hens pretend not to notice grand gobblers on fire and expanded for them to see.

Hawaiian gobbler taken by Jay Cassel during a Hawaii media hunt. From left, our guide and friend, Jon Sabati, Jay, Linda Powell of Mossberg, and Gordy Krahn of *North American Hunter* magazine.

The Gould's in Mexico responded no differently than do the other subspecies of turkeys.

You might find it interesting that I utilize the same techniques and hunting strategies everywhere, on all these subspecies, and I call exactly the same—except for the ocellated turkeys in the Yucatan. The males sing, and the hens whistle, but they still act like all turkeys. I don't change anything. If there is any difference in hunting any of the subspecies of turkeys, it isn't the turkeys themselves, but the multitude of terrain variations. A hunter will simply need to adjust setups and how to move on gobblers dependent on the features of the hunting terrain.

The hunting strategies and calling tactics I employ in the Missouri Ozarks are the same ones I utilize in north Missouri, Alabama, Mississippi, New York, Pennsylvania, California, and Hawaii. It's my experience that all turkeys are just turkeys everywhere. So don't get confused when someone says, "Oh, you might do that where you've hunted, but you can't do that here."

Another thing you should remember when you hear turkey hunters say, "Merriam's are easy," or "Rios in Texas are easy" is that these subspecies may *seem* easy only because they are relatively unpressured. The fact is that any subspecies of wild turkey, anywhere, whether it's the Eastern, the Osceola in Florida, the Gould's in Mexico, the Rio Grande, or the Merriam's, will become more "difficult" if the birds receive a lot of pressure. I do not like to use the phrase "hunting pressure" because it really all comes down to people pressure.

When I first hunted with my great friend Jon Sabati in Hawaii, he located turkeys with a turkey call no different from the way we do back in Missouri.

Rios on this Texas ranch were supposed to not like calling, but as with turkeys everywhere, calling was very effective.

Excessive human activity in any hunting area creates a lot of pressure on birds; it will shut birds down, period. It doesn't matter where you're hunting, pressured birds are pressured birds. But the way I hunt turkeys and the way I call turkeys are the same tactics I use everywhere I've ever hunted wild turkeys.

Case in point and a great example comes from back in the early 1980s during an outdoor writers' hunt in western Oklahoma. After arrival at camp for our first hunt with this particular outfitter, our writers were broken into groups of three. After our camp rules session and hunt plan meeting, our appointed guide drove us out to the area scheduled for our group for a little scouting prior to the next morning's hunt. Our guide explained that we would be hunting with rifles, because these turkeys are different. Turkeys in this part of Oklahoma just do not like calling, he said, so our outfitter had three blinds set up in places where turkeys will walk by, at around 8:30 AM. Now, while I am very opposed to rifles for turkey hunting, I'm not completely opposed to hunting blinds. One must understand that this hunt took place a long time before today's blind mania, before hundreds of styles of manufactured blinds were available, and my successful hunting style for many years was always "run and gun," and I'm very dependent on calling to make things happen.

But being outdoor media and having an agreement with the outfitter to help promote his business with magazine articles, we agreed to start our hunt in the outfitter's blinds, though we would much rather have been hunting with our shotguns. The outfitter agreed to allow us to hunt with our shotguns, but continued to stress that we should not call, because turkeys in this area would not respond to calling, and he actually suggested we leave our turkey calls in camp.

After our early morning arrival at the hunting area, our guide drove us down a narrow sand road, dropping us off one at a time at the three individual blind assignments. I was the last hunter he dropped off, and he wished me luck, saying he would be parked out at the main gate if we needed him. I guessed that for the guide, this "drop off and sit in a blind" was a good way for him to catch up on his sleep. After I settled in, first I checked my calls—yes, I had my calls with me. Then, after carefully loading my gun, I leaned it safely in the corner of my blind and quietly awaited daybreak.

The first gobbler rattled while it was still dark as the inside of a tractor tire, but as the light gradually increased, so did the gobbling, and it was really unbelievable. Gobbling started in the northeast, to my left, then rolled like thunder down a river bottom and all the way around to my right. I was not sure how many Rios roosted in these river bottom cottonwoods, but as a Missouri boy from the Ozarks, I had never heard anything like this before. There was no way I could sit in this blind until 8:30, so I grabbed my gun and stepped out of the blind. Even at over 300 yards away, I could plainly see the river bottom trees were full of turkeys.

After stepping up and standing on a slightly elevated hump for a better view of the roost, I made a mental plan of attack for the best approach to close the distance. Watching turkeys fly down, I planned a setup in the same direction of travel as the gobblers flying from the roost to my left. I decided to owl hoot, before I dropped off into the drainage to hide my movement to the northeast.

I owl hooted about as loud as I ever have, because of this wide-open country, and the response was nothing short of amazing. Gobbling started to my far left and came down through the river bottom like the wave of 50,000 fans in a football stadium. As I moved down the ditch, ever closer to the river bottom, hens, jakes, and gobblers were really blowing it out. They made every vocalization I've ever heard from a wild turkey—nonstop yelping, cutting, cackles, gobbles, kee-kee runs, gobbler yelps, fighting purrs—I got to tell you, for turkeys that did not like calling, these turkeys seemed to really like doing a lot of it.

As the ditch became deeper and began to widen, and I approached

My buddy and turkey hunting "brother" Paul Butski with me in Montana during a television shoot for *Turkey Revolution*. Merriam's turkeys in Montana respond to our calling just as well as anywhere else.

a slight rise in a clearing, I checked for any sign of birds in the clearing and then climbed up onto the rise. Spotting a small grove of trees about twenty yards to my left, I quickly moved low and to my left, and plopped down against the biggest tree while digging out my calls. There was a good-size clearing out in front of me, a sand-covered hump out toward the middle, and a row of trees running from my setup and angling back toward the turkeys' river bottom roost, about 150 yards away. Turkeys were now yelping and gobbling 180 degrees out in front of me. I rested my gun on my knee and hammered yelps and cutting from my old box call, and the response was unreal, both gobbles and yelping. So I heated up my mouth yelper, and even before I finished my first series of yelping and cutting, right out in front of me, four large, white-tipped fans appeared from just over the sand-covered hump.

Pulling my gun tight against my cheek, I yelped and cut like a dominant hen that's mad at the world. All four strutting toms immediately folded up, and the race was on, sprinting across the sand with bodies rocking in a mad dash toward my hiding place. As the four amigos slowed their stride at twenty yards, I aimed at the bird on the right just as he dropped back in strut, putting loudly on my mouth call. His head went up, my gun went bang, and it was over.

This was unreal. Even before the sun broke the horizon, here I was heading back to my blind carrying a western Oklahoma Rio, a hunt with a kill taking less than ten minutes from start to finish. I decide to detour on my way out and stop by one of the guy's blinds, and as I approached holding up my gobbler for him to see, I asked Ben how much longer he was planning to stay in his blind and wait for a turkey to walk by. I knew his answer when it didn't take him very long to be standing next to me. I lay my tagged bird in his blind, and we took off in the same direction I had just come from. We hadn't gone very far when we heard our first gobble about a hundred yards to our left, in a low place among a grove of trees. After a quick setup, my first series of calls was greeted with an excited gobble from the grove of trees. But as I aggressively cut on my mouth call, a gobble exploded directly behind us. We quickly spun around and Ben just barely got the gun up before a fast-walking Rio appeared less than thirty feet from our setup.

Ben slapped the trigger, and the tom folded in a pile. Ben fell backward on the ground laughing hysterically—the hunt had maybe taken about five minutes. Our third hunter, Mike, was standing outside his blind when we returned, and was more than willing to take a break from his sit-and-wait tactics.

Well the short of it is, Mike killed his gobbler a half hour later, and we decided to walk out to the road instead of waiting on the guide, and I am glad we did. The entire old roadbed along the river bottom was covered with morel mushrooms. We filled every turkey vest, took off T-shirts to tie into bags, and even filled an old bucket we found in a shed.

Arriving at the gate to the main road around 9:30, we saw our guide asleep in his truck, and as we climbed the gate, the outfitter pulled up in his truck. Climbing from his truck he proudly stated, "See, I told you they would walk by at 8:30." As both he and the guide admired our turkeys, they claimed the mushrooms we picked were poisonous, so I told him that's okay, we would take care of these "poison" mushrooms.

"And, no," I said, "we didn't exactly wait until 8:30 to kill these turkeys— we called them." Yeah, he was a little mad at first. But then he asked how I called the turkeys, and I quickly pulled out my calls for a little calling demo. The chances of what happened next were pretty low, but three different turkeys back in his lease gobbled at my calling demo. The outfitter asked me what sound I'd made and how I had made it.

Outdoor writer Mark Strand with a Wyoming Merriam's that reacted to the same calling Mark uses in his home state of Minnesota.

And the rest is history. Now the outfitter has his guides hunting with calls we supplied, and after a few lessons, they changed to calling turkeys instead of waiting for them to walk by, and his hunter success rate went way up. The rest of the story on the mushrooms is that we cleaned and fried some of our bounty in his camp. Our outfitter, his guides, and friends and neighbors came to watch, all the while telling us they were poison. But it didn't take very long for them to realize what they were missing out on.

But the rest of this story is even better. Leaving Oklahoma for our Ozarks camp on the Mineral Fork Creek, we brought the rest of the mushrooms along with us for the ride. That spring was not a good year for morels in Missouri. Very few people found any, and we were having a late spring. Our first night in Missouri camp, we had a big, old-fashioned mushroom fry for our local hunters and our outdoor writers. The best part was, when asked where we found so many mushrooms, we just pointed to the national forest ridges next to camp. I'm not really sure how long those people searched the woods for those Oklahoma mushrooms.

A more recent example that turkeys are just turkeys comes out of the great state of New York. I flew into New York State several years ago to run camera, field produce, and call turkeys for a scheduled hunter for a national television show on Outdoor Channel.

As with almost everywhere I work, the first thing I heard from the local guide was, "Okay, our turkeys are different. I'll do the calling, because the way you call in Missouri will not work here. You just run that camera. I'll take care of the rest." The first morning of our hunt, I remained quiet, but I ran camera for interviews and for scenic shots for a B-roll, because our guide didn't get a turkey even close to any of our multiple setups to film one.

This included a total bust at daylight. You see, he didn't roost turkeys, and gambled on a setup where he'd observed birds several weeks previously. The second day was pretty much like the first, except that we walked a lot more, with more setups and calling sessions than on the first day. However, during both days I kept a mental note on distant gobbles and areas with good signs, and learned the lay of the land. On the afternoon of the second day, I reviewed my camera footage and listened to turkey audio to get a better idea of where I needed to take my hunter the last morning in this camp and in New York.

The highest concentration of gobbling in the distance that first morning was way across a valley about a mile away, so I checked the outfitter's topo maps to check out the terrain and to make sure it was part of his property; it was. I told everyone in camp I would not make dinner and had some work to do and I would see them all later that evening. I drove my rental car close to the ridgetop location on a county road, grabbed my camera, and walked across a long wide field to the timber's edge. I moved inside the cover checking for signs as I moved and called to locate gobblers. On my third setup, I heard two gobblers just up the ridge from me. Grabbing my gear, I moved up the ridge closer to the corner of the field. By checking the map and by looking across the valley, it was clear I had found the area where I'd heard birds from a roost the first and second mornings.

As roost time approached, I really got on my call. Gobblers, jakes, and hens opened up just below the ridge, and continued right up until they flew up to roost just below me on a big bench of the main ridge. I waited until dark and slipped out. On my return to camp I first told my hunter I'd roosted some turkeys and he was very excited and happy, but our guide was not so cool with it. However, the outfitter, who depends on TV coverage to help promote his business, wasn't quite as upset as the guide, and gave the OK for us to hunt my roosted birds at daylight.

Our guide, my hunter, and I all moved in to the roost early the next morning. Of course I would have liked this deal much better if the guide slept in or stayed in camp, but we had to have a guide with us when hunting the property. After we quietly made our way across the field in the dark, I asked the guide to stay back a little as I set up our hunter. After setting up my hunter just out in front of me, so I could shoot video just over his right shoulder, I set up my tripod, camera, and microphones, and then settled in to wait for daylight.

The magic time was close. I was running camera to record morning nature sounds and to capture the morning wake-up calls of the turkeys, when I heard something in the leaves behind me. Turning slightly, I barely saw the guide slowly crawling toward me, so in a whisper I asked him what he needed. The guide scooted up close to the back of my tree and told me, "Okay, now listen—you're not in Missouri anymore, and these turkeys do not like that pop, pop fancy calling crap you do. First of all, you are way too close, and your loud calling will blow them out. Best if you stay quiet, and I will go back about a hundred yards and call."

"Okay," I said. "You go back behind us a hundred yards or so and call, and I will take it from here." Now that is the most intelligent thing he said during this entire hunt—the part about him moving back a hundred yards, that is—so I could now do what I needed to do to kill my hunter a turkey, and get a TV show. But the coolest part of this whole deal is I have evidence, everything he said to me, recorded on both my lavalier and shotgun microphones to prove my case to my boss, and the outfitter, about what I'm dealing with out here to get a TV show. When will they ever learn that the camera is always on?

I will not bore you with the details, but those New York turkeys were no different than Missouri turkeys. Right from the start at first light, until my hunter pulled the trigger, those New York turkeys seemed to like my pop, pop fancy calling crap just fine.

Then there was yet another Florida nightmare, and one of the wildest, most bizarre hunts I have ever experienced. I was scheduled to field produce,

If there is any slight difference in hunting the subspecies, it isn't the turkeys, it's the terrain. How you adjust your setups and move in on the gobblers depends on the circumstances.

run camera, and call for hunters for a national television show. The flight to south Florida started this entire chain of events, when it was first delayed, then canceled, then rescheduled, with us finally arriving in Florida at midnight.

With long lines at baggage claim, and Disney World–type lines at the rental car counter, I didn't get to my car until 2 AM. About a half hour out into my two-hour drive to a camp, I realized I didn't have the paper with the directions and the contact phone numbers. So I turned around and returned to the airport. Unbelievably, I found my paperwork on the floor in the rental car garage. Bottom line is that I didn't get to or find the camp (this is another story) until after the hunters were loaded in the truck to go out to hunt.

Climbing into the truck without any sleep, the first thing I heard is, "These turkeys are different and do not like calling." Great. Just what I wanted to hear.

Once in the field, we were instructed to sit in a blind and face only in one direction—and of course, not to call. The guide would call when necessary. At first light I heard gobblers behind us and to the south. I asked about moving on them—that would be a no. I asked about maybe turning around in the blind? No. The guide finally yelped softly and whispered for us to sit still because turkeys would arrive soon. Yeah, right. I couldn't stand it any longer and broke out my call; however, I asked if he minded if a called a little. After cutting and yelping I saw the look of horror on his face—even with gobblers now coming quickly from behind the blind—so I suggested we turn our shooter around. No.

One of the gobblers walked up maybe several feet behind our blind, then quickly retreated. The next several days were pretty much the same, but now with coolers and food, we set up in a clump of trees in a cow pasture at 4:30 AM, and sat all day and did not leave until after dark, the idea being that sometime during the day a turkey would walk by. Oh yeah, did I mention that the guide crawled up to me at first light and told me, "Do not call—I will be watching you."?

I called my boss that night and said I was going to pull the plug and catch a flight back home, but I was assured things would get better after a phone call to the outfitter. The last evening we were directed to set up between an orange grove and a roost. Diesel pumps were running close by—not a good thing for shooting for TV—but the good news was that it was just me and my hunter; the guide had another hunter somewhere else in the area.

I broke the rules. I quickly left just before dark, and went to the place where I'd heard gobblers on the roost that first morning. Once there, I quickly located a gobbler with my turkey call, and roosted him, and we were set for the last morning's hunt. That is, if I could talk the guide into allowing us to hunt the roosted bird.

The next morning I told everyone I had "roosted" a gobbler, and we needed to set up on him. The guide was not happy, but finally agreed, but insisted that he would sit with me. We set up, I started the gobbler, got on the call with one mad guide, but my hunter killed the bird and I had a TV show. Did I mention that when he dropped me off at my rental car for my mad dash for the airport, he spun his tires and threw gravel against my rental car?

We have great success with outdoor media hunts and TV shows because we hunt hard, we get after the turkeys, we're not afraid to call, and we learn as much as we can about turkeys in the areas during the time we are hunting them. And we always have a good time doing it. So don't believe some of the stories you hear, "You might be able to do that where you're from, but it won't work here, 'cause our turkeys are different." Because I'm here to tell you that the tactics I share with you in this book have worked everywhere I've ever hunted.

11

What's Wrong with the Turkeys?

BY TODAY'S STANDARDS, SPRING HUNTERS JUDGE TURKEY hunting seasons as "right," "good," or "quality" seasons solely if everything is just right, a perfect world with bluebird skies, nonstop gobbling, a majority of hens on the nest, and two-year-old toms running to the gun. If anything is outside of this perfect world, then something is wrong with the turkeys.

So, what is wrong with the turkeys? As I've mentioned previously, not a thing—they're just out there being turkeys and going about their turkey business. But to understand why they're not gobbling, or why they're not racing to your every call, it's important to understand more about the wild turkeys and their habits than what occurs just within the short timeframe of the turkey's spring mating season. However, this perfect world is only a very narrow window of opportunity, and with so many hunters today dealing with limited time to hunt, it's very rare for this "perfect world" to fall into place during those few days that many hunters have available to hunt.

Yet another side of the equation is that, as I mentioned earlier, generations of hunters are programmed with information and tactics for use only during this short period of opportunity. This is why it is so important for hunters to expand their turkey hunting knowledge, calling, and hunting tactics. Outside of this perfect world, on mornings with little gobbling and turkeys ignoring hunters' calls, many hunters become frustrated with the lack of success and begin pointing fingers and complaining about the turkey season. It is during this time that hunters scratch their heads and ask, "Why are they not responding to calls?" and "Why aren't they gobbling?" and "What's wrong with the turkeys?"

So why are many of today's hunters experiencing less gobbling than in past years? Through the years, hunters have come up with numerous reasons for less gobbling. Turkey hunter excuses include blaming fish and game agencies, conservation restoration programs, live trapping of turkeys, the weather, other hunters made 'em call-shy, and that the season is off. But

We have very successful media/outdoor writer hunts and television shoots because we have always taken the issue of "people pressure" head on.

none of this is new, and is something I have witnessed for many, many years.

One of my all-time favorite explanations of less gobbling is a quote from my old friend, and one of the greatest turkey hunting legends of all time, the late Ben Lee. Many years ago while we were working a seminar together, the moderator was fielding questions from the audience. He asked Ben why he believed there was less gobbling now than during past years. Ben calmly took the microphone, and in a booming voice he said, "Because we done went an' killed all the stupid ones."

So, what is wrong with your turkeys? It could be the weather, time of year, cycle, or seasonality of area turkeys. All of these are factors in if and when turkeys gobble. Another thing I've noticed with turkeys everywhere is that sometimes they just seem to gobble better on some days more than others, and as I always like to say, only the turkeys know why. From my many, many years of research and turkey hunting experience, I have found several factors or reasons outside this "perfect world" of turkey hunting why gobbling intensity has decreased over the years.

If we look closely outside this small window of opportunity, reasons include an early season, when gobblers are still in flocks together, during the mating peak and a time toms are covered up with hens. The end result from all of the above is very little turkey response to a hunter's mating hen calls, little gobbling, if any, at daylight, and then the dreaded quiet time during the remainder of the morning.

Yet another factor has everything to do with the area's turkey flock. After several years of low hatches, there are fewer two-year-old gobbling turkeys available, hence there is much less gobbling. The sad thing is that part-time hunters end up playing the turkey-gobbling lottery, hoping to win big on just the few days they have available to hunt. With fewer gobbling two-year-olds available, and with two-year-olds normally the highest percentage of a season's harvest, hunters are now dealing with three-, four-, and five-year-old mature gobblers, a whole different animal than a two-year-old kamikaze.

Another reason for silent days, with today's expanded, large population of turkeys, is that there are more hens readily available throughout the gobbler's daily routine. So if a tom is not breeding, he is strutting nonstop or very busy running lesser toms away from his hens. In today's turkey's world, with so many hens available, a dominant gobbler wakes up in the morning with hens in his tree, or if not, he gobbles a few times from his roost as hens run or fly quickly to him. A tom simply drops out of his roost tree with his hens and begins his day by making baby turkeys, totally ignoring the hunter's pleading calls. The frustrated hunter then curses the day the gobbler was hatched, and tells everyone he encounters that the gobblers are all "call-shy" and "henned up."

Another reason is that many of today's hunters are afraid to call, or call very little, and set up way too far away from turkeys, which results in very little gobbling response from turkeys. Calling with realism, emotion, and feeling works turkeys up, hence turkeys work up other turkeys, and this results in turkeys gobbling, something hunters will not experience with soft, laid-back calling.

From my observations and from detailed information from a working-man hunter with limited time, usually only a weekend, his typical setup is way too far from a gobbling turkey. Many choose to set up two hundred yards or more from a gobbling turkey, and yelp softly every thirty minutes by their watch. This has absolutely no effect, because turkeys just continue with their normal daily activities.

To expand your calling knowledge, learn from the experts—the wild turkeys. There is no better teacher than the experience gained by interacting with the birds. "Listen to the turkeys," my grandfather once told me. "They will tell you what they want and how to call to them." I never stopped listening to the turkeys and still follow this simple but sage advice. Whatever the turkeys are doing, imitate it—but with more intensity and emotion.

Next, learn tactics from turkey hunting pros who begin their season the first of March, and hunt through the first of June. Unlike many turkey hunters, who only have a little time to enjoy a hunt with friends and family, the pros are at work. They have to produce, day in, day out, regardless of the weather or seasonality of the turkeys. Because of years of hunting experience, pro turkey hunters have developed hunting tactics during all phases of the wild turkey, during gobbling days and nongobbling days.

Take pecking order, for instance. This is something every pro takes advantage of during every hunt. Every turkey has a role in the social hierarchy of the flock. When a dominant hen turkey hears a new voice (a hunter calling) she's either curious or furious, and it is the dominant hen's business to find out where this new voice fits in the pecking order. By the hunter calling to these dominant hens and playing to their natural instincts, they can't help but come to investigate—possibly bringing a boyfriend in tow. So what calls do you use to get this hen interested? You challenge her status in the pecking order with aggressive yelping and cutting, something that soft, laid-back calling will not accomplish.

But one of the most critical factors in less gobbling is "people pressure." Excessive human activity in any hunting area shuts turkeys down, period. This is something I've battled for more than thirty years, and everywhere I've hunted. Public hunting grounds are a great example and reflect the effects of human pressure. These areas also receive additional numbers of hunters with the highest percentage of nonresident hunters.

We have very successful media/outdoor writer hunts and television shoots because we have and always have taken "people pressure" head on. (People pressure is also known in turkey hunting circles as "call-shy" or "henned-up" and "They know we are here.") Allowing hunting areas to rest for several days, alternating hunting areas, locking gates, and restricting vehicle traffic in hunting areas, all factor in less pressure and help produce successful hunts. Hunting from blinds in open country or on smaller tracts of land also results in less pressure and more gobbling during the season.

On this subject of "what's wrong with the turkeys," in my home state of Missouri during a recent spring turkey season I worked all season researching why many hunters today experience less gobbling. However, my

Press photo showing the late Billy McCoy, Paul Butski, the late Ben Lee, and Ray Eye.

completed research from Missouri is more than applicable for turkey hunters everywhere.

After a final sunrise and the last gobble of a recent Missouri spring turkey season slowly echoes away in the distance, Missouri turkey hunters reflect on their past season. For many, this is of what could have been. Mass confusion runs rampant through the ranks of these thousands of unsuccessful Missouri turkey hunters. Griping and complaining grows louder and louder to whoever will listen. The interesting part is, for those who didn't get a turkey, the season was terrible; for those who took gobblers, it was the best turkey season in years.

The season is off, the season is too late, the season was too early, and gobblers are "henned up" are the main topics in every camp, coffee shop, and sporting goods store. But after the Missouri Department of Conservation check-in process is completed, the final tally reflects a pretty successful season. The spring season's harvest total is the fourth highest kill ever, even with 3,000 fewer permits sold.

As much as I hate to say it, things are changing in my home state. For many years, no state could compare to Missouri's quality hunting and intense gobbling activity. Well, turkey hunters, Missouri is beginning to experience what hunters from other states experience each spring—little or no gobbling. To further study and gather additional information, I scheduled hunts across our entire state. I hunted the Ozarks in southern Missouri, central Missouri, and north Missouri. In addition, I hunted both the east side and the west side of the state.

In addition to my personal observations, I worked very closely with professional guides, outfitters, outdoor writers, and other television crews hunting all across our state. I kept in close contact throughout the season by cell phone and e-mail, receiving daily turkey reports from their areas on gobbling activity, or lack thereof, hunting pressure, and weather.

So what was wrong with the turkeys this past season? Well, sorry, but nothing; they were just being turkeys: roosting, eating, pooping, and breeding, just like every other spring.

From this research, past years of research, and from years of my turkey hunting experience, I have to conclude there are several factors or reasons for all the complaining and decreased gobbling intensity in Missouri and elsewhere as well. Both Missouri hunters and nonresidents who experienced our Missouri wild turkey boom of the 1980s and early 1990s are the hunters who complain the most. Why all the complaining? Missouri hunters are just not experiencing the gobbling activity they did during those glory years.

This "perfect world" of turkey hunting is exactly what we all experienced in the 1980s and early 1990s, during a time when Missouri wild turkeys were expanding into new habitat, the state's flock was on the move, growing by leaps and bounds. Brood hen hatches were going through the roof, and gobbling was nonstop all morning and most of the day. Wild turkeys since that time have reached their maximum expansion within our state, with virtually all prime habitats holding birds. High hatch counts and excessive gobbling activity are directly related to the growth and expansion of the state's flock during the restoration era.

Public hunting grounds, national forests, and state lands all reflect these effects, and are perfect examples of "pressure." These areas also receive the highest percentage of nonresident hunters, although numbers were down this past season with only around 10,000 nonresident permits being sold. Public land hunters complain as much as anyone, and I have to agree with them. There is usually less gobbling on public ground. In addition, southern Missouri hunters complain more than northern Missouri hunters. Naturally, gobbling activity was very good on some private lands with little or no hunting season pressure.

Missouri, like many other states, experienced a low hatch. This is something that also contributes to less gobbling. After several springs of bad hatches, two-year-old gobbling turkeys were at an all-time low, and were directly responsi-

ble for a lack of gobbling during the spring hunting season. In addition, because of low numbers of two-year-old gobblers, hunters are dealing with three-, four-, and five-year-old mature gobblers—totally different animals from two-year-olds. These old gobblers do not gobble much, if at all. Instead

Jay Cassell with his beautiful Hawaiian Rio Grande, during a recent media hunt.

the hens run to them, and these old toms strut and breed all morning long, with little if any gobbling.

But a major factor is that, overall, wild turkey numbers are at an all-time high and there is more hen competition than ever for hunters to battle. With so many available hens staying with gobblers, this also equals little gobbling, because with so many hens, there is no real reason for toms to gobble.

Last but not least, and I have to repeat myself, the most critical factor in the cause for less gobbling is hunting season pressure. Excessive human activity in a hunting area shuts turkeys down, period, and this is something I experienced more than thirty years ago.

This is a true scenario, something I witnessed many years ago on a farm next to our north Missouri camp, something that applies all across America, providing an answer to the question, "What's wrong with the turkeys?"

In early April, gobblers began their courtship on an old, 200-acre abandoned farm. Each and every day the wild turkeys gobbled, strutted, and did what turkeys do, without any interference from people. But as the turkey

season approached, a group of ten hunters arrived two days before the opener, and ran all through the property on ATVs in the name of "scouting." Our hunters set up camp right in the middle of prime turkey habitat, loud rock music blasted, and laughter filled the air as they cut and hauled in camp firewood.

The morning before opening morning, our ten hunters walked throughout their entire hunting area, drove their trucks through fields and down every woods road, while others ran loud ATVs wide open every-

Field & Stream's Anthony Licata with a northern Missouri gobbler taken during a high wind in the early season.

where on the farm until after dark. The next morning, late on opening day, after experiencing little gobbling and with little success, and after returning to their campsite, our ten hunters were involved in deep discussion. "What's wrong with the turkeys, why aren't they gobbling?"

So with my extensive research, you might ask, "What's wrong with the turkeys?" Well, nothing. Sorry, but they are just out there being turkeys. And there is something hunters have known for decades: Turkeys are the most frustrating bird there is to hunt on the planet and this is one of the main reasons we really love to hunt them.

12

The Role of People Pressure

I HAVE BEEN TALKING FOR MANY YEARS ABOUT HOW WILD turkeys become people-shy. I often receive ridicule from pointing to this factor when hunters complain that turkeys are "call-shy." The term itself and most of what you'll read here are the guiding principles that drive the way I hunt and guide others. For many early years of hunting for myself and guiding friends and family, directly from the realization that people pressure in one's hunting area shuts turkeys down, not calling, my turkey kill success rate went way up.

Hunters seem to have a hard time fully realizing what they can and can't get away with out in the turkey woods. Even hunters with experience and successes under their belts make mistakes left and right when it comes to what they let the birds see and hear. Even if you are amazing in the woodsmanship department yourself, it's still important to keep in mind the people pressure factor beyond your control and what it can do to your hunting area. People pressure causes turkeys to get quiet, and commonly causes them to move.

Whether people pressure comes from hunters or ATV riders or Boy Scout pack movements or farmers fixing fences, it usually results in turkeys temporarily moving somewhere else. How long they stay somewhere else depends, among other things, on whether the new place has what they need, and whether the people pressure is sustained. As I mentioned earlier, many hunters have no idea that their extended activity in an area has shut turkeys down and moved the birds from their normal activities, especially on a large tract of land, either private or public. During late winter and into the spring season, turkeys just go about their business with little or no interference from people.

Then, as hunting season approaches, hunters arrive to scout and upset the daily turkey activity with people disturbance, something that is nonexistent prior to the hunting season.

Almost always, wild turkeys are ever-vigilant and ready to quickly go somewhere else if they pick up on the presence of something that could be evil. They're dang good at picking up on movement, and are justifiably famous for leaving first and wondering what it was later—if ever.

The bottom line is that turkeys hear and see better than we do, and they naturally move away from even subtle pressures that do not ring true to their ears and eyes. They are sometimes willing to freeze in place and wait to see what is coming at them, but it better look like a deer or a fellow turkey when it shows up.

So much depends on what options the turkeys have. If it's painless for them to move, they will slip, run, or fly away from pressure. Even oft-bumped wild turkeys might hang around—but they will probably get much quieter, at least for a while.

From my early days in the Ozark hills and up to more recent years on properties in northern Missouri, it became very apparent that, with controlling the human activity (or with less human pressure) on our hunting properties, our success rate went up as we killed many more turkeys. But the best news and results were with the great gobbling that continued throughout all three weeks of the season, even after the first week, when other properties in the same area went silent.

During later years, on our controlled hunting area of 2,500 acres in northeast Missouri, I aggressively studied the impact of people pressure with extensive in-the-field research before, during, and after turkey seasons. During this five-year research project, through my national media hunts and outdoor television shows, we documented turkeys' responses from calling versus human activity.

Later in this chapter I will outline my documented findings from my research in regard to people-shy versus call-shy, but first let's discuss the basics of the people-shy factor, how it affects you as a turkey

During a five-year research project conducted in Missouri, we documented the effects of calling versus human activity on turkeys.

hunter, and what you should do to cut down on spooking turkeys in your hunting area. While I am not an outfitter and I do not guide the hunting public anymore, I have guided and hunted with people from all walks of life for the past forty years, and even with guiding professional outdoor writers, there is not much that surprises me anymore in the many ways hunters can mess up a turkey hunt.

Today, by adding a video camera into the mix—well maybe a few things do in fact surprise me—it is amazing the number of ways hunters blow opportunities to kill a gobbler. When shooting TV shows, I recorded hunters blowing all types of opportunities, and all of these are great teaching tools for use in my seminar programs. During my turkey hunting seminars, I show all the really dumb things hunters manage to do to scare the crap out of the wild turkeys, and it has become a very popular segment of my presentation.

As a great teaching tool, I took the video thing a step further with a "gun cam" attached to the hunter's gun. This is now the best teaching aid to show what hunters do when they take the shot. I now have a library of gun cam footage that is absolutely amazing and tells the real story of why a hunter misses the shot—something that is always different from the hunter's own explanation.

There are a lot of reasons why hunters spook turkeys in their hunting areas. One is that many hunters are always in too big a hurry. In a world of

everything "right now" and "I have to have it now, fast-food, drive-thru service," hunters expect the same thing when turkey hunting. We all live in a very fast-paced world, but wild turkeys remain on "turkey time." I have guided very few hunters who do not express their desire to have it "right now"—they have to kill a turkey, and the sooner the better. They have no patience for anything, especially if a bird is not gobbling. But most important is that many hunters just cannot

Our aggressive calling methods, combined with avoiding "people pressure," netted success.

This is a successful television shoot in Wisconsin, but this is not always the case. By adding a video camera into the mix, it is amazing the number of ways I record that show hunters blowing opportunities to kill a gobbler.

sit still, nor do they have any idea what sitting still really means.

Very few hunters I've guided seem to have any woodsmanship skills whatsoever. They never pay any attention to their surroundings or have any idea what is going on around them. They move too much, make unnecessary noise, and wear noisy clothing and accessories. They have absolutely no knowledge of how to walk quietly, continually bob their heads, talk loudly, slam guns shut when loading, and slam truck doors—and these are outdoor professionals doing all this.

Hunters have no clue when it comes to judging distance, both for shooting and the distance of a gobbling turkey, and they rush forward, shutting the turkey down. While binoculars can be effective in open country and in some other situations, from my experience witnessing hunters running turkeys off, many turkey hunters would be better off leaving their binoculars (and rangefinders) in the truck—or better yet, at home.

Here is a short list of reasons why hunters shut turkeys down during a hunt:

1. On a setup, breaking limbs. Walking in the open completely upright to a tree, to set up with a gobbling turkey at fifty yards. Making a "nest" before sitting down, then head-bobbing and arm-waving like there's no tomorrow, after they finally sit down.
2. Walking—no, stomping—and moving toward a turkey, skylined all the way to setup.
3. Talking loudly, slamming doors, slamming guns.
4. Absolutely zero knowledge of the wild turkeys or how to hunt them.
5. Judging distance.
6. Knowing more than their guide or God himself about hunting turkeys even though they have never killed a bird, or maybe killed only one bird, which was one I called in for them the year before.

Woodsmanship

You have to use a combination of all your hunting skills to become a better turkey hunter. I've heard some hunters say, "Well, I'm better at woodsmanship than I am at calling." Well, become a better caller. Learn to call. Let's go back to what I've talked about, in that hunters seem to be afraid to call. Combine calling skills with woodsmanship skills, the ability to sit still, learn about the turkeys, learn the lay of the land and the terrain features where you're hunting. It's a combination of these many things that will make you successful; so don't try to just get by with minimal calling skills, or just woodsmanship, or just knowing the ground, or just learning about turkeys. Combine those factors to become a better-rounded and more proficient and effective turkey hunter.

I'd like to talk to you a little bit about woodsmanship skills. Yes, it's important to know basic skills in hunting turkeys. A lot of the turkey hunters I grew up with hunted squirrels and other game and they were very proficient in the woods because they knew how to move quietly from place to place, and not disturb wildlife. What happened with today's turkey hunters is they live in a very fast-paced world where everyone is always in a hurry.

When you get into the turkey woods, you're on "turkey time." You're not on your time. The first thing you need to do with your woodsmanship skills is slow down; slow way down; take your time. After the first couple of days' turkey hunting, you'll notice a difference. At first you'll be bumping turkeys or you'll have squirrels scurrying off. Once you slow your pace down and learn to move quietly, to not step on and break sticks, to not bob your head around and make sudden movements, to not talk loudly and slam truck doors, things will change in the woods, and you'll notice a huge difference.

First of all, you'll see a lot more wildlife, and second, you'll be a lot more successful with the turkeys. Most of the turkey hunters I've hunted with over the years have never learned the lesson to slow down and basically just be much more quiet. Don't make any sudden movements. Don't turn your head quickly. Don't walk where you will be skylighted, where a turkey can see you; if you're walking a ridgetop and they're positioned below you, yes, you are skylighted. Avoid those situations.

Another important woodsmanship skill when you're approaching a gobbling turkey is never taking a direct route toward the turkey. Use the terrain to your advantage. Stay low, stay hidden, and circle around the turkey to make your approach. If a turkey is walking away from you, gobbling, it's probably best to go around that turkey and get on the other side. Use the same direction of travel the turkey is going in to set up before you call.

Those are just a few basic skills. But I just have to say again, what I see most often is that hunters move far too much. They make too much noise. When I tell hunters to sit still, they don't understand the term of "sitting still." Turkeys are trying to survive. Everything in the woods is trying to eat them, and when they see movement, to them that's danger.

Turkeys don't know you're a hunter or you're calling them or trying to shoot them. Turkeys just know they don't want to be anywhere around any sort of movement because it could be some kind of predator. So if you stick with the basics in woodsmanship—how you walk, where you put your feet down, take your time, put your foot down slowly, feel what's under your feet and move quietly, slowly, from place to place—you'll have much more success.

Years ago it was a common belief you had to run to a gobbler. I've had hunters run past me many times, going to a gobbling turkey. You don't want to run in the woods. The turkey's not going anyplace. He lives there. They're going to be there. Take your time to get to them. But movement is the essential part to avoid. So many hunters make the mistake that, once they get set up, they turn or look, or rise up and try to see the turkey, and end up moving too quickly.

You can actually raise a shotgun on a turkey, if you do it very slowly, and you watch the turkey. Too much quick movement spooks birds. So learn to walk quietly, do not talk loudly, and slow down. You're on turkey time; you're not on people time. Don't get in a hurry. Be as quiet as you can. Sit still. I mean, sit *still*. You cannot make any sudden movements. If you'll just put those basic ingredients with calling skills, your success rate is really going to go up.

Let's review a recent magazine article written by my good friend Mark Strand on the subject of people pressure, after hunting on of my media hunts. Here is what Mark has to say about this subject in his piece:

"In open country, the importance of minimizing people pressure can be everything to sustaining good hunting. Back in the 1990s, Eye was conducting media turkey camps in an especially open section of rolling hills in northeast Missouri. Knowing what he was dealing with, he thoroughly scouted each spot and constructed tall sided blinds that he insisted head-bobbing outdoor writers and camera men, myself included, approach quietly and settle into.

"When the writers listened to him and stayed put, spectacular shows of strutting and gobbling were the norm. When they broke from the playbook and wandered the open hills, the result was the same as stomping through a dry fly stretch and expecting the trout to keep rising.

"'Use whatever terrain features are available to stay out of sight,' says Eye, a piece of advice we have all heard before, but one that gets overlooked constantly. 'Don't walk across the top of the ridge, even in the dark. Hunters silhouette themselves against the sky when they walk in, and then they wonder why turkeys don't respond when they call.' They don't respond, in a lot of cases, because they're not there anymore.

"As a side note, and a case for realistic and excited calling, it seems possible to get away with more of the wrong kinds of sound and movement when turkeys are really fired up. Last spring in Wyoming, Ray had a small band of gobblers so drunk on their own testosterone supply that one of them can be clearly seen strutting out in the open as two hunters walk out to claim the dead one that Mossberg's Linda Powell just shot. (It's all on video, and these were not pen-raised turkeys in somebody's back yard.) That which is absent from most of us mere mortal turkey callers, though, it remains best practice to sound natural and remain unseen."

Many hunters try hard to do everything right at the beginning of the day, then as they get tired, hot, hungry, thirsty, and frustrated, they turn into monsters leaving destruction and fleeing turkeys in their wake as they head back to the truck. We are all guilty as charged, at least at times. People pressure on turkeys will move them, plenty far enough to screw up your future hunting prospects on a piece of property. For the sake of your own hunting fortunes, and especially for those who will hunt the same ground after you, make stealth a priority, until you start the truck and head for town.

Gunfire, in and of itself, does not drive turkeys away. Sure, some birds

Last spring in Wyoming we had gobblers so drunk on their own testosterone from calling that they continued strutting at forty yards even as Mossberg's Linda Powell retrieved her gobbler.

might be spooked by a super-loud noise, at least momentarily, but they usually gobble at a gunshot or will be mostly unaffected by it. Loud bangs are part of the natural ambience. Think about thunder, which occurs frequently in the turkey's world. It's not the noise all by itself that creates a spooking response. It's the movement of the gun-holder, the shuffling of the butt cushion under leaves and rocks, throat clearing, arm or hand waving, all revealing the large, unknown form, that triggers the flight response.

For too many hunters the immediate reaction to dropping a gobbler with a well-placed shot has come to simulate baseball players clinching the World Series: The hunting spot becomes a locker-room celebration, with jumping up and down, hollering, in-your-face turkeys, who cooks for me, rushing out to the fallen prize, with other nearby turkeys almost puking from the adrenaline rush associated with getting away from whatever the hell that all was.

This doesn't mean that they'll never come back. But in deference to those who will come after you (especially if it's members of your own party who haven't filled their tags yet), why not err on the side of keeping quiet until you get back to the truck? Go ahead and celebrate quietly and take pictures and stuff like that, but at least wait until the other turkeys go out of sight before you start the festivities.

One of my outdoor writer turkey hunts in Illinois in the mid-1990s is a perfect example of people pressure. As with any of my spring turkey marathons in April, after hunting Kansas, South Dakota, and Nebraska, and hunting only a short time in Missouri, I'm scheduled to hunt three days in Illinois with three outdoor writers, then I have to turn right around and drive back to my Missouri camp to finish the season with another group of writers.

With many states scheduling concurrent season dates, to make hunts work, I deal with a crazy and ridiculously tight schedule. I depart from my northeast Missouri camp at 1:30 AM to drive to Illinois to make it to the hunting area before gobbling time. This first morning is to scout with my Illinois host while hunting, and to set up our camp for my writers arriving later that day.

After a very early morning arrival at the Illinois River Hills hunting area's locked gate, already wearing my pajamas and house shoes from the drive over, and now with a little time before meeting my host, I decided to take advantage of some much-needed sleep in the backseat of my truck.

Waking up at first light to songbirds singing, at first I had no idea where I was. As I was looking around, with drool running down my chin, a turkey gobbled fairly close but there was no sign of my Illinois host. I hadn't spoken to anyone about the hunt for several weeks and decided to drive into town and call him from a pay phone to find out what was going on with our hunt.

After backing out of the gate and heading down the road toward the main road, with my window open to try to stay awake, I heard a turkey gobble, so I pulled over, stepped out of my truck in my pajamas, walked to the back of my truck, and gave owl hoot. A turkey somewhere up the steep ridge and just down from the gate gobbled. With no time to get properly dressed, I grabbed my gun and a couple of shells, crossed the fence, and climbed the hill.

After reaching a small flat just below the main bench, I paused, cutting and yelping on my mouth call. A hen cut me off, coming my way and yelping as she came. I quickly moved up slightly, and with no place to set up where I can see, I stood up next to a tree, and called again. This time a gobble just above me just about blew my cap off.

I first saw the hen when she reached the edge of the bench and, as she ran her neck up to look for the source of my calling, a big turkey fan appeared behind her. As I slowly rose to aim my gun, the hen flushed, cackling as she went up through the treetops. The gobbler hesitated for just a second, and I pulled the trigger.

Small limbs, weeds, and tree bark flew everywhere as the gobbler went down, but only for an instant, as he quickly recovered and now was airborne, flying to my right. I pulled in on him for the second time, and slapped the trigger. This time he folded like a cheap card table and crashed through the tree limbs and hit with a thud on

As with every spring's crazy turkey marathon, I'm scheduled to hunt with three writers in Illinois, then turn right around and finish my media hunt in Missouri.

the road right behind my parked truck. This had never happened before, and probably will never happen again.

I had to laugh out loud about this crazy scene, the turkey folding and dropping on the road, hunting in my night-nights, and I could only imagine what this would have looked like if someone was watching from the gate. When I reached the road, there was still no one waiting for me at the gate, so I picked up and tagged my gobbler, loaded him up, got myself dressed, and drove to town.

When I called from a gas station pay phone, I woke my guy and he told me he called late last night and left a recorded message on my camp house answering machine—a message I didn't receive telling me not to bother coming over because it's over, the turkeys are done and not gobbling, and they are all call-shy.

We decided to meet for breakfast and talk it over, because there was just no way I would tell my scheduled writers to go home. After meeting in the café parking lot, I told him I had something to show him. Opening up the back of the Suburban, I pulled out my turkey. He asked if I killed the turkey in Missouri, and why would I haul it all the way here?

Well, not exactly, I told him. I killed this turkey this morning at your place while I was waiting on you. He just couldn't believe it, as those turkeys at his farm were done, it was over, and they had the worst case of call-shy in years. Over breakfast he told me a sad tale of nongobbling turkeys, whereas earlier in the season there were many. The only turkey they killed, they located deep in the woods and away from the best part of his hunting ground. As his story progressed, I began to understand what was going on with his turkeys and was able to put the puzzle pieces together, concluding that this was nothing more than a people pressure problem.

So, read this carefully and take it all in. What I am about to tell you is a very common occurrence just about everywhere with turkey hunters. Few understand that their actions are the reason the turkeys in their area shut down like those Illinois turkeys.

I managed to extract the following information from our breakfast conversation. Just before the opening of the Illinois turkey season, turkeys gobbled all over the property, but after several days of scouting with a four-wheeler, there was much less gobbling, especially toward the front of his property. But the most amazing part was how disappointed my friend was after he, six of his friends, and several family members hunted this property on opening morning without hearing even a single turkey.

However, they did not arrive at the farm until right at first light, they drove two diesel trucks (they are farmers, not turkey hunters) through the gate, up the road, and across the pastures—a farm with ridgetop fields, with all timber sloping away from the hilltop. Driving across the hilltop pastures, dropping off hunters, they talked loudly, slammed truck doors, and were skylighted as they approached timbered areas from above.

The few turkeys they actually did hear gobble were later in the morning and deeper in the woods, and did not respond to their very soft calling from 300 yards away. Subsequently, he believed that his turkeys were all call-shy, the season was off, it was all over, the turkeys were not acting like turkeys, and there was no reason to hunt this farm again this season.

But the best news during our entire conversation was that no one had been on or hunted his farm for several days. After my writers' arrival, I decided it best we not go in to roost, but wait until morning. In addition, with a good topo map, my Illinois guy pointed out every place they had heard and seen gobblers last season, prior to this season, and while farming.

There was a change in plan. Early the next morning we parked our trucks at the main gate, and we walked in an hour before daylight. Yep, all three of my writers killed turkeys that first morning, and I also called a turkey for my host. That, including mine, totaled five gobblers in two mornings, in a place where "it's over" and "the turkeys are call-shy."

Back at camp, as I loaded my truck for the long drive back to Missouri, I overheard my Illinois host talking to someone on his camp house wall phone. Yep, he told them they were going hunting again tomorrow, because the turkeys are now acting like turkeys again.

But there is something else really funny, and that is so true with turkey hunters everywhere: As I said my goodbyes and thanked everyone for a great camp, I looked him in the eyes and said, "I bet after I leave here, you will tell everyone you called in all those turkeys we killed."

And this is what he said to me: "When you leave here, your truck tires won't even be warm on the blacktop yet, when I tell everyone I know I called those turkeys—even the one for you!" Oh well, at least he's honest about it.

Okay, let's summarize what we have learned. You have to do your best to avoid creating unnatural sounds when you walk and to avoid letting birds see you for what you really are. As you enter a hunting spot, or as you move from one calling position to another, keep in mind that wild turkeys live there. That all the natural sounds of animals coming and going and singing and grunting are everyday ambience. Adult wild turkeys have lived out there long enough to "just know" what it's supposed to sound like.

Squirrels scurry through the leaves and jump from tree to tree. Deer, and fellow turkeys, unless they're spooked and running for their lives, move with a methodical cadence, usually a few steps at a time, maybe followed by pawing at the leaves to uncover something to eat.

Geese fly over and honk their heads off, wood ducks whistle with their wings and voices, owls wonder who is cooking for whom, and the list goes on. This all sounds "right" to a turkey's ears. Then along comes you. If you don't pay attention to the details, it's easy to fail to notice that your pant legs are swishing together, that the bottoms of your boots are scraping the ground, and that you're crunching leaves underfoot with every step. You don't have to hit turkeys over the head with making the wrong sounds. Turkeys are not amazingly smart, but they instinctively know when something just doesn't sound right.

It might not sound loud to your ears, and it might not be, but the black-berry bushes scraping across your vest and the cling-cling-cling of your sling against the metal adjustment thingy on your vest is not the kind of sound that attracts wild turkeys. Even when turkeys cannot see you (yet), these careless sounds cause them to take notice. In most cases, they move away from the source of the sounds—doing a much better job of being quiet about it than you are. They don't gobble to tell you they're leaving. They just leave. You stop and call, get no response, and continue farther into the spot, making all the same mistakes every step of the way.

If it looks like you, it's game over. (And you probably never even knew the game started!)

Showing yourself to turkeys causes a predictable response, especially when it's preceded by bad walking. Birds that are already wondering what kind of aliens have invaded are not predisposed to dealing with seeing a human form. The pressure does not have to be glaring to be impactful. Foot traffic accompanied by showing yourself to wild turkeys equals unfilled tags, no matter where you do it.

So, bowing to the idea that people pressure has a huge impact on where turkeys go, how long they stay there, and how vocal they are likely to be, what's a hunter to do? After all, you can't levitate as you move from spot to spot. And even if you could slip silently, there's this little matter of turkey eyeballs spotting your silent movements and them boogeying off into the distance.

There's no need to be absolutely silent in order to avoid spooking turkeys. But your movements should sound natural. Practice sounding like a deer or turkey as you walk. One key is to resist the weight of your foot as it comes down. We don't do this when we're walking out to the mailbox, so it takes practice. Set every step down, quietly, heel first, rolling forward toward your toes. With a little practice, you can learn to feel what's under your boots as your foot is rolling forward. If you can't, get different boots. This is going to sound goofy, but you can develop the ability, even as you walk fairly quickly, to detect sticks that are about to snap, and roll back onto your heel to avoid making sharp, snapping sounds.

In reality, there's no way to completely avoid snapping sticks. We all snap a million of 'em every day. The definition of sounds that sound "natural" to a turkey's ears can get into some debatable areas, but there is a difference

On one of our last big hunts on this managed property, we invited personally selected outdoor writers with a history of promoting our sponsors and telling the story as it happens. We built huge, tall blinds in key areas that the turkeys had actually showed us. (If you're curious about the guy in the barn, read Jay Cassell's testimonial in "About the Author.")

between what a twig sounds like when it snaps under a deer that's been spooked, even if it's just walking quickly, and what that same twig sounds like when a deer steps on it while moving at an unhurried pace.

When we walk through the woods, we should try to sound like deer—or, better yet, like turkeys that are calmly going about the business of eating and looking for girlfriends. Again, you can't be dead silent, but you don't have to be. Instead, try to sound like an animal moving through the woods. Take a few steps; stop; take a few more. Choose the quiet way, by looking ahead of you and picking a path with fewer sticks to crunch and less brush for you to come into contact with. Stay in the shadows, in or tight to cover, and below the crests of hills. When you sit down against a tree, do so quietly.

Now it's time to review my extensive people-shy versus call-shy research. From the late 1980s into the 1990s, while hosting America's leading outdoor writers during my Missouri whitetail media hunts, I found it important to keep hunter activity to a minimum so as not to change the habits of deer. By keeping people activity to a minimum with locked gates, no truck or ATV traffic in hunting areas, allowing areas to rest, keeping bedding areas off-limits, and never having an organized deer drive, our kill rate went up and we were taking bigger bucks.

In those days you could lease large sections of ground all year, for very little money, and this would give you complete control of the property. To manage it in the best possible way to improve the deer hunting, I would scout from a distance, watch and log all deer movement, place twenty-five to thirty deer stands, and build ground blinds as well.

We would only hunt stands according to the proper wind, and always let areas rest several days after hunting a stand. Leaving beans and corn standing after harvest and planting food plots and winter supplementary feeding were other methods we utilized. The results of our whitetail media hunts were amazing, so one day it just came to me: Why not do this same program with turkeys?

In the mid-1990s we moved our hunting operation farther north, close to the Iowa border. At the time I was working for a muzzleloader gun company that had purchased 2,500 acres in one chunk, and asked me to manage the land and set it up strictly for outdoor media and hunting industry buyers. While whitetails were the main focus, the management program I instituted benefited other wildlife, including turkeys, and so I began managing the turkeys as well.

By implementing less people pressure with no driving in the hunting area, all gates closed and locked, alternating hunting areas and allowing areas to rest, the quality of the hunt and the kill rate went off the charts.

With managing turkeys we ceased shooting jakes, we implemented wintertime supplementary feeding by spreading feed in 100-yard strips of field edge cover, planted food plots, and left corn and beans standing in fields after harvest. We implemented policies including a locked gate, no driving in hunting areas, alternating hunting areas, and allowing areas to rest after hunting. All this improved our kill ratio. We experienced more gobbling, and the quality of our turkey hunts went off the charts.

As a call manufacturer, I also used this program as a testing ground for turkey calls. It became very apparent early on that you could call to turkeys every day, as long as you did not spook them, bump them, or walk and drive all through the property. Calling, in and of itself, had absolutely no negative effect on the turkeys.

I would test new calls on winter roosts, utilize calling with an approaching spring season to document gobbler counts, locate turkeys at different times of the day—all from a distance, and without people pressure on the property. When outdoor writers arrived for the season, we outlined rules on keeping human pressure off our turkeys but allowed them to call at will. We usually ended the season with a 100 percent kill success during these media hunts.

So with all these successes with turkey management, in the late 1990s, we decided to take it a step further by building blinds in key areas, and cease all "running and gunning" activity, and only hunted from blinds to further our research. By watching and listing and calling to turkeys closer to the season, we would decide on blind placement. However, we did not build blinds until after dark, after the turkeys were a safe distance away and on the roost.

We alternated writers in our hunting areas during the season, and let areas rest for several days. We were very strict with outdoor writers to go only in the dark, and not to leave until all turkeys were gone from the blind area after a kill. We did not allow any vehicles in hunting areas, and all gates were locked to prevent any ATV or truck access.

This blind hunting was not very popular with the outdoor media, especially with Southern outdoor writers, but this research was going on years before the popularity of today's easy-set-up mass-marketed, manufactured blinds.

What many of our out-of-state hunters just did not realize was that, in this open-country hunting, bumping turkeys was very easy, simply by walking into an area, much less their "running and gunning" behavior. The downside is that even after writers were killing turkeys, we received very little publicity about our program's effectiveness. It was always something about my scouting and knowing where turkeys were on the property, instead of focusing on the people-shy issues and effective turkey management. And of course, even after being one of the early days "running and gunning" guys (which I was condemned for at the time) now I was a blind hunter, like it was somehow a bad thing.

On one of our last big hunts on this managed property, we invited several personally selected outdoor writers with a history of promoting our sponsors and telling the story as it happened. We built huge, tall blinds in key areas in which the turkeys' own activities had shown us just where to place them.

From late March up until the late April turkey season, we called to turkeys every day, from gates, roads, and inside blinds, to shoot TV show pre-roll and turkey footage. I would call from pasture hilltops to log-gobbling and gobbler location, at all times of day, all without putting people pressure on the turkeys.

One morning a friend and National Wild Turkey Federation officer was in my area for the upcoming turkey season, and I asked him to join me for

We called to turkeys through the late April turkey season, all without putting people pressure on them.

a morning gobble count. Once on the pasture hilltop, to hear the twisting creek bottom roost areas, I asked that he step away and listen to help me get an accurate count. But when I hit my mouth call with some aggressive yelping and cutting, well, even as a guest on my place, he went absolutely nuts, and ran up to me yelling at me with, "What in the hell are you doing? I can't believe you're calling before season!"

I calmly asked him to be quiet and just listen to the turkeys gobble, adding that I had done this for years and it had no negative effect on turkeys—other than eventually killing them.

My guides and I continued our calling right up to our outdoor writers' arrival. We then separated them into groups and loaded them up and drove main roads to show them their blinds from a distance. Four of the five areas already had turkeys strutting in front of the blinds.

The next morning and the day before the opener, with strategically placed living room sofas in pastures at a distance from creek bottom roost areas, we parked at the road, walked our guys in, placed them on the couches with coffee and snacks, and let them hear the rewards of our intensive turkey management. After fly-down, we slipped everyone out, went to a cabin, and cooked a large breakfast. There were spotting scopes set up on the porch for viewing strutters in bottom fields around their blinds.

Well, the bottom line is that we had a 100 percent kill: twenty writers, twenty dead gobblers, and the gobbling was intense and unlike anything they had ever heard anywhere. And so it continued for the remainder of the season, all three weeks, and all due to our management program and keeping people pressure off the turkeys.

The only downside was that again we received little coverage of what this hunt was really all about—that it's people pressure, not calling, that shuts turkeys down. That turkey management works, and hunting from blinds will increase your odds during the length of a season, without shutting turkeys down. But instead I then became known as a "blind hunter," which is kind of a funny thing in many ways.

However, maybe you, as turkey hunters, should try what we learned from our research in your own hunting areas, big or small, though these techniques will prove especially useful on smaller tracts of land, so your birds do not go silent by the second day.

Yep, turkeys definitely become people-shy, not call-shy.

13

Scouting and Roosting

IF YOU'RE GOING TO GO TURKEY HUNTING AND EXPECT TO shoot a turkey, it's important that you find the turkeys through advance scouting in the area you will be hunting. It may sound a bit difficult, but it's really not, especially if you have time to actually watch turkeys in your hunting area.

Observing turkeys in your hunting area is really important in the spring of the year. During the gobbling, get out there undetected, and at a distance, and listen to turkeys gobble. But don't just listen at first light—also listen after daylight, especially after the birds fly down. Very important information can be gathered later in the morning, such as: What direction do gobblers travel after fly-down? Where do they go later in the morning and gobble? Dependent on the terrain you're hunting, do they then move into a field? Do they go to a woodlot somewhere on the property, or do they leave the property?

By watching and listening, you will gain knowledge of the daily direction of their travel and if your gobblers go somewhere in particular to meet hens. Of course it's also important to scout your area to learn the lay of the land. Learning terrain features will help you hunt, call, and kill turkeys later. However, it's not just the lay of the land, but a question of where do your turkeys hang out later in the morning?

If you have the time, you probably should apply scouting basics as well. Of course, you look for scat, feathers, scratching, dusting bowls, and things like that. I was never one to get into too much specific detail, so just remember, if it's large scat, it's probably a large tur-

The best locating call to scout with is your turkey call. I locate and roost turkeys with cutting and yelping simply because it works.

I locate how many gobblers are on the farm I'm hunting simply by using cutting, right at dark and at roost time, or early in the morning at first light.

key, and if it's small, it's more than likely a smaller turkey. If it's a large track, it's a large turkey; if it's a small track; it's probably a small turkey. But more important for me is that the hottest track in the woods is the one with a foot still sticking in it! No amount of sign locating is ever as effective as actually watching and listening to the turkeys in your hunting area.

I return that late afternoon and watch and videotape turkeys in the creek bottom crop fields until dark, then follow them to the roost, and choose my setup for the morning.

Now it's time to connect all the signs you found with terrain features of the area you're hunting, and go the next step; now it's time to call. You can owl call to locate turkeys, or you can use a crow call, but the best call in the world to scout turkeys, to find turkeys, to get turkeys to react, is your turkey call, and the one that I love to use to locate and roost turkeys is with cutting and yelping. I also locate turkeys throughout the day by cutting and yelping. Now I'm not talking about calling them up and spooking them off, or going in, moving around, and letting the turkeys know I'm there.

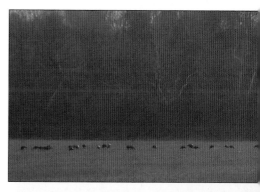

It's okay, take a deep breath.

I've called turkeys during scouting and roosting for thirty years, because it really works and because calling doesn't negatively affect turkeys in any way.

If you have time, apply the scouting basics. They will give you an edge.

Calling does, however, provoke them to react, and turkeys react better to a turkey call during scouting than to an owl call or a crow call. A response from my calling is what I use in order to locate them, to see how they react to the call, to know what direction of travel they take, and also to achieve a pretty accurate gobbler count in my hunting area.

I figure out how many gobblers are on the farm I'm hunting simply by using cutting right at dark and right at roost time, or early in the morning at daylight. Later in the morning, I'll move and call—not spooking turkeys, not putting pressure on turkeys—just using turkey vocalizations, sounds that turkeys react to, and it has absolutely no effect on shutting down turkeys in the place you're hunting.

Using your turkey call for scouting and roosting will make you a much better turkey hunter, and you will know what the turkeys are doing, what time they're doing it, and their direction of travel. You can learn all this just by calling, watching, and listening. Turkey calling helps me get an accurate gobbler count as well as their roost locations, and after fly-down, their direction of travel. I have to tell you it is very effective, and calling prior to season or even the day before a hunt has absolutely no negative effect on turkeys, and we have had great success killing turkeys later when hunting these prescouted areas.

Of the hundreds of examples I could use to illustrate scouting and roosting with a turkey call, I will tell you of three: one in New England, another in Missouri, and one in South Dakota's Black Hills.

Toward the end of my whirlwind turkey hunting marathon, we usually finish up in New England, the last of May or the first of June. Roosting is also a camp tradition in most of my out-of-state hunts, especially in New England, where it is a big event and something we have done for over twenty-five years, and the result, more often than not, is a dead turkey. But on my arrival, I was greeted with the common saying, "It's over and all the turkeys are call-shy." But I only had limited time to complete a TV show and had to rely on what always works for me—calling.

I arrived in Massachusetts late on a Sunday morning. The season opened on Monday, so late afternoon and into the evening on Sunday, we drove dirt roads in our hunting areas, stopped and called, moved on, stopped and called, until we located gobbling turkeys. After striking several gobblers with my turkey call right before dark, I followed them to roost, found my setup for daybreak, and we killed a bird early the next morning. And that is how it works for me, with limited time to make it happen.

In Missouri I had a media hunt scheduled on Monday morning. I arrived in camp late Saturday night, never having seen the property or set foot on the location I would be hunting. In such situations, calling becomes even more important to my success. The first order of business was reviewing a topo map of the farm. I quickly eliminated open pasture areas and zeroed in on a creek bottom with crop fields and big, timbered ridges. Next I asked the landowner where he typically saw and heard turkeys.

Early Sunday morning, I sat back from creek bottom fields and ridges, and listened, documenting all of it on my video camera. After locating roost areas and fly-down locations, I carefully moved in closer and called to get a gobbler count and direction of travel from their roost. I hung out until around 10 AM, just watching, calling, and listening. I returned late that afternoon and watched and videotaped turkeys in the creek bottom crop fields until dark, then followed them to the roost and chose my setup for the next morning. I returned to camp for dinner, organized my gear, then returned to the farm way after dark and quietly set up my blind, just inside the field edge between roosted gobblers and the field—a location chosen from my extensive but necessarily brief calling-and-scouting excursion.

My blind setup covered two directions: the back of the blind overlooked a creek bottom timber and roost area, while the front of the blind covered a corner of the field. This field edge is where I'd observed a gobbler enter the field at daylight and then leave the same place at dark. Now, there were two reasons why I set up the blind in this way: First, the woods were extremely open, and of course we were hunting open field country in north Missouri;

and second, I had a total of four people and two video cameras to conceal. Early the next morning, we quietly and carefully set up in the blind about an hour before first light, and I have to tell you that showtime at daylight was amazing. I captured gobblers on the roost, flying down, flying across a creek, and marching in to the gun, with an awesome on-camera kill.

My Missouri blind setup covers two directions.

The late Denny Dennis and I carefully set up in the blind about an hour before first light. We captured gobblers on camera flying down from the roost, flying across a creek, and then marching into gun range for an awesome video kill.

One additional reason this worked so well is that, besides my scouting with a call, watching the turkeys, and roosting, we were in the zone—in tight with the turkeys, where calling is so much more effective than from a distance.

Roosting is one of the most important factors for you, and especially for my media hunts and television success, roosting is what makes it happen. I have roosted turkeys in forty-three states and in Mexico, all with great success, and often on the sly, as some outfitters and hunters claim that roosting does not work in their state or their hunting area. Roosting tactics may vary, depending on what part of the country you're in and the terrain features. Watching turkeys in open country, from a distance, then following them in to the roost, and choosing the setup the night before, has always worked very well for me. In more timbered areas, I like to start fairly early, especially if I just arrived from out of town and have no knowledge of the local turkeys.

This is a time when I really get on my turkey call, to start a gobbler before dark and keep him going as he goes to roost, with me following close behind. I now know his direction of travel to the roost, and I do not just find his tree, but I also want to know which limb he is on for my morning hunt.

I'm sure most hunters have heard the term "roosted ain't roasted." Well, I have always disagreed with this, because roosted for me is usually a roasted turkey. Now, when I say roosted, I am not talking old-school roosting, standing in a road ditch right at dark and owl hooting, hearing a gobble a quarter mile away, then high-fiving while leaving. I am talking about what many call "radical roosting," because

This New York gobbler was taken because of roosting.

when I roost with someone new, my roosting tactics freak them out, mainly because I use a turkey call with aggressive yelping and cutting to roost turkeys. I absolutely love to roost birds with hen yelps, rather than an owl hooter or crow call.

Now, the reason I love it is because it works. Turkeys always respond better to other turkeys than to owls or crows. I want to get the gobbler worked up before he goes to sleep. I want to be the last thing he hears at night, and the first thing he hears in the morning.

I put in the extra effort to find where and in what direction the gobbler pitches up to the roost, not only where he's roosting, not just the tree, but the actual limb he is sitting on. Locate the spot he pitched up from, and be set up on that spot the next morning. There is a reason he flew up from that side, usually because of easy access to the roost. Chances are very good that he will pitch back down to that same spot the next morning, and I believe it helps if he thinks the girls are there waiting for him.

During a recent television shoot with *Winchester Turkey Revolution* in the Black Hills of South Dakota, roosting was the main element for us completing a show. The weather was cold, with wind, snow, and sleet, and most hunters at our camp not only stayed in camp that evening, but remained there the next morning as well. After arrival at camp the evening before our hunt, we drove into the hills to see our hunting area and to locate turkeys for the next morning's hunt. We finally located a big flock with multiple strutters in a low valley, located somewhat out of the wind, and between huge hills.

We watched the turkeys until dark, and as they drifted to the south and moved up on a pine-covered ridge, I followed close behind. Once they flew

up, even in the high wind, the turkeys gobbled nonstop to my cutting and yelping. After dark we met back in the canyon, where the strutting gobblers and hens were before going to roost. We set up two blinds on an elevated pond dam, overlooking the

Snow and cold wind are parts of early season. This gobbler was taken because we roosted him the night before, then set up close to his roost in the morning, and started yelping.

This Florida Osceola is a perfect example of aggressive yet successful roosting and calling tactics.

valley and just below the roost. The next morning, the wind continued to blow, with sleet changing over to snow, but our aggressive calling lit up the roost with gobbling. It was not long before we had several flocks out in front of us, including groups of hens, a group of pushing and shoving lesser toms, and just to our right, six big toms strutting with the girls.

This story had a wonderful ending, with two on-camera kills and a completed TV show, even in terrible weather—and all because of scouting by watching, locating and roosting with calling, and setting up tight on the roost. Roosting is how many other pros and I consistently kill turkeys; record awesome roost footage; locate the why, where, and how to set up; and utilize aggressive, often criticized—yet extremely successful—calling tactics.

So, here's one final note worth mentioning as you get ready to hit the woods. Make a concerted effort to roost your birds. As the season finally arrives, in timber, listen in late evening to locate where they roost. Always work to find the roost, and always roost the evening prior to a day of hunting. In open country, watching turkeys and following them to roost works extremely well. All this will help you to become very consistent with killing gobblers, regardless of the weather, time of year, or of people pressure or gobblers being with hens.

14

The Final Approach

NOW WE'RE GOING TO TALK ABOUT ONE OF THE MOST essential elements in turkey hunting: the final approach. Your setup, where you sit, how close you set up, and how you set up will make or break your hunt—whether you tote a turkey out over your shoulder or sit in the woods with your face in your hands. In this chapter we cover field hunting setups first, then timber hunting setups, but before we get into field hunting and timber hunting, let's cover a few rules of engagement during a gobbler's final approach.

I grew up hunting in the heavily timbered Missouri Ozarks national forests. It was guerilla warfare, with plenty of hunter interference. To kill a turkey you had to get there first, get really tight, and get the bird on the ground flopping before some clown came in behind you and scared your bird away. I quickly found in later years that the Ozark timber setup tactics I'd learned didn't apply in open country, and especially out West.

One of the most important things I have taught over the years for hunting success is to get in really tight on turkeys—use the terrain to get as close as possible to set up. Gobblers react better to your calling if your setup is in close. Try to locate a tree wider than your shoulders to help you blend in better, but do not sit too low. Sit up a little so that you can see well out in front of you. You should sit on a small seat to help elevate yourself slightly. Pull your knees up, and if you're right-handed, put your left shoulder in the direction you think the turkey will approach from.

For years in seminars and in our writings, pro hunters have taught basics and given hunters guidelines to follow, but we ask that you be willing to adapt to a situation. Think for yourself and use common sense. I have witnessed way too many hunters who will only employ tactics exactly as they read or were told. During one of our hunts, a hunter in a blind in a big field didn't shoot a gobbler at ten yards because the tom was in full strut. He simply let the turkey strut away and go out of sight. The reason he gave was that he'd read you should not shoot a gobbler in full strut.

It is critical that you pattern your turkey gun prior to hunting, with the proper loads, choke, and sighting system to match the terrain you're hunting.

On another hunt I was guiding in Iowa, we were moving up on a gobbling turkey. We ran out of timber and moved up into a pasture to the crest of a hill. When I hit my call to check on the bird, several turkeys gobbled just over the rise, and the top of a fan appeared out in front of us. I told my hunter to raise his gun and shoot the gobbler as soon as he topped the rise. But I was talking to air because the hunter had just turned around and run back some forty yards to the woods' edge to find a tree wider than his shoulders, to sit against.

Okay, you do not always have to sit against a tree—sometimes you may have to stand up to see and kill a turkey, and I have certainly killed a lot of turkeys while standing. In other situations, I've told a hunter to stand up from a sitting position to kill a turkey that's in range but that we cannot see. Wow, this really freaks them out, but it works. That is, if you can get them to do it.

For the final approach, it's very important that you always make it easier for the turkey to come to your position, possibly someplace he wants to go anyway, rather than you going to him. A good setup is one where you can't see him until you can kill him. This could be a bend in an old logging road or a little rise in a hill. If you're on a bench on a big ridge, with heavy steep timber and the turkey is roosted up high just off the edge, set yourself up where he has to come over a little rise to find the hen he thinks he hears calling. If a turkey is able to see a long ways and does not see the hen where the sound is coming from, this causes a hang-up of a gobbler that refuses to come the final distance needed to kill him.

In other hunting situations, on a turkey's approach, at the last minute, and maybe when he's almost within range, you suddenly realize your setup isn't going to work out. I've had many hunters in a setup who needed to change positions, maybe heading just three feet to another tree so they could make the shot, but they stood up to move, and it was game over. You have to stay low. You can't make sudden movements, like quickly standing up, or it just doesn't work. If you need to change positions, stay low. Stay down in the cover and watch the turkey when he struts. If he goes behind his fan or goes behind a tree, that's the time when you need to move, and stay down low. Don't try to rush to the next tree—get down low, and instead just ease over to where you can take that better shot.

There are so many scenarios and so many situations you're going to encounter that you must remember something: The level of turkey hunters' skills will vary according to their hunting experience. If hunters are really new at turkey hunting, they can only talk about what has actually happened with them, so they really do not know how turkeys will react to other tactics, such as those a more experienced hunter might employ. It's a continuing learning process, the elimination of mistakes such as learning when not to move, working on your calling, improving your setups, and more.

But one of the simplest mistakes I continually see hunters make is that they are in too much of a hurry. If you slow down, let events unfold, think clearly and carefully about what you're doing, and take a little time, good things will happen. Both my grandpa and my dad always told me, "You're in too big a hurry, stop rushing everything, if you'll just slow down and enjoy the woods and take your time, the turkey will come."

Hunting Fields

If you take the time to scout and watch turkey activities in the field you're hunting, the turkeys will pretty much tell you where you need to set up. If I have the time, I observe turkeys in the evening before a hunt to see where they exit the field. If you have an opportunity to see where they enter the field, especially in a big, open field, you will often find a low place away from roads where there's not a lot of activity, or maybe a narrow place in the field. The turkeys will usually roost just off the field, and this would be your best setup area.

Use a tree wider than your shoulders to help you blend in, but do not sit too low. Use a small seat to elevate yourself slightly, and pull up your knees.

My setup for open country is a very tight choke, heavier size shot, and a low power scope sighting system. A set of shooting sticks or a bipod is also a good choice in open country.

Sometimes with field setups it's best not to set up right on the field, but in the woods between the roost and the field edge, and then call the turkeys as they leave the roost to come into the field. If this doesn't work out, you're already in cover, so you can maneuver around the field for a new setup.

But one of the best field tactics is to roost turkeys near the field. So, for your field setup, if you roost turkeys in the evening, watch them from a distance. Now, I'm not talking about going in right at dark as they're flying up, but going to watch them earlier while they're still in the field you're going to hunt. Observe their movement, where they go to roost, where they fly up, and your best setup is going to be somewhere relatively close to the turkeys' fly-up point.

There's a reason why they fly up from there into the roost trees—easy access to the roost. There's no reason for the turkeys that fly up from the field to fly down the next morning into the thick stuff, or timber. They easily pitch and drop right back out in the field and continue their activities from the day before. By where you locate your setup in a field you'll improve your odds of killing turkeys, because when you're scouting turkeys, they will tell you where you need to be sitting on the field. It's really quite simple. If you watch turkeys on a field in the evening and they fly up on the right side of the field, there's no reason for you to set up across the field on the left and attempt to call them all the way across a big field.

So watch the turkeys and carefully choose your setup. If your setup doesn't work, find out where turkeys come into the field in the morning. If I go to a new place to hunt field country, and the turkeys come into the field a long ways from where I'm sitting, you can bet I'll be sitting right there the next morning. As long as you don't put a lot of pressure on turkeys and continually spook the birds out of the field, after hunting a field for several days until you are tuned in to exact turkey movement, you will kill a turkey.

This is the view from blind three toward the creek bottom woods, an awesome setup.

It is also important to note that in open country, big fields, and especially hunting in the West, your gun, ammunition, and choke must match the terrain. There was a time when I would never tell anyone to shoot a turkey at over forty yards, but times have changed, and with modern turkey guns, ammunition, and choke tubes, clean kill shots out to fifty yards are not uncommon.

It is critical to pattern your turkey gun prior to hunting with the proper loads, choke, and sighting system to match the terrain you are hunting. My gun setup for open country is a very tight choke, heavier shot—like #4, which retains energy out to longer ranges—and a low-power scope sighting system. A set of shooting sticks or a bipod is also a good choice in open country. This setup is sighted in at center of pattern density dead on at fifty yards.

Timber-Field Setup

We talked a little bit about field hunting. Now there's timber hunting, and there's timber hunting with broken fields and small openings. There are a lot of

This is the shooting lane toward the field from blind one, and is where I set up the decoys.

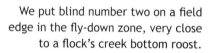

We put blind number two on a field edge in the fly-down zone, very close to a flock's creek bottom roost.

areas in the country where you'll hunt with strips of timber, such as northeast Missouri, southern Iowa, or even Illinois. If you have a place where there are fields that connect strips of timber or old roadbeds, these are all ideal setups.

Of course all this is dictated by turkey movement—where they go during the day. But an ideal setup most of the time (because there's nothing definite about turkeys) is where an old field joins a strip of woods; for instance where an old farm road connects to another field. Just as in deer hunting setups, anywhere different types of structure come together is a good setup where the terrain dictates the movement of turkeys. The gobblers like to go from opening to opening to strut and display.

If you scout your area and notice turkey movement, find an area where the field edge joins a little strip of timber with a roadbed that leads to another opening. This is an ideal setup—in a narrow place on the edge of an old field where you have timber, back up and get inside the timber. Of course, where the turkeys roost is really going to help you, so roosting is really important on a setup. A roost determines where I'm going to sit the next morning.

Blinds are very efficient in a small hunting area in order to keep pressure off birds, and to keep us dry in the inclement weather.

Blind number three is my favorite set up. This blind covers both the field edge and the creek bottom woods where gobblers fly down and strut from the second roost.

My scouting paid off, and we took one of the gobblers—a 23-pound bird with a 10-inch beard and 1-inch spurs—even before the sun came up.

After I watch where turkeys fly up and their direction of travel as they go to the roost, I carefully choose my setup very close to the fly-up point and on the side of their direction of travel to the roost. But the real secret to taking a lot of turkeys is to set up as tight as the terrain will allow you. If you stay back two to three hundred yards from a flock of turkeys with several gobblers or even one gobbler, the chances of calling him in are slim. Too many things can happen at long distances, so get in tight whenever the terrain allows it. I like to be at sixty yards, fifty yards if possible, and I like to be in the area where they pitch down from the roost. You need to get to him quick, and get to him before the hens. So in any open area with strips of timber, look at the terrain, listen, and watch the turkeys and your setup will make all the difference in the world in taking a gobbler.

My gun choice for this type of terrain is a tight choke, #5 shot, and either a red dot or open sights.

For close-in timber hunting, I prefer a more open choke, such as the H.S. Undertaker, with No.6 or 7 1/2 shot and open sights. It's dead on at 25 yards.

My gun choice for mixed field and timber terrain is a tight choke (less restriction than an open-country choke) #5 shot, and either a red dot or open sights such as TruGlo. The gun is sighted dead on at forty yards.

Timber Setup

Setting up in heavy timber like that in the Missouri Ozarks, Massachusetts, or upstate New York is a different game. Of course, you can't see as far in timber and you can't hear as well, but the terrain will also dictate the turkeys' movements. But what I've always taught is in the timber, try to set up on a turkey as close as possible and in the direction of the turkey's travel.

Let's talk about roosting first—if you roost a turkey, this is a major benefit. A good rule of thumb in the ridge country is that if a gobbler goes out the end of the ridge and flies up to roost off a point over a steep hollow, nine times out of ten he's going to pitch back down the same way he flew up. The ideal setup is on the same ridge with the turkey, not on an adjoining ridge or below the roost. Turkeys will go uphill, or they will go downhill—they go wherever they want, because they live there!

But your best bet for your setup is to always make it as easy as possible for a turkey to come to your location and get in as tight as you possibly can. So get on the same ridge, at the same level if possible, where you know he's going to come in because he went down the long ridge to go to roost on the end of the ridge.

Now, if there are a lot of flat woods it may be a little bit different, but again it depends on the terrain and where you're hunting. If it's near water—as it often is in the South—most of the time turkeys will roost over the water. If there's a place where they flew up from the night before, just set up near the same place, because that's where they'll likely fly down the next morning. Wherever you go, turkeys are turkeys.

You have to keep exceptionally still on timber turkeys, especially turkeys in state and national forests, because they have a tendency to come up just under a rise and raise that head for a look around before they commit. But if you sit extremely still, and talk to that turkey, you're in tight, and get to him before the hens get to him, with a good setup, you will kill a lot of timber turkeys. Now, what is a good setup? Twenty-five or thirty yards from a break in the hill or a bend in the road, we have killed literally hundreds of turkeys over the years. Get tight, get close, don't be afraid to call, and sit still. You're going to get a lot of great action and kill a lot of timber turkeys.

For this close-in work, I prefer a more open choke, like the H. S. Strut Undertaker, or a standard full choke. I shoot #6 shot, and sometimes #7½ shot. And I recommend open sights, with the gun patterned dead on at twenty-five yards.

Blinds

Another tactic that has now become very popular is hunting from ground blinds. Blinds are a great choice on smaller tracts of land, to keep pressure off the turkeys. Blinds also work well to conceal multiple hunters and TV camera crews, not to mention being a great choice in inclement weather.

I often utilize blind setups for youth hunts and media hunts, depending on the hunting situation. During my 2011 Chasing Spring™ hunts, blinds were

necessary for my Kansas hunt, which took place in open country during bad weather. In the Hunting for A Cure youth benefit in Tennessee, blinds were the only choice. But blinds in Missouri on a small tract of field and timber strip country, in the early season, and to keep pressure off

The author and Peanut—who gets her own little turkey blind—return to the Missouri Ozarks for a special turkey hunt.

Blind set up on a small tract in Missouri, to keep pressure off the birds.

We set up blind number one against a tree and along the edge of the biggest field, where hens were feeding and gobblers fighting.

the birds, were also very important. Blind setups depend on the area and the turkey's movements, and we have had great success using blinds, much more than if we had attempted run-and-gun tactics.

Ground blinds really help a lot of turkey hunters who have a problem sitting still or setting up in the right place. However turkeys can still detect movement, and a lot of these blinds have windows all the way around. You must close the windows behind you and to your sides, and open only the front of the blind where you're going to take the shot. But you still have to sit still, even inside a blind.

In blinds, too many hunters still make too much noise and move around too much. Yes, you can get away with a little more movement inside an enclosed blind than sitting out in the open, but it doesn't mean you can just move from one window to the other and bob your head around. Blinds can work for you—but you still have to keep still and you still have to be quiet and not make a lot of unnecessary noise.

15

Early Season

OVER THE YEARS EARLY SEASON OR A "LATE SPRING" SEEMS to occur more often than an early spring, perfect weather, or perfect timing with gobbling at its peak. During my 2011 Chasing Spring™ expedition, late spring followed me from Florida to New England. I found open woods, cold wind, rain, and even snow. In more or less every state, on every hunt, turkeys were in the early phases of the mating ritual, thus rendering the old-school "soft yelp, call very little, wait thirty minutes" tactic completely useless.

Many hunters face late spring or "early season" when their state's hunting season opens before there's been much in the way of springtime green-up, and area gobbler flocks haven't broken up yet, or for that matter even partially broken up. Now, early season can be really tough for many hunters when gobblers are bunched together, but in this chapter I will teach you how to call and kill gobblers during this early season phase.

With gobblers fighting within the flock for social status, hen yelps are not as effective during this phase; a hunter must be willing to change his or her calling to challenge a gobbler's status within the pecking order. During this timeframe, I gobbler yelp to call and kill gobblers, and I challenge their status with aggressive yelping, purring, gobbler cutting, and even gobbling.

Now, while it is usually tough for hunters during early season with gobblers still grouped together, it just doesn't have to

Many hunters face late spring or "early season," when their state's hunting season opens, before springtime green up. Area flocks frequently haven't broken up for the mating season, yet.

For duplicating gobbler yelping, a box call or a good slate or glass offer excellent choices.

be this way, because gobbler yelping will change the game in your favor. I utilize my fall turkey calling skills—I call tom-to-tom with gobbler talk, and for more than thirty years I have killed gobblers all across America with this tactic. A good friction call (like a box call or a good slate or glass) is an excellent choice to duplicate gobbler yelping. Just lengthen your yelp more than hen yelps, and use a slightly slower rhythm. Don't worry, gobblers know what it is. The reaction to challenging toms with gobbler yelping is actually pretty much the same as a hunter using modern male strutting and jake decoys, and both are good when used in conjunction with gobbler yelping. It's also important to roost early season birds, get in tight, and call aggressively to challenge a gobbler's status in the pecking order of the flock.

I'll use an example with the Merriam's turkey simply to make the point that the gobbler yelping I've used successfully for years with Easterns also works with all subspecies of turkeys. During a recent media hunt in Wyoming with the Solitude Ranch, we faced quite the challenge with an early season. On our morning setups, the daylight roosts were full of both hen and gobbler flocks, and there was plenty of live hen competition, as well as gobblers more interested in fighting with their buddies than coming to our hen calls.

During this media hunt, I hunted one at time with my editors and outdoor writers from start to finish, as others remained on deck for their turn as

Early season outdoor media hunt on the Solitude Ranch.

This northern Missouri gobbler was taken during early season by roosting, getting in tight in the dark because of open woods, calling aggressively, and challenging the hens.

the shooter. This was just the case after a morning kill with Gordy Krahn of *North American Hunter.* Up next was my longtime turkey hunting buddy Karen Mehall of NRA's *American Hunter* magazine, and she was more than ready for her afternoon hunt.

After several hours of driving the ranch with our super guide Jay Norman, Jay Cassell, and my hunter Karen, we were having little success at first with calling and starting gobblers. But when we finally struck a gobbler late in the evening, we quickly realized that in this wide-open country it would be quite the challenge to move in to set up and call. We drove quite a ways around to park behind a large hill to hide ourselves and our truck, and then it was a forced march to close the distance and set up before our bird disappeared into the late evening hills. After little response to our hen calling, I opened up with a barrage of gobbler yelping and cutting. The response was better than I expected, with return gobbler yelping and gobbling.

A really nice gobbler with a dozen jakes in tow managed to get by our setup, but reappeared in the bottom pasture. Jakes yelped at my every call, and the big guy gobbled and strutted, but it was apparent that, with their movement across the valley, they were heading for a faraway roost site.

Finally, after another pleading yet challenging run of gobbler yelps, with a couple of jake gobbles thrown in, we heard a gobbler to our right, then he appeared in full strut on his way to whip me. But he didn't quite make it, as Karen took him out of the gene pool with one well-placed shot. This was an incredibly cool hunt, and since it may be difficult for you to understand the gobbler yelp in the writing on these pages, Karen's hunt is on my *Calling is Everything* DVD, where you can hear gobbler yelping and watch turkeys responding to gobbler yelping.

Early season in your hunting area may also fall at a time when gobblers are covered up with hens, but the mating ritual is not yet in full swing, with hens paying little or no attention to gobblers. This is a time of frustration for hunt-ers—gobblers pay little heed to calling because they just follow hens every-where in an attempt to impress the nonresponsive ladies. It is during this phase when a hunter has set up and called to a gobbling tom at daylight, but the hens lead him away and the hunter curses the day that gobbler was hatched.

There are also several tactics you can implement during this phase. The first is to use the pecking order again, but this time by challenging the hens, not to call to the gobbler, but call to the hens, challenge hens, call aggressively, call however the hens call but with more feeling and emotion. Call in a yelp-ing, mad hen, and many times the rest of the flock and gobblers will blindly follow her right up to the business end of your gun barrel.

I could cite hundreds of examples of this tactic's success, from my early Ozarks days all the way to my 2011 Chasing Spring™ hunts; however, I am going to tell you about calling hens on that same recent media hunt in Wyoming with Merriam's turkeys. After roosting a huge, early season flock of turkeys the night before on a steep Wyoming rock bluff, our guide set up our group in the dark the next morning, below the roost in a creek bottom, about 300 yards from the turkeys. This is not where I would have liked to set up—I'd have liked to be much closer, but I also realized that our guide knew these turkeys' travel route after leaving the roost.

On an early season Merriam's roost like this one, turkeys wake up with some chatter. Toms gobble for a short while, then hens fly down and start their day, moving away from the roost and feeding as they have done for weeks, then more or less just vanish to somewhere that only the turkeys know. As for the gobblers, after their fly-down, the strutting begins, the gobbling ceases, and they simply follow unre-sponsive hens for the rest of the day. This is when calling becomes very important, especially while the tur-keys are still in the roost. Working

This early season gobbler was taken in North Missouri by Bob Whitehead of *Outdoor Guide* magazine by roosting, setting up tight, and getting on the call even while gobblers were still on the roost.

Brother Marty with a early season Ozarks gobbler. An early season usually has little green up with gobblers either still running together or covered up with hens. This gobbler was taken by challenging and calling in the hens.

up the hens with calling and challenging their status in the flock with a new voice, a different turkey, really works them up. As hen yelping and cutting increases, so does the gobbling, and all turkeys in the roost get worked up into a frenzy. But you really have to pour it on—besides, what do you have to lose? They will simply walk away with the gobblers if you hold back on calling or wait until fly-down to call.

This turned out to be an amazing early season hunt, with hens yelping nonstop and marching 300 yards to the gun, and multiple toms strutting as they followed the hens right to our setup. It's important to realize that the gobblers couldn't care less that we were calling. They did not respond to our calls, but the hens sure did, and it cost one of those gobblers his life. This incredible hunt, with unbelievable turkey vocalizations, is also on my *Calling is Everything* DVD for you to hear both the hens' and our calling, and see our hunt unfold with a kill by calling the hens in the early season.

Let's review everything we've covered about hunting an early season, with how-to information to consistently call and kill early season gobblers. Hunters pursuing springtime gobblers are programmed from years of turkey hunting lore to hen-yelp a gobbling tom within a short timeframe of the mating season.

Early season hunting prior to mating or even during mating equals plenty of hen competition for gobblers, thus making life miserable for turkey hunters who rely only on the hen yelp made to responsive, lonely, lovestruck toms.

Hunters facing a late spring or "early season" many times have their season arrival before spring green up, gobbler flocks either haven't broke up, or have partially broke up. With gobblers fighting for social status within the flock, hen yelps are not effective during this phase; a hunter must be willing to change his or her calling to challenge a gobbler's status within the pecking order.

The reaction from challenging toms is actually much the same as using today's male and strutting decoys, and these decoys are very good when used in conjunction with gobbler yelping. It's also important to roost early season birds, get in tight and to call aggressively.

There are several tactics to implement during this phase. The first is to use the pecking order again, but this time by challenging the hens. Do not call to the gobbler, but call to the hens. Challenge hens, call aggressively, call however the hens call, but you should call with more feeling and emotion. Call in a yelping, mad hen, and the rest of the flock and the gobbler will follow.

The next tactic is to bust the flock, scatter the hens from the gobbler, either from the roost or later in the morning, set up in the direction of the gobblers' escape and call with excitement, and more often than not, the gobbler will return quickly to rejoin his hens.

The next phase of early spring is the actual mating process, a time when hunters hear little gobbling because toms are strutting for the girls. Roosting is very important during this time. Set up tight to the roost, be the first hen he hears at daylight, get him down, and kill him before most of the hens are even out of the roost. Scattering and gobbler yelping can also be utilized with great success during this time. Hunters need to adapt to the situation, the time of year, and be willing to try something different to become consistent turkey killers during early season.

16

Breeding Season

WE'VE COVERED EARLY SEASON AND SEVERAL TACTICS TO utilize during that time. The next phase that presents problems for hunters is the actual mating process, a time when hunters may or may not hear much gobbling, because toms are strutting and hanging with the girls. Many times a hunter's season opens when turkeys are in the middle of mating and few hens are on the nest.

Before we get into tactics, let's first review turkeys' seasonality during the mating phase of spring turkey hunting. Now, just a little later in an early season as the day length increases, gobbler activity increases, with gobblers strutting and displaying in an attempt to attract hens for mating. During break-up, lesser birds are pushed out of the area, and a dominant gobbler is involved in the majority of the mating and gathers and protects the hens.

When the turkey flocks begin break up, they disperse into other areas. The dominant gobbler has a particular territory where he struts and displays for the hens, but it's the hens that actually dictate the gobblers' movements. Gobblers will follow the hens. So where there's good cover, good nesting, and decent food sources, that's where your gobblers will go for the mating season, simply because they follow the hens. Eventually, dominant gobblers will hold the bulk of the hens in an area and perform the majority of the mating.

Once the hens are with the gobblers and they're in the middle of the mating, when hens become responsive and toms are actually breeding the hens, it's a very difficult time for you as a turkey hunter to call a wild turkey—they're with the real thing.

With the dominant gobblers strutting and displaying with the hens, your lesser birds are on the outside of these areas, gobbling. Many hunters call these "satellite gobblers," and they respond very well to calling, so you actually imitate a hen that wants to get with a gobbler—but instead you play "hard to get," and lure the gobbler. A two-year-old will come to the call and he'll try to slip in and get over there and get involved in the mating because the old gobbler's getting all the girls.

This Wyoming Merriam's was taken during breeding season by using the proven tactics of setting up really tight and calling in the hens.

Of course this all depends on turkey populations in your area, and as has been the case the past several seasons, after multiple bad hatches, those two-year-olds are nonexistent and hunters are dealing with older gobblers covered up with hens. That's why during this mating phase roosting becomes ever more important. Set up tight on the roost, be the first hen turkey he hears at daylight, get him down from his roost in front of you, and kill him even before most of the hens fly out of the roost.

I have hundreds of examples of roosting scenarios from over the years that ended with the killing of nongobbling turkeys covered up with hens in the heat of mating, however, given limited space, I will recall for you several exceptional situations of taking gobblers during this very difficult time of henned-up gobblers.

In northeast Missouri during one of our sponsored outdoor media hunts, the weather was terribly cold, with wind and rain, but turkeys were acting even worse than the weather as hens became receptive right before our writers arrived in camp. With fifteen writers in our camp, without any morning gobbling, with pouring rain and high winds every day, and to add to the mix, the hens were running and flying to

Carman Forbes of Hunter's Specialties took this Eastern gobbler with the author in North Missouri for the *HS Outdoors* TV show. Moving and calling until finally striking the bird and moving in quickly, they were able to kill the gobbler before the hens moved in to the gobbler.

any tom that gobbled. Our hunters really faced a challenge, and we had our work cut out for us.

During a rainy late afternoon, from a distance I watched a big strutter and his partner display with a flock of hens in a big cornfield. Once the turkeys went into the woods right before dark, I made my move, carefully easing in and following them up the ridge to the roost. The hens flew up first on the edge of a bench, leaving their strutting lover boys alone on the forest floor. The gobblers moved across the bench to the head of a deep holler and flew up into a big oak. I yelped on my mouth call, and the hens quickly yelped back. I turned it up a bit, and when the hens came back more excited, both toms gobbled, and I paused for a second and threw out an excited fly-up cackle, to which both the hens and gobblers lit up.

I backed away, made a circle under the ridge, and came up just below the gobblers' roost. I studied the bench above me and noticed another big oak on the bench just up from the gobblers. But more important, my morning setup would be between the girls and the boys. As I slipped back down the hill, I paused and hit my call again, and both toms gobbled "good-night." I wanted to be the last hen they heard at night, and the first hen they heard in the morning.

Jon Sabati killed this Wyoming gobbler by challenging the hens with his calling during the breeding season.

We were up really early the next morning. Well, that is, I was up with my hunter, Scotty Rupp from *Petersen's Hunting*. All the others grumbled, and chose to stay in bed a while longer. The rain had finally let up after midnight, but the creeks would still be up, and a challenge for us to cross in order to get up on the ridge with the turkeys. We had to park out on the road because of muddy fields, and we knew it would be best to keep the noise of a truck out of the bottom below the roost.

Once across the bottom field, I had to search for a place to cross the swollen creek. Finally locating a big log in a narrow place, we made our way across the creek and started up the ridge. About 100 yards short of the roost, we paused, lights out, no talking, and we slipped out of our boots and slowly and quietly worked our way to the big oak.

Now I told Scott I had roosted some turkeys and that we would be set up tight, but he didn't have any idea what "tight on the roost" means with me. Holding his shotgun under his coat to muffle any sound, he loaded his gun, and while we quietly waited for first light, the rain started again. Then, just after the first songbirds began to greet a new day, the drumming from the big oak came loud and clear. Well, Scotty now knew the meaning of "tight." I whispered to Scott to hold his gun to his shoulder and aim on the bench just out in front of him—and no matter what, do not move. Out of the corner of my eye, I could see both birds strutting on the limb, doing a little preening, and then heading back into strut. The hens called first, so I replied with a little pert-pert and soft yelping. The hens yelped back and both toms gobbled. And I gotta tell you, at about twenty-five yards, they were really loud.

Scott was mumbling under his breath something about, "Are you kidding me, holy crap," or something like that, when I noticed the bigger of the two toms start rocking on the limb to fly down. It was now time. I cut hard on my call, both toms gobbled, the hens came to life, and soon that ridge was really rocking, when the big gobbler pitched down and hit the ground right in front of Scott at about ten steps. His gun roared, and it was over.

We were the only team in camp—out of fifteen hunters—to kill a gobbler that morning, and the reason was roosting, setting up really tight, getting between the gobblers and the girls, and calling, both with roosting and at first light.

You see, when gobblers are covered up with hens during this mating phase, roosting becomes ever more important. Set up tight on the roost, be the first "hen turkey" he hears at daylight, then get him

Ozark gobblers taken by Marty Eye and Ray during the breeding phase.

down quickly and out in front of you, and kill him before any of his hens are even off the roost.

Several years later, I witnessed another unique roosting event. Not unlike during Scott's hunt, the turkeys were in the middle of breeding, and the hens would more often than not lead your gobbler away from your calling. My hunter came in for my media hunt on the last leg of his Grand Slam, and he was pretty pumped to kill his Eastern. But this would not be an easy chore, as turkeys were really tough at the time of his hunt.

But I had a plan. I really watched and listened to the turkeys on my place, and I knew that if we did it right, we would get him his Grand Slam. In the back section of my farm there is a big creek bottom field, and up on top of the main ridge, three ridges come together. This is an area I had let rest for three days, and only watched and listened from a distance.

The hens fed in the field in the evening with strutters in tow, and then went up the ridge; the hens roosted on the middle of the main ridge, and the gobblers would separate and roost out on the three adjoining ridges.

But the interesting part of this whole deal was a high-pitched, clear-voiced hen I heard at daylight during my scouting. When she yelped, the gobblers would go crazy. It didn't matter if other hens yelped, the toms ran to her, and she was not shy about calling. The night before our hunt, with my hunter relaxing back at camp, I roosted the birds from the field edge next to the creek. Then after dark and when the gobblers were tucked safely in bed out on the three ridges, I climbed the steep ridge and flushed my clear-yelping friend from her roost on the main ridge where all three ridges met.

Now with a TV crew, way too many people, and a really fidgety, out-of-shape, and noisy hunter, there was no way we would make it in for a setup from below, and up the steep ridge, without blowing out every bird on the property. So on my way back to camp, I stopped by my neighbor's to ask permission to cross his property from above in order to go in on my ridge to set up.

We loaded up extra early with five people and drove through to my neighbor's on an old ridgetop logging road, about 150 yards from my fenceline and our tree. It was better to sit in the dark for an hour with all these people than to ruin the hunt before it even got started. We were in place and ready to go at first light. Our three gobblers opened up, the others across the valley and down the creek bottom opened up, and I knew I had to get them in quickly before our hen returned and led them away. I was using my Wood Witch glass call this morning, because with it I could duplicate the hen's clear, clean yelp. I have to tell you, my yelping from the hen's roost area, just like her, tore them up. We had gobblers closing fast from three sides, even before we had enough light for the camera.

I shifted my hunter to the south, as two gobblers coming from that ridge were about to join us on the main ridge. Once the camera dude gave the okay on the light, I wore that call out just like that hen called, and we had a gobbler and a Grand Slam on the ground even before 6 AM. Guess who's buying breakfast?

Now, none of these hunters had any idea how much time and work I put into their hunts, or how much research and planning I went through. They just thought I was magic, and that's OK. I actually like it better that way!

During the breeding phase, a tactic utilizing gobbler yelping to challenge a gobbler's social status is very effective, with a history of great success. Yet another tactic during this time is scattering hens and gobblers from the roost. This is a fall hunting tactic, to bust the flock, scatter the hens from the gobblers, either from the roost or later in the morning from in a field.

First is the roost scatter, in open country following a gobbler and hens to the roost, or roosting in timber using locating calls or turkey calls, then waiting until dark to walk under the roost and scatter them everywhere. The next morning's hunt is usually a wild one with hens calling to regroup and the gobbler breaking his neck to rejoin his hens; this is a time your calling will really work effectively. The key is to set up in the direction of the gobbler's escape and call with excitement. More often than not, the gobbler will make every effort to return quickly to rejoin his hens.

Some years back in northern Missouri, after an unsuccessful morning in another area, after driving back to our main camp, we spotted a strutter with a dozen hens in our bottom field. We quickly slipped through the cover to close the distance, and once I was fairly close, I ran out in the field and scattered turkeys everywhere. The good thing for us is the hens flew across the field and a big creek to a big ridge, but the tom chose to run in the opposite direction into a little patch of hillside cover. My hunter had just sat down and was loading his gun when the gobbler, in a fast walk, broke from the cover into the field. On my first call, the hens immediately called from behind us and the gobbler broke into a full run, right at us. It was all over in less than five minutes.

Radical roosting and setting up tight put these two Ozarks gobblers in the bag for Gary Lee and Marty Eye.

The high population of hens is the biggest difference in my overall turkey hunting experience. When I started turkey hunting years ago, there wasn't as much hen turkey competition or as much hunter competition as there is today, especially on public ground. But your biggest competition as a turkey hunter is the hen turkey itself, because there is such a large population of turkeys today.

We have more turkeys now than we've had in the last hundred years. With a lot of turkeys, gobblers don't have to travel very far to find hens. Usually they wake up with hens, so your competition is the hen turkey, and this is why you have to get in tight on turkeys. That is also another reason why I teach calling. You really need to learn to call with feeling, with enthusiasm, and get turkeys worked up, because you're competing with the real thing. Another point is that a hen turkey can walk to a gobbler—you can't. So call excitedly, get in tight, try to get to him before the hens get there, do not be afraid to call, and call aggressively.

With high populations of turkeys, the hunting tactics have changed over the years. I feel, if the correct term is "aggressive," that we have to get more aggressive and call more than we did just twenty years ago, if you're going to have any success with today's hen turkey competition. It all comes down to hunters having to adapt to the situation and the time of year, and be willing to try something different to become consistent turkey killers during spring mating season when gobblers are covered up with hens.

17

Late Season, Post-Breeding

AFTER BREEDING, MOST OF THE HENS IN YOUR AREA GO on the nest. Of course, calling and killing turkeys during this time also works best when there are a lot of two-year-old gobblers. It all depends on the turkey population during the time you're hunting. But if there are a lot of two-year-old gobblers, they make up most of the turkeys taken during the spring season.

This is a time in the phase of turkey's seasonality when almost all turkey hunters shine with their calling—gobblers will literally knock down other gobblers to race to whatever might even slightly resemble the squeaking sound of a willing hen. Now this is a small window of opportunity, and it's what most turkey hunting—well, all turkey hunting—is judged by. Outside of that window of opportunity it becomes very difficult for a lot of hunters to kill turkeys, but I will tell you later in this chapter how to do just that.

The older, dominant turkeys are very used to the hens coming to them, but when they run out of hens and they still want to breed and you sound like a hen playing hard to get, sometimes they'll break, because they're frustrated and worked up with calling.

Now to the old question: "Are you reversing nature when you call a wild turkey in the spring of the year?" Well, yes and no. It depends on what's going on with the turkey flock at that time, wherever you may be hunting. Your old gobblers, your three-, four-, five-year-old dominant birds, call the hens to them. That's what they do. That's why they gobble. They attract the hens. You will see hens running to gobblers. You'll see hens *flying* to gobblers. And it's really tough to hunt turkeys when all the hens are going to the gobblers. However you still have those lesser birds to the pecking order like the two-year-olds and some three-year-olds that've been pushed from the flock. They will investigate a hen call, and come to the call, so it really isn't "reversing nature."

Also, it's very natural for tom turkeys to go to a hen when they hear a hen calling because hens will often answer a gobbler but then go on about their daily business and not pay any attention to the gobbler. Gobblers will respond to your calling especially if hens are not interested in breeding so that gobblers become frustrated and will go to the "hen" to try to court her. You just have to stay with it because some gobblers will continue looking for hens and they will peak and gobble again, as there are some gobblers that continue looking for hens that haven't been bred.

Listen to the turkeys, watch the turkeys, and they will tell you how to hunt them and how to call them. If you hit that small window of opportunity when everything's right, the hens are on the nest, gobblers respond, and that's great.

It all depends on the turkeys, but you need to adjust your hunting tactics and learn to adapt. Change your tactics and how you call your turkeys depending on what the turkeys are doing. How do you know what the turkeys are doing? Watch them; listen to them and adjust your hunting tactics depending on what the turkeys are doing at the time you're hunting them.

After mating, when a lot of hens are on the nest, you get another, later peak of gobbling. That's when toms are getting back together, regrouping, and rebuilding the social structure of the gobbler flock. Sometimes during post-breeding you'll hit a period when all the breeding is done and there's not a lot of gobbling. But there's going to be another peak of gobbling sometime during the post-breeding phase. Many hunters say that when gobbling is over, turkey season is over. But it really isn't that way at all.

Spring turkey seasons run into the first week of June in some places. This is especially true in the Northeast, but don't be fooled by the old myth that springtime love begins in the south and runs north into June. I've found that hunting Old Mexico's Sierra Madre during the first week of June was actually very good on several trips. We called in many gobbling Gould's turkeys to the gun, and this kind of blows holes in the old myth that "It's over in the South after the month of March."

Late in the season, both hunter and hunted are driven by the hope that spring can be called back up. But late season may also be the only free time you

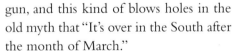

As you can tell by the high grass and thick tree green up, this is late season. This Illinois hunt was successful due to watching, listening to the turkeys, and adjusting calling and hunting strategies accordingly.

When hunting the Sierra Madre during the first week of June, we called in many Gould's turkeys.

have available to hunt, so it is important to be willing to learn as much as possible about late season hunting. If you are either forced or just choose to chase late spring gobblers, you are admitting up front that you share something with the bird you pursue: a hopeful nature that ignores reality. Both of you should grow up and move on, but can't.

Think about it. Hens, by and large, are no longer available to gobblers. Hunters, long ago, should have been tending to lawn work, gone back to their real jobs, or at the very least become serious about fishing season. Trees have now leafed out, and the grasses are tall enough to hide a standing turkey. Tent caterpillars drop from the trees, sounding like rain. Mosquitoes swarm in droves. Poison ivy is in full bloom. But, thank the Lord, boy turkeys can't let go of it, either, and they gobble back with a gusto that's often missing during the peak of breeding. And that's what makes late season hunts possible.

Let's call it what it is: early summer turkey hunting. Back during the actual breeding season, grand and glorious specimens—the biggest, baddest gobblers of all time—were fooled into believing that hen turkeys were actually interested in seeing them fight off rival toms, and flexed in the aftermath, stomping around the pasture as if they just won a loser-leaves-town cage match. The myth is given wings when, in a fit of female hormones, the hen allows the triumphant tom to climb all over her back and do what he's been preoccupied with for most of his life. Then, long after hens have resumed normal self-control (and in fact are beginning to take care of babies in some cases), foolish strutters remain convinced that if they gobble with enough bravado and tuck their heads in tight against their chests, it will be April again, and they might get a second date.

The truth of the matter is that those boys turkeys are allowed to stand around field corners and strut because the turkey world does not have a legal system complete with child support mechanisms. Otherwise, boy turkeys would be punching a time clock and having their wages garnished, instead of dragging their down-stretched wings across the ground until the tips are squared off. In our wonderful land of shared fantasy, we end up in the same places every May, those of us who look away and pretend spawning crappies don't exist, and testosterone-laced wild turkey gobblers, so perfectly single-minded that they give us hope that today could be the day.

Late season turkey hunts are a time to take on birds you would leave for somebody else earlier in the year. That big tom that owns the ridge, always surrounded by a bevy of prying female eyes as he pitches down among them, becomes a possible target after he finds himself without the entourage. After all, once a star, always wanting to be a star again, is what I always say, and in many ways that turkey is most vulnerable after breeding, refusing to relinquish the crown of king of the whole area until somebody rubs his face in the dried leaves and makes him cry uncle. He is huntable now precisely because he was once king of a court that has now moved on, and he clings to yesterday in much the same way you do.

There would be no way to prove it in a court of law, and no way to describe it to anybody, but you know his gobble when you hear it. You might not be able to distinguish human voices on the phone, but his gobble is very obvious. When it comes to hen talk, you know what he likes, evidence enough that you probably should be home planting the garden, but there you sit in the dark, listening to the wind through the new leaves, waiting for the show to start. It's a tragedy and a comedy and a natural desire impossible to break rolled into one great hunt after another. He wants to come to you so badly and you want to get a shot at him, and yet both of you retain just enough disparate strengths and weaknesses that you usually repel each other right at the moment of truth.

He wants to believe you are a real hen, his ears hearing overtures that turn back the clock, so he glides in strutting at daylight, as if it were six weeks ago. Despite the hormones, he retains instincts honed by avoiding coyotes that like the taste of turkey, so he stops and looks in at the source, and sees you move, and

Ralph Duren with his late season Kansas Rio.

has no choice but to drift away without a sound, gobbling a retreating invitation when you call again, and you wonder why he does this every time. Why, he must be "call-shy."

You want to hear it one more time, another gobble, so even when you don't get the one you want, you hunt out the morning. Marshall McLuhan, famous for his studies of human culture, claimed that language is man's richest art form, something that distinguishes us from animals. If that's true, then it would be on a technicality. Because our words will never compare to the gobbler's voice, when the measure is our emotional response, and the way it keeps us in the woods after we can't even see through them anymore. A gobble rings all the way through, unhooking the part of our brain responsible for reasoned thought.

On plenty of our turkey hunting days, late season included, we walk miles, and end up back at the truck with little to show except muddy grass stuck to the bottoms of our boots. In fact, the grass eventually gets long enough that we have to paw through it to find our slate call and striker before moving to the next promising spot. There are other things you can do with your time after the world greens up completely, but nothing replaces one last hunt. Being able to drink coffee out of a mug with strutting turkeys on it might serve as an oxygen mask, but it's nothing like leaning your head back and connecting with that familiar feeling of tree bark. It says a lot about the pull of the sport when we remain in love with every tortured bit of it, until long after it should have been over for the year. Or maybe it's much simpler than that. Maybe it does come down to the remarkable similarities between turkey hunters and turkey gobblers, both choosing hope over a long look in the mirror.

The hardest day of any season is the last day. I can't speak for the birds, but only by filling the final tag or coming to the actual end of the line, by the legal definition according to the calendar, am I willing to hang it up until spring comes again, if it ever will.

What Makes Late Season Gobblers Tough for Hunters?

If birds are tough during late season, it's usually from pressure on the turkeys. Of course it depends on where you are hunting, but weeks of people activity, vehicles, ATVs, hunters bumping birds, and disturbing roosts all take a toll on gobbling. Turkeys will change their normal habits dependent on the amount of people disturbance, time of year, weather, seasonality of turkeys, late spring, and early spring. All of these factor into how you should hunt

In addition to weather, hunting success also depends on the turkey's cycle or seasonality.

late season. A hunter needs to read the turkeys, watch, and listen to what the turkeys are doing at the time he is hunting them.

If you are fortunate to have a hunting area where turkeys have had no pressure, just hunt the way you always have during regular season. Now, once again, spring turkey hunting is measured, determined to be "right" only during a small window of opportunity, when there are lots of gobbling two-year-olds, many hens are already bred, most hens are on the nest, and gobblers readily respond to a hen call. Anything outside that window and people say the season is off and birds are call-shy, which is of course all a fallacy.

Turkeys are turkeys, and they act like turkeys by doing what they always do and have done for thousands of years. Many times late season is best (dependent on pressure) because of less hen interference. Late in the season, breeding is sometimes over and reestablishment of the pecking order is going on. Gobblers fight for status as much after breeding as they do prior to breeding.

I have in my possession valuable, incredible video footage of gobblers displaying, gobbling, pushing, and fighting into June, July, August, even all year long—so it is never really over, despite what some hunters like to say. So during late season fall, hunt those gobblers, challenge them with gobbler yelps. I kill more gobblers all across America with gobbler yelps than I do with hen calls. I have been doing this for thirty years, and today, hunters are finally starting to realize this. That is why there are so many strutting decoys. They challenge gobblers, just as I do with my calling. Always use a strutting decoy in late season. I will also sometimes scatter a gobbler with hens or a flock of gobblers, either from a roost or a field and call again, get to a tom before his hens get back to him, or kill a bird as the gobblers try to get back together.

What is Your Single Best Hunting Tip for the Late Season?

Hunt like it's opening day, adapt your calling and hunting style dependent on what turkeys are doing in the area you are hunting. Get tight, and call hard.

How Many Calls Will You Carry in the Late Season?

Same as I do anytime: mouth calls, glass or slate, and always a really good, loud, great-sounding box call.

How is your Calling Game Plan Different in the Late Season Versus Early Season?

Problem is, this is a loaded question, and it all depends on what is going on—seasonality, weather, early, late spring, hunting pressure. However, I usually go to challenging gobblers instead of hen calling for mating.

What is the Best Time of Day and Ideal Conditions to Hunt Gobblers in the Late Season?

When the season is open, anytime you can be out there is the best time. I'm not sure if there are ever any ideal conditions. For years and years I have continued to like hunting the roost at daybreak. I always roost turkeys. If I can roost a late season gobbler, I know what tree he is in, what limb he is on, and his direction of fly-up. I get really tight and call hard, and many times I carry him out and I'm having breakfast by 7:30 AM.

It's the Last Day of the Season, and Time is Winding Down: What's Your Last-resort Tactic?

Not sure if I have one of those. I just go with what is working. I always say hunt the last day no differently than the first day. Stay away from peer-pressure thinking and "time is running down, I have to kill a turkey" attitudes. Just hunt hard, never give up, and let things unfold as they will. And just go until the whistle blows, kill or no kill.

What is Your Favorite Way to End a Successful Turkey Hunt?

A big breakfast.

18

2011 Chasing Spring™ Hunt Breakdown

IN THIS CHAPTER I BREAK DOWN SOME OF MY 2011 CHASing Spring™ tour, and explain weather, turkey seasonality, tactics, what worked, what didn't, and why. It would be impossible to cover every hunt, so I have chosen some of my most memorable hunts to share with you. I am very proud to have been chosen by *Outdoor Life* magazine to host their Chasing Spring™ website.

Outdoor Life Partners with Ray Eye For Chasing Spring™, a One-stop Turkey Hunting Destination

"New York, NY–*Outdoor Life*, The Source for Hunting and Fishing Adventure, announced today a new partnership with legendary turkey hunter Ray Eye. Chasing Spring™ will offer readers the ultimate turkey hunting destination through a dedicated blog, video, and photos that will follow Ray Eye as he turkey hunts all over North America. Chasing Spring™ will also be covered in *Outdoor Life*'s print edition and highlighted on the Ray Eye radio show and during his traveling seminars.

"Chasing Spring™ is really going to highlight the best and most exciting aspects of turkey hunting. Ray is one of the world's most renowned turkey hunters and his knowledge and passion for the sport will be great for our turkey-hunting fanatic readers.

"Beginning in February, Eye will set out on the ultimate turkey hunting road trip, starting in the South and chasing turkeys north through mid-June. Along the way he'll visit some of the most renowned turkey hunting locations, chronicling his hunting and calling and, with a little luck, taking gobblers all across the map. Throughout the journey, Eye will offer readers the best turkey hunting tips and tricks, from the best calling techniques to the gear needed to get the job done right.

"As Eye hunts his way though Missouri, Massachusetts, Florida, Illinois, Wyoming, Kansas, Mexico, and more, he'll share his professional turkey

Today's modern turkey gun, with a Nikon low-power turkey scope, is good medicine for Florida osceolas.

hunting secrets with readers along the way. Eye's advanced turkey tactics will arm readers with the knowledge they'll need to enhance their turkey hunting success no matter the conditions, including hunting with limited time, hunting without preseason scouting, hunting early season and late season, hunting pressured gobblers, and more.

"From where to go to what gear to use, Chasing Spring™ is a one-stop shop for turkey hunters. There really isn't a better person for the job than Ray Eye. With his support, Chasing Spring™ is going to be a place to get inspired and also to get advice from a turkey hunting legend on what works."

South Florida Early Season

Chasing Spring™ embarked on its first turkey hunt of the 2011 season, and as you will see it was an overwhelming success. Our journey began early

Our crew, from left to right: Stephen Mitchell, Eric Zinczenko, C. J. Davis, Greg Gatto, me, and Brian Lisankie.

On the job, and just another day in the office. C. J. and I hunted together to try to get some gobblers on camera. We did.

Here's C. J., Brian Lisankie, and me, with C. J.'s long-spurred south Florida gobbler.

Capturing the morning as it unfolds. This is my early-morning camera setup, between the roost and the orange groves.

Sunday morning, March 6, at 3 AM. After loading my old green Suburban, I headed off from home at 4 AM for my drive to St. Louis for a 6 AM flight. I was flying to Florida to hunt the wily Osceolas with the boys from *Outdoor Life* and C. J. Davis from Nikon Hunting.

On arrival in Fort Myers, I was greeted by Stephen Mitchell, *Outdoor Life's* sporting goods manager, and as we loaded my bags and camera gear, Stephen caught me up with news of intense gobbler fights he'd witnessed near the area we would be hunting. We quickly drove to the ranch to meet the other hunters for our first afternoon in the Florida swamps. After we got to camp, I paired with C. J. Davis of Nikon and Brian Lisanke of Aimpoint for an evening pasture camera setup, deep within the ranch's hunting area.

We didn't hear any gobbling or see any bearded warriors during our first set. We only spotted a couple of hens and enjoyed an unbelievable barred owl serenade at dark, but my first whip-poor-will song and firefly show of a new spring sure made it all worthwhile. This was not your typical spring hunt with receptive gobblers running to anything that resembled a hen call. This hunt was actually one of the toughest spring hunts I've had in Florida in many years.

Outdoor Life publisher Eric Zinczenko took his gobbler with stick and string.

As we witnessed turkey flocks still in the middle of spring break-up, this was going to be an early season hunt situation, and just as Stephen had witnessed, we saw plenty of gobblers shoving, fighting, and jockeying for position within the social structure of the flock. We did see a few strutting toms with eight to ten hens, but it was not the norm, and during one evening of intense roosting, even after covering lots of ground, our owl hooting and hen cutting did not produce a single response from any turkeys.

The following morning was not much better. There was limited distant morning roost gobbling, and it became very quiet later into the morning. However we knew we had to adapt to the current situation. After watching large gangs of meandering jakes, longbeards still in flocks, and the gobblers chasing jakes we knew how we would have to hunt these turkeys. Challenging toms with gobbler yelping and calling in the jakes with gobblers in tow were keys to this hunt's success.

With long hours in the field, intense patience, perseverance, and adjusting our hunting strategies to focus more on the pecking order than on mating urges, all our guys prevailed with a 100 percent kill rate during this hunt.

South Carolina Low Country

There was little time for recovery following our first Chasing Spring™ hunt of the season in Florida. To say the journey to South Carolina was a wild adventure is quite an understatement, and it began as soon as I walked out the front door. The 4 AM drive to the airport came complete with intense rain, sleet, and finally some serious snow. Traffic was slow, cars and trucks lined the roadside ditches, and I was thankful for my four-wheel-drive as I fought my way around slow cars and up steep ice- and snow-covered inclines.

By the time I parked at the airport, snowflakes the size of golf balls were falling from the sky. I won't go into all that went so terribly wrong, but suffice it to say that my 6:30 AM flight was delayed, then delayed some more, then de-iced, turning it into an 11:30 AM flight complete with missed connections.

Here's our crew with Tony Chachere of Creole seasoning. Tony's posing with his gobbler in the middle of the gang. He and Steve Cobb did a cooking segment for NWTF TV during our hunt.

Lori Smith Bell Johnson sitting with Mark McBride on our first morning hunt setup.

But Chasing Spring™ is aptly named: I witnessed spring arrive in state after state while hunting gobblers. My flight landed in 86-degree temperatures, with blooming flowers and budding trees. My destination was Deux Cheneaux Plantation in Walterboro, South Carolina. The lodge was awesome, the food was off the charts, and our hosts, Allen and Susan Bell, were terrific. This Low Country hunt was set up by old friend Steve Cobb and filmed by NWTF TV cameraman Brian Combs. Another great guy, Tony Chacheres of food seasoning fame, was in our camp and he took a nice gobbler on camera. I hunted with Lori Smith Bell Johnson, a great gal who hunted hard, never complained, and finally took a gobbler during the last hour of the hunt.

Every camp has a unique person and our camp had little Jimmy Andrews. Here he is holding court with yet another story. Jimmy is the funniest guy I have ever met at a hunting camp, and that's saying a lot.

A late afternoon set up as Lori waits and watches for turkeys. Lori sat better than some 20-year turkey hunting veterans that I've hunted with.

Success! Lori took this gobbler on the last day and last hour of our hunt. Lori was a trooper and a true pleasure to hunt with. She never gave up and hunted as hard as any man I ever hunted with.

Like Florida a week ago, this early season proved tough with very little gobbling, Boone and Crockett skeeters, gators, and long hours in the field. I rate calling Low Country gobblers right up there with south Alabama turkeys as far as difficulty in closing the deal. Persistence, patience, roosting, scouting, and observing turkeys habits at the time of the hunt along with a lot of aggressive calling, were all key to Lori taking her first turkey.

This was truly a wonderful hunt. An awesome camp with great fellowship with old friends and new friends, and for me, the turkey hunting was secondary to spending some time in this turkey camp with so many fun and wonderful people. I am truly blessed to be Chasing Spring™. Our next stop is Tennessee.

Tennessee Kids Hunting for a Cure (KHFAC), St. Jude Children's Hospital

I met some of the coolest young hunters ever assembled on a recent Kids Hunting for a Cure event in Tennessee. KHFAC leads kids, many with

Ray's brother Marty Eye, with his hunter, Bailey Carpenter.

Our crew: Amy Carpenter, Brent Carpenter, Blake, Bailey, land owner Donnie Covey, Stan the man, me, Marty Eye, and outdoor writer and photographer Steve Felgenhauer.

terminal illnesses, on organized hunts to raise money for cancer research and to teach them that they can make a difference. Rain, wind, and cold could not dampen the enthusiasm, eagerness, and spirit of our kids during the hunt.

Guide Kelly Cooper drove all the way from Pennsylvania, Von Eubanks flew in from California, and Terry Phillips, Don Shipp, and Mike Miller came in early on Tuesday just to help scout hunting spots. My brother Marty and I met with our kids when we got there. I hunted with twelve-year-old Blake Carpenter, and Marty hunted with Blake's ten-year-old brother Bailey. They are two great kids, and we all had a lot of fun together.

Marty and I scouted our farm earlier in the day, and we set up blinds for Blake and our cameras. Marty opted to run and gun with Bailey in his area of the farm. Even in the rainy, blustery conditions, we managed to hear gobbling and call in turkeys. But for our group it just wasn't in the cards. We only had the chance to hunt on Saturday and had to deal with some less-than-ideal weather conditions. But even though we didn't take a bird, it was still a great hunt and one I'll remember for a long time.

Unfortunately, Blake missed an opportunity to take a gobbler. He got off a shot at a nice tom at about thirty yards, but it was a clean miss. Bailey didn't get a shot at a gobbling turkey that closed in on Marty's calling in thick cover at seventeen steps. But this hunt was about more than just killing turkeys. The four of us all had a great time, and I think Bailey and Blake are now hooked on turkey hunting.

As of Saturday afternoon there were twenty-two birds harvested and twenty-three reported misses. We only got to hunt for one day. However, my longtime friend

Our double blind setup worked well with the cold and rain. We put hunters and guides in one blind and the camera crew in the other.

Blake and me ready to depart for the midday hunt.

and fellow road dog, Terry Phillips, hunted our area Sunday morning and took a nice gobbler with his hunter Trent Kelsey.

Fostering an appreciation for the outdoors in the next generation is a primary goal of Kids Hunting for a Cure (KHFAC), which was founded in 2007 by Dr. John Waples and Dave Norval. "When you take them out, their eyes sparkle," says "Super" Dave Norval. Based in Tennessee, KHFAC is entirely volunteer-run, but there's no problem getting people to donate time, land, and knowledge. "Successful hunters love to teach," said Waples. "Getting them to take kids out is easy. You just need an organizational base. We provide that platform."

KHFAC has raised approximately $240,000 nationally through organized hunts, auctions, and cookouts. The organization currently operates in seven states and aims to have at least seventy chapters by the end of 2011.

Kansas Governor's One-shot Turkey Hunt

I'm thinking about renaming Chasing Spring™ "Chasing Storms." We arrived in El Dorado for the Kansas Governor's One-shot Turkey Hunt with rain, hail, and high winds. But it was such a fun event with old friends, new friends, banquets, fundraisers, and auctions that the weather didn't really matter much anyway.

A few of the great programs were the Get-acquainted Social and Celebrity and Guides Meeting, the Big Tom Social Hog Roast, and, on Saturday night,

the One-shot Banquet and Fundraising Auction. Our morning began with a 4 AM breakfast, always great food, hot coffee, fellowship, and storytelling. Then it was into the kids' sandwich making line to pick up our field

Just before 7:00 AM, in heavy winds and rain, my guide Steve Seymour and I connected on a nice Kansas tom.

I had plenty of turkeys to hunt, and friends to meet, like Bass Pro Shops RedHead team member, Rob Keck.

The girls having some fun as I point out my name on the celebrity hunt list. Becky Wolfe, shown kneeling, is someone who never slows down and makes things happen during the One Shot, while One Shot CEO Janet Post is shown standing.

lunches. This year was a little different from last. This time I was hunting as a celebrity guest and had an opportunity to take a turkey myself for Chasing Spring.™

I made the best of the opportunity with the help of my guide, Steve Seymour, who did a tremendous job of scouting and preparation. Rain, wind, and hail couldn't dampen our spirits, and by the end of the event everyone was more of a family than friends. The current Kansas Governor, Sam Brownback, was on the hunt, and country music star Brian White, who's had more than six number one songs on the country charts. Eighty hunters in all braved the elements during this awesome event, including the high school winner from the NWTF Essay Contest.

Preseason scouting by our guide, a carefully selected blind location from observing recent turkey activity, and a lot of hard, aggressive calling made this hunt happen. Next, Chasing Spring™ was headed for battle with Missouri gobblers.

Chasing Spring™ Supports Our Troops During a Hunt at Camp Hope with Our American Warriors

After our central Missouri KFNS media hunt, Chasing Spring™ loaded up immediately for the drive to the Ozarks in southeast Missouri for our next

These are my soldiers, Crystal Dagget and Shane Rapsey. Even though we didn't get a turkey, we had a great time hunting together.

Sgt. Erin Bell, stationed in Fort Knox Kentucky, is a serious turkey hunter.

American Warrior Bobby Licek returns to Camp Hope each year as a guide, to help with the hunt.

The campfire was a great place to visit and get to know the soldiers.

hunt with Camp Hope, where veterans heal up by fishing, hiking, four-wheeling, and hunting.

Camp Hope was founded by William White, who lost his twenty-three-year-old son, Christopher Neal White, in Iraq in 2006. He decided to memorialize him by buying 170 acres in Missouri, naming it Chris Neal Farm, and dedicating it to wounded vets. Today, there are more than 2.3 million combat-wounded veterans in the U.S. These brave men and women have

Our official 2011 Camp Hope group photo.

sacrificed much to ensure our safety and freedom. The number of combat wounded veterans is growing each day as the War on Terror continues. All these veterans had dreams about the future, but many of these dreams were dashed due to injuries suffered in the line of duty.

White believes the best healing comes with a good deer or turkey hunt. And there's no substitute for just sitting around the campfire to share experiences with good friends. When veterans gather around the campfire to share experiences, the camaraderie of being together, being able to discuss some of the issues in their lives, and being able to forget what's been going on can work wonders. Veterans can participate in hunting, fishing, canoeing, shooting, hiking, and relaxing in a peaceful setting at Camp Hope.

Camp Hope needs help in supporting our men and women in uniform. Your donations help create cherished moments and help them to a full and speedy recovery. A simple monetary "thank you for your service" goes a long way toward bring us closer as a nation in repaying these great patriots for their service and sacrifice. Camp Hope is a nonprofit 501(c)(3) corporation. Your donation is therefore tax deductible. Please mail donations, no matter how small or large, to:

Chris Neal Farm
PO Box 52
Farmington, MO 63640

Crystal Dagget on the hunt.

We were not finding any turkeys, so we did a little owl hooting to our owl friend who followed us during the hunt.

Soldier Rye Boruff (center) was our only hunter to take a gobbler.

New England has no shortage of trout streams.

You know you're hunting Massachusetts, Connecticut, or even eastern New York, because of the sheer number of rock walls.

The prevalence of streams can make it difficult to hear a gobbler or to make your way to a gobbling turkey.

Jamus Driscoll and Tony Caggiano with a pair of New York gobblers.

New England Hunt

With Chasing Spring™ completing Missouri and Illinois turkey hunts, it was time once again for my yearly trip to New England. This year with Chasing Spring™, we first hunted in New York State, then, as many years before, make our Mother's Day journey to our New England turkey camp in the great state of Massachusetts.

This year, all of New England was experiencing a late spring.

The *Chasing Spring* camera strikes again in New England.

Roosting is one of our longest-running traditions in our New England camp, and one of the main reasons for years of successful hunts.

Massachusetts is one the prettiest timbered states I hunt. Many hunters only think of New England as being associated with New York City, but most places I hunt are very remote and close to wilderness, in areas that hold both bear and moose.

Ralph and Gerry. We have taken many pictures over the years in front of this blooming bush.

Just three weeks earlier, there were several feet of snow on the ground. My prehunt turkey report was not promising, with reported sparse gobbling, and little response from turkeys to calling.

However, after a late night (early morning) arrival in New York State and with little sleep, we pulled off a double on–camera kill our first morning. This was due to my host and friend Tony Caggiano's great job of scouting and roosting.

This year's Massachusetts camp was small compared to earlier years' large outdoor media hunts. In attendance was camp host Gerald Bethge of *Outdoor Life,* Chasing Spring's™ Alex Robinson, Rick Story, old friend Ralph

Stuart, and me. I had never experienced a New England spring this far behind during turkey season, so I knew our hunt would be a challenge. However, there was so much more to our annual turkey camp that just hunting turkeys. Our camp was always a good time, with great food, fellowship, and lifelong friends who always make this camp especially enjoyable.

Not unlike the past twenty-five-plus seasons in New England, with just a couple of mornings available, I depended on hard work, determination, watching and listening to local turkeys, and roosting and calling skills to make something happen.

Second Annual Old West Invitational Turkey Shoot

The Old West Invitational is one of my favorite hunts, and I really love hunting Merriam's turkeys in the shadow of Devils Tower. Weather was a factor, with cold, rain, sleet, snow, and wind, as spring was once again way behind schedule. Local guides and hunters were quite concerned with unusually quiet gobblers, birds still in flocks, and little response to calling.

This Old West Invitational was held in Hulett, Wyoming. The event's signature sponsor, Remington Outdoor Foundation (ROF), teamed with the Wildlife Heritage Foundation of Wyoming (WHFW) to raise funds to conserve Wyoming wildlife. Event co-hosts, the WHFW and the Greater Hulett Community Center, welcomed celebrities and special guests for a weekend of turkey hunting. A portion of the proceeds from this event was used to help fund research, education, and habitat projects that benefit Wyoming's game and nongame species.

Will and me, with our teamwork gobbler.

My home for several days, the Hulett hotel in downtown Hulett, Wyoming.

Early morning hunter and guide meeting place for breakfast and hunt snacks.

Guide Will McAmis lighting them up with his box call.

Old West Invitational Turkey Shoot guests enjoyed a first-class event consisting of two days of turkey hunting in northeast Wyoming, home to Devils Tower. Western hospitality was provided by the Greater Hulett Community Center, a nonprofit organization with a mission to transform the former Hulett School into a community center. Hulett residents helped coordinate guides, lodging, meals, and transportation. During the event, local landowners offered hunting opportunities on private land, where only guided hunts are traditionally allowed.

Auctions, dinners, and a host of other activities ran throughout the weekend in support of conserving Wyoming's more than 600 different wildlife species. My team, with me, Will McAmis, and our first-time hunter Kurt Milne from California took third place out of thirty-seven teams in the greater Western Celebrity Turkey Shoot via the NWTF turkey scoring system. My guide, Will, and his dad, the ranch land-owner, both really nice guys, were called up at the big event Saturday night and were awarded nice belt buckles and other assorted prizes.

Our success was due to our guide Will, who really knows his turkeys. He gets in tight and calls aggressively, challenging the pecking order of both hens and gobblers. My kill came about from several tactical moves to close the distance on a tom that

Wyoming is a beautiful place to hunt turkeys, even with adverse weather conditions during our hunt.

Will and Kurt with his gobbler.

hens were pulling away from us. Once reset very tight, we called the hens to the break of a hill with the old tom in tow, and he gave his life to score third place out of eighty hunters.

Campeche, Mexico—Ocellated Turkey of the Yucatan Peninsula.

Chasing Spring™ departed Hulett, Wyoming, leaving behind rain and frigid temperatures for the warm weather of the Yucatan Peninsula and the city of Campeche, Mexico. Campeche City, the capital of the State of Campeche, is an incredible region in southern Mexico for hunting, fishing, sightseeing, or a long family vacation. The Yucatan peninsula and Campeche have been unfairly judged unsafe because of media reports of violent crime on the northern border and in central Mexico. Chasing Spring's™ time in Campeche found those reports to be untrue. Campeche is a safe, wonderful place with friendly people and an incredible number of things to see and do.

Chasing Spring™ was in Campeche hunting for the ocellated turkey and fishing for tarpon, and of course the Mayan ruins were also on our list of things to see. My final goal in turkey hunting was to hear the love song of the ocellated turkey in the jungles of the Yucatan. I was not disappointed, and it was one of the biggest thrills in my turkey hunting career.

Like many other hunters, I misjudged the ocellated turkey as not really being a turkey at all. After hunting them, I discovered they are in fact turkeys, not unlike the other five subspecies of turkeys. The ocellated turkey's loudest call is his song, a mate attraction song of the adult male, which corresponds to the gobble of our wild turkey. The local Spanish-speaking guides call a singing male a *cantador*. These *cantadors* sang from the roost at dawn, and from time to time during the day. When they went back to roost in the evening, the males sang until dark, or sometimes even after dark.

The ocellated turkey exists only in a 50,000-square-mile area comprising the Yucatan Peninsula, including the states of Quintana Roo, Campeche, and Yucatan, as well as parts of southern Tabasco and northeastern Chiapas.

Ocellated turkeys are known by several different names that vary by Central American locale: *pavo, pavo ocelado,* or its Mayan name, *ucutz il chican.* Ocellated

Our base camp, close to the hunting area.

turkeys are considerably smaller than any of the five subspecies of North American wild turkeys. Adult hens weigh approximately eight pounds just prior to egg-laying and nesting and about six or seven pounds the remainder of the year. During the breeding season, adult males weigh approximately 11 to 12 pounds.

The ocellated turkey is easily distinguished from its North American cousin in appearance. The body feathers of both male and female birds have a bronze-green iridescent color mixture, although females sometimes appear duller in color with more green than bronze pigments. Unlike North American turkeys, the breast feathers of male and female ocellated turkeys do not differ and cannot be used to determine sex. Neither male nor female birds have beards.

Both sexes have blue heads and necks with distinctive orange to red, warty, caruncle-like growths, called nodules, but these are more pronounced on males. The head of the male also has a fleshy blue crown behind the snood, which is adorned with yellow-orange nodules similar to those on the neck. During breeding season, this crown enlarges and the coloration of the nodules becomes more pronounced. Ocellated turkeys also have a distinct eye ring of bright red-colored skin, especially visible on adult males during the breeding season.

Tail feathers in both sexes are bluish-gray in color with a well defined, eye-shaped, blue-bronze colored spot near the end, followed by a bright gold tip. The tail feather spots are similar to those seen on peacock feathers, which once led some scientists to believe the ocellated was more related to peafowl than turkeys. In fact, these spots helped give the ocellated its name, as the Latin word for eye is *oculus*. The legs of ocellated

Our other guide and my buddy Margarito Campos Dzul, who has worked for Jorge L. Sansores B. of Snook Inn since he was nine years old.

Bill Cooper and our guide, Aurelio Sanches Hernandez, with a Campeche ocellated turkey. The ocellated has the most brilliant, beautiful colors of all wild turkeys.

The Mayan Ruins were amazing.

turkeys are shorter and thinner than those of North American wild turkeys and are deep red in color. The legs of adult males also have pronounced spurs, longer and more attenuated than those of North American gobblers. Spur lengths in males over one year old average at least one and a half inches. Spurs longer than two inches also have been recorded.

I learned a lot about the ocellated turkey and our guides during our Campeche adventure. The ocellated is in fact a turkey, and acts no differently than other subspecies. I assure you that when I return to Campeche next year for another round with *pavo* or *ucutz il chican,* I will call him in to the gun just as I call the Gould's in the Sierra Madre,

You can hunt for more than just turkeys. Here, Bill and Mikie admire a tarpon.

the Rio Grandes in Hawaii, the Easterns in the Ozarks, and the Merriam's in the shadow of Devils Tower.

For more information on hunting the ocellated turkey and tarpon fishing in Campeche, contact:

Jorge L. Sansores B.

snookinnjorge@hotmail.com

www.snookinnhunting.com.mx

phone: 001 52 (981) 813 1047

For tarpon fishing, contact:

Capt. Miguel Encalada

www.campecheflyfishing@tarponbay.com.mx

"*Chasing Spring*™ really highlights the best and most exciting aspects of turkey hunting, and turkey hunting legend Ray Eye is one of the world's most renowned turkey hunters and *Chasing Spring*™, with his knowledge and passion for the sport, is just the thing for all turkey-hunting fanatics everywhere."

—**Outdoor Life** *magazine*

19

Storytime with Uncle Ray

WELCOME TO STORYTIME WITH UNCLE RAY—BUT BEFORE you read the six stories in this chapter, first let's cover a little history of these stories, storytelling, and how my stories originated for purposes of entertaining both live and outdoor radio audiences, and now do the same within the pages of this book.

My early-days hunting adventures are a collection of turkey stories I presented during my early barnstorming seminar days. I quickly learned that if you expect to teach live audiences how to hunt turkeys and hold their attention, then you'd better entertain them and also inject a little humor, if you'd like them to remember what you tell them.

These stories are an assortment of those told at seminars, around campfires, on radio shows, and also some I've written for publication. Most are true hunting adventures that I like to employ in teaching as well as entertaining live audiences. Each is designed for a particular part of my show, and they address setups, locating, and proper equipment, all used to explain tactics. They not only contain hunting how-to information, but also have a moral.

Back in the day, boring seminar speakers didn't last long with the crowds of roughneck turkey hunters who made up any audience attending shows given in barns and taverns, and at county fairs and archery clubs, and in the basements of sporting-goods stores. As a traveling seminar speaker back then, you had to have a really thick skin. Especially in the South, during rural programs, a wire cage like those used in bars to protect bands from hand-thrown objects would have been a welcome addition to my program.

For instance, one of the toughest crowds I ever had was in the state of Louisiana, a big seminar crowd of over four hundred, in a huge, concrete-floored building. I was the final speaker of four, and by the time it was my turn to speak, clear liquor in Mason jars was flowing freely, and the crowd was growing ever more restless.

But I was "the man" everywhere I traveled that year, as I was the only seminar speaker on the road with a modern slideshow. Just as I was wrapping up, right before closing, and after rocking the house (well, not exactly . . .) I clicked to my last slide: a pretty gruesome photo of a turkey hunter in a hospital bed with hundreds of holes in the right side of his face, as if a swarm of hornets had nailed him. This was a real gut-wrencher in every other one of my seminars—but not in this one.

With the nasty slide remaining on the big screen, I paced back and forth, preaching the gospel of gun safety, hunting safety, positively identifying your target, and reciting several mistaken-for-game accidents as cautionary examples. In closing, all the while pointing to the shot-in-the-face shotgun victim, shaking my head and with a short pause, and proceeding in a lowered voice, I stated carefully just how lucky the individual was to be alive. This dramatic moment was short-lived, however, because of a booming voice from the back of the room that broke the silence, commenting, "Nice pattern!"

Yes, it really did all go downhill from there.

"Storytime" (on KFNS 590, The Fan, St. Louis Missouri) is the most requested and listened-to segment of my *Eye on the Outdoors* radio show. As such, it would seem only right to make it a part of this book.

As a longtime storyteller, and from my many years of working live audiences, I found storytelling a real challenge, especially during live radio programming. Missing are the facial expressions displayed when vocalizing bird and animal sounds with my voice, or with props of plastic guns, forked sticks, turkey heads, hand grenades, and turkey feathers. Also missing is the

"Uncle Ray" and Peanut.

nonstop arm-waving and body language. But more important, missing is the live audience reaction, something I feed on and that really helps me get into it and really tell a story with enthusiasm.

So, as an alternative to telling live stories on radio, and as was my practice with my seminars, I presented Storytime as a live reading to my listeners, and the rest is history. This remains the most popular segment during my live radio programming.

Live audiences and radio programming is one thing, but to have an impact with my stories, to relay humor in the pages of a book, becomes yet another challenge to pull off. Although some of my stories were published in my first and second books, I really didn't have much input into how they were presented, and never quite felt like these earlier books did them much justice. They seemed to lose energy, somehow, especially with losing the punch line, possibly due to the lack of proper sentence structure, spelling, and grammar.

My publisher at the time exclaimed, "You sound like a hillbilly!" Oh well, I am a hillbilly, and this is what makes my stories exactly what they are—*me*. Writing this book, I have much more leeway, and this time appearing in print they're pretty much as I tell them to live audiences.

In my second book, one of my stories is the "Store-bought Mouth Yelper." Its original name was "Three Piles of Puke." (Guess it's easy to see why the name changed?) Anyway, this story is one of my first seminar stories, and became a real classic. I told this story in one of my first "set-down" seminars in 1977, given in one of the very first Wal-Mart stores in my area, and from the roar of the crowd at the finish, I knew I was on to something good.

I always presented this story during "Calling Devices," a part of my show in which I teach hunters the importance of learning to properly use a mouth diaphragm turkey call, long before the arrival of the hunting season. This story was actually born of several true events. The first, from my Uncle Lee making fun as Ole Joe choked on a mouth call; and the second, from a friend of mine who did in fact swallow one. Thus the phrase: "Don't swallow 'em, they're

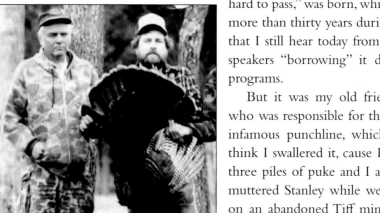

hard to pass," was born, which I used for than more than thirty years during my shows, and that I still hear today from younger seminar speakers "borrowing" it during their own programs.

But it was my old friend Stanley King who was responsible for the ending, and the infamous punchline, which is also true: "I think I swallered it, cause I've been through three piles of puke and I ain't found it yet," muttered Stanley while we hunted together on an abandoned Tiff mine. He was deter-

Stanley King with me after an Ozarks turkey hunt.

mined to use a mouth call for the first time, but this effort met with really disgusting results.

During later years, Stanley was always in the front row of my early seminars, and every time I told the story he laughed more than anyone else in the room. This story also worked well during turkey seminars with a crowd of all guys, beer drinking groups, archery range groups, or local NWTF functions, even with a mixed crowd at school gyms in rural America.

On a seminar, in-store promotion, and product promo road trip to Denver, Colorado, back in 1986, I experienced this lesson, and I really went down in flames. After several sporting goods store seminars, my sales rep and I attended the very first NWTF Colorado state banquet. The NWTF chapter president asked me to come up front and say a few words during dinner. Though not aware of it at the time, I now realize I was kind of out of my element, and a long ways from the Ozarks.

I jumped from my seat and briskly walked up in front of the roomful of new NWTF members: doctors, lawyers, bankers, new car dealers, none of whom had ever turkey hunted, much less knew anything about a "mouth call."

I leaned into that microphone and told my story, while gobbling, spitting, and with some of my best gagging sounds ever, just as I really nailed the punchline. But as I stepped back from the podium to take in the laughter and thundering applause, the only sound in the room besides crickets was the gasping for air and groaning of hundreds of people shaking their heads in disgust as they pushed their dinner plates away.

Oh, but there was laughter in the otherwise quiet room, and it was deafening. It was from only one person, my Hunter's Specialties sales rep, who was basically on the floor in a knot during a fit of laughter, not so much from me nailing the punchline, but from my ever-faster fiery spiral into the ground, after my weak attempt to try and recover by quickly telling my "Poop in the Woods" story.

However, I guess I just had to learn the hard way there is much more to storytelling than just content, delivery, and timing. After Three Piles of Puke miserably failed for the second time during the St. Louis Boat & Sportshow, I finally learned my lesson on how speakers should read their audience, where and when a story is effective, but especially, when not to use it.

Another one of my original stories was "The Cow Suit," though later on I renamed it "The Monarch of Sutton's Pasture." I wrote this story back in 1976 as an opener for my programs. It was one of my very first live-audience stories, and without question one of my best all-time seminar stories.

I found early on that a humorous story at the beginning of a seminar is perfect for seizing audience attention, and to keep people's interest during the remainder of the program. Like so many of my stories, this story also came to life from a combination of several actual events that took place during my early turkey hunting experiences in the Ozarks.

I included it in my second book, but it was retitled by the publisher as the "Cow and the Gobbler." Originally it was another Uncle Lee and Ole Joe story, but at the time of the writing of that book, I inserted two of my good hunting friends to be the "cow suit."

This story has always been a very successful component of my seminar programs, and not just for humor or entertainment value, but as a lesson for hunters to always be willing to change, be innovative, and to try something different if what you're doing is not working.

During later years, my Cow Suit story still worked very well and was always a huge hit during conservation group fundraising banquets. It was very easy to also involve the audience by including the evening's celebrity guest or local dignitary in the story, by placing them inside the cow suit during my telling of the story.

As a mainstay of my programs, I told this story for many years in small towns across Missouri, and at small hunting clubs, taverns, and local sporting goods stores. During later years, as my seminars expanded into larger venues, I took my road show into the bordering states of Illinois, Arkansas, Kansas, and Iowa.

During the early to late 1980s I presented programs for national seminar tours throughout America, all across the Southern states to Florida, then worked my way up to New York, then back across the country on to the West Coast—Oregon, Washington, and California. It was not uncommon in those days to be on a "suicide" road tour, not unlike a traveling rock band, and to present anywhere from seventy-five to 150 seminars per year.

The downside of all of this is that I decided to discontinue telling my own cow suit story at the beginning of the 1990s. I began to notice little reaction to my story anywhere I traveled, and audience members would then tell me they'd already heard the story, and I should feel bad for taking the story from whoever they heard it from.

It seemed as if anyone who ever stood in front of a crowd with any type of turkey hunting program stole my story and used it in their seminar as if it were their very own. This included small-time local area speakers as well as regional- and national-level speakers, including big-name speakers of the time such as traveling NWTF staff and even a big-name speaker on the NRA Great American tour. They all used my story as their own.

In recent years I worked a NWTF banquet in Minnesota. As I was preparing to take the stage, one of the state officers before me told my cow suit story. After the show, this same guy came up to me with my book he had just purchased and asked me to sign it for him. "No problem," I said. I then opened the book to the right place and signed my name across the first title page of my story.

One of the most arrogant examples took place at the NWTF national convention. During the Saturday night banquet, a guy dressed like a back-woods goober stood up in front of 2,500 people and told my story, knowing very well that it was my story and that I was sitting in the audience. I guess what all this really proves is that my cow suit story I told to hundreds of thou-sands people over the years, a story that served me so well to entertain live audiences everywhere, is one hell of a good story. After all, imitation definitely is the sincerest form of flattery!

For this story, I have a shorter version for seminars, and a radio show ver-sion as well, and with so many versions, variations, and imitations of this story in circulation, I decided to include the story in this Storytime chapter, as it was written, in its original full-length form.

Well it's time to dive, so let's start with the "Monarch Of Sutton's Pasture" and then we'll continue with our Storytime reading in this chapter with the others. And as I say on my radio program: Okay, boys and girls, it's time for Storytime with your Uncle Ray.

The Monarch of Sutton's Pasture

In southern Missouri, along an Ozarks river, there is a wild turkey gob-bler roosting high on a river bluff. This gobbler is huge for an Ozarks bird, his beard as thick as man's wrist, and his spurs the size of golf tees.

At first light each morning, this gobbler sails from his roost, and on set wings, glides across the river, then lands in the middle of a big pasture next to a cattle pond. Every day it's the same thing. Out there, strutting among Her-eford cows smack dab in the middle of the field, he gobbles nonstop for the hens to come on over for a little early morning lovemaking.

Missouri Ozarks turkey hunters are seasoned timber hunters, their expe-rience gained from hunting mountains with steep wooded ridges and deep hollers. But with the expansion of cattle ranching in the 1970s, along with clearing of large areas of bottomland timber for pasture, a new situation was created, something few had any knowledge or experience of: hunting turkeys in vast, open fields.

Donnie Sutton, the owner of this pasture, allows locals to hunt so just about everyone from the surrounding area has given this old tom a try, all with little success. During a spring turkey season, hunters from miles around try to kill this gobbler of Sutton's pasture, so the conversation at the local café consists of tales of woe and frustration from every failed attempt..

Hunters have tried every conceivable calling setup, on the edge of the pasture, hiding under the river bank, in the woods on the opposite side. They hen call, they gobble, and jake yelp, but nothing works, this gobbler always holds his ground. He just stays in the middle of the field and struts.

One hunter had a plan to sneak in before daylight and set up on the field edge, for the bird usually leaves the field at midmorning; he did, for eight hours, but all in vain as the gobbler, for the first time, departed the field in a new direction.

One innovative hunter came up with something unheard of at the time; he took a modified goose decoy body and covered it with turkey feathers, one of the very first turkey decoys. Other turkeys came to his homemade decoy, but the big strutting gobbler in the middle of the pasture wouldn't even look his way.

As the turkey's reputation grew, interesting stories begin circulating around town. Billy Johnson from down on Lost Creek supposedly asked the landowner if he could dig a pit in the middle of the pasture to lie in wait to ambush that elusive gobbler. Mr. Sutton told him no way was anyone digging a hole in his field. But the best story ever was about this out-of-state hunter, who asked Donnie for permission to hunt from his pond, to lie submersed in the cattle pond with a snorkel and his shotgun inside a plastic bag.

I too tried my best to call in that turkey and kill him, but just like everyone else, this legendary gobbler made a fool out of me time and time again. But I was not alone; this field-strutting turkey made every hunter in the county who ever owned a turkey call look really bad.

Word traveled quickly that the old pasture tom just couldn't be killed, so bets and wagers started flying, a jackpot of money from everyone who purchased a tag was set up, winner takes all. With the possibility of countywide, maybe even statewide fame, along with cash thrown in, my Uncle Lee and his partner in crime, ole Joe, claimed they had a plan with a surefire and legal way to kill that old gobbler.

While sitting around a campfire during our last night in camp, Uncle Lee explained his well-devised plan to take that turkey out on the last day of the turkey season; they had designed and built a custom cow suit, head and all.

You see, Uncle Lee noticed the cows didn't spook the gobbler, so he figured they'd just ease out into the field like a cow and put the hurt on him. Then from Joe's old truck he brought out a big tanned cowhide. His plan is just like Indians of long ago; they would cover up with an animal hide and advance across the field and kill that turkey. The plan was for Uncle Lee to be the front of the cow and Joe the back of the cow. Uncle Lee would hold the barrel of the shotgun with Joe aiming and pulling the trigger.

Long before dawn the next morning they stood at the edge of the cow pasture with their custom cow suit, then both giggling like schoolkids, they pulled their cow suit into place. Discussing their plan of attack, they decided that when they got close enough, they'd slide a shotgun forward and torch the gobbler, they would be famous, and a big pile of money would be theirs.

Sure enough, just like every other morning, at first light that turkey gobbled on the roost then sailed down into the middle of the pasture and began his daily ritual of strutting for the hens. Lee and ole Joe started by easing out into the field, walking real slow while mooing like a cow.

Bent over in the back of the cow and unable to see anything, ole Joe asks, "How far is he? Where's he at?"

"He's still about seventy yards out," Uncle Lee whispered. "I don't want to head right at him; let's just take our time and get closer 'cause he ain't even lookin' at us."

Moving real slow and easy, then a little faster, step by step, they moved ever closer to the strutting prize.

Joe whispered again, "How we doing? Let's hurry and make him jelly head so I can get out of the back of this cow suit and straighten up."

"Just be patient," Lee said, "He's about forty-five yards out. I think this is going to work. He's totally ignoring us. Just fifteen more yards and we'll smoke him."

As the fake cow steadily inched across the pasture closer and closer, suddenly Uncle Lee abruptly stopped, causing Joe to slam into his back.

"Why'd you stop? Come on, let's get a little closer and kill 'im."

But Uncle Lee whispered, "Uh, there's a big bull standing over here; he's looking right at us."

"Don't worry about no damn bull," muttered ole Joe, "I don't care about any old bull. Keep moving so we can kill that turkey."

The hunters and the cow suit began to move forward, but Uncle Lee abruptly stopped again with Joe slamming into his back.

"What's wrong now? Why did you stop this time?"

"Uh-oh, that big ole bull is all bug-eyed, pawing the ground, and slobbering, and now he's coming fast, marching right at us with a glazed look in his eye!"

"So," ole Joe asked, "What we gonna to do now?"

Uncle Lee came back quickly in a high-pitched, squeaky voice, "I don't know, I'm not sure, but I'm not going to encourage him by looking at him, I think I'm gonna eat some grass, but you'd better brace yourself!"

The Gift: A Story of a Little Boy's First Gobbler

The gobbler is close; I clearly hear drumming with wings dragging through leaves on the forest floor. I yelp softly with my voice, a booming throaty gobble rattles directly below us; suddenly, a glowing white head floats across a small opening. I quickly assist my young hunter to raise his single-shot 20-gauge and with my thumb over his, I help him pull the hammer back until it clicks.

I'm guiding a youth hunter on his first turkey hunt in the Missouri Ozarks. This is the first opportunity for this little guy to go turkey hunting. He has an ailment in his hip socket at the joint called Legg-Calvé-Perthes syndrome. He's doing better now, but for the last several years he was forced to walk with crutches while wearing a sling device with his small leg strapped tight up against his body. He hails from a family of five boys and one girl, and his daddy works two jobs to support and feed his growing family.

The odds are certainly stacked against us on this morning; turkeys are very difficult this season, there is little gobbling at daylight, and turkeys show little interest in calling. We're having a late spring, and with little green-up, the Ozarks hills are extremely open. Despite a difficult turkey season, the little guy is having a great time and enjoying quite an experience camping out for turkey season. We're sleeping in an old camper in the middle of thousands of acres of national forest. We have a big campfire at night; we go fishing in the afternoon, hunt mushrooms, and enjoy great meals cooked outdoors.

The timbered ridges, hollers, and old fields around our camp have received a lot of hunting pressure this season, so early this morning, I make the decision to hunt a different area in an attempt to change our luck. In the early morning darkness, we load up my Jeep and drive about fifteen miles out on the hardtop road to a very remote area called Peter Cave Hollow. The owls and whip-poor-wills are calling on this frosty cool morning as we quietly make our way through the darkness to where the ridge edge narrows.

As we settle in awaiting daylight, I clearly hear his teeth chattering. My little hunter is cold, so I wrap him in my hunting coat. Much warmer now and fighting sleep, he lies down in the leaves at my feet and nods off.

At first light I hear a distant gobble in response to my owl call, across the valley, about a mile away on the far mountain; it's the only bird that gobbles on this morning. I have a decision to make; with extremely open woods, and a small hunter who is not capable of walking very far in this steep, rough country, we will have to stay right here. As the little turkey hunter continues to sleep, I call to the distant gobbling bird. I shake my head in disbelief as the gobbling grows ever closer. With steady gobbling, the turkey hurries down the side of the distant mountain and is quickly coming across the valley.

I decide to wake my hunter when the gobbler is at the base of our ridge. I certainly didn't think the bird would actually climb up the steep ridge in front of us, but the gobbler is quickly climbing our ridge.

The bobbing white head now appears much closer. I yelp, and a booming gobble almost causes the little hunter to drop his gun. I shift my young hunter to the right, with the turkey out of sight again, I whisper for him to follow the crunching sounds of walking in the leaves with his gun barrel. The sound grows ever louder as the Ozarks Ghost walks from left to right, straight up the steep hollow rim.

With my arms around him supporting his trembling body, I tell my heavily breathing little hunter to shoot. But before he can pull the trigger the gobbler steps behind a tree in half strut, folds up and continues up the hill out of sight.

Finally, the big tom appears from just under the ridge, as he stands straight up at a mere ten feet away, looking for the hen he knows is right here. As the bead finally settles on the turkey's wattles, I frantically whisper for him to shoot. With the roar of the little 20-gauge gun the gobbler collapses in a wild frenzy of flopping and rolls all the way back down the steep embankment from which he came.

Old newspaper clipping account of my little brother's first turkey: the "gift."

The author and little brother Marty Eye after returning to their Hillsboro, Missouri, home, with the "gift."

A GOOD EYE — HILLSBORO—
Hillsboro was a successful turkey hunter during
completed gobbler season. Here he is pictured with a
bird he killed near Johnston Mountain in Iron County.
had two beards. Young Eye was assisted by his older b
who called the turkey for him.

All is quiet now with the exception of squirrels barking and the echoing sound of the gunshot fading away across the mountains and steep valleys. My hunter's teeth are chattering and his little body is shivering with excitement. I shake his hand as I hug him, and tell him over and over, "We got him."

We carefully make our way down the steep ridge using small saplings to keep us from tumbling all the way to the bottom. The old bird now lies still at the very base of the ridge with a trembling, giggling little boy standing over the magnificent four-year-old gobbler.

It really is something to witness this small, thin little turkey hunter, wearing a coat that hangs to the ground, wrestling with a turkey that's bigger than him. Just as early morning sunlight spills into the valley and reflects multiple colors from the turkey's feathers, I lift the gobbler across his shoulders and this turkey covers his whole backside.

I explain it is important that he alone should carry his trophy back to the Jeep; he needs to climb the ridge with his first gobbler all by himself. I tell him I will wait here and hold his gun; as the little man turns away to take those first steps with his first turkey, he can't see the tears welling up in my eyes.

I really believe this gobbler is a gift, something very special that was meant to be. That old gobbler with razor-sharp, long spurs and a double paintbrush beard marched from a mile away, down a mountain, across a valley, and straight up that steep ridge and stopped right in front of a very special little man's battered single-barrel shotgun.

Yes, this is a very special hunt, one that I will always remember as my most cherished youth hunting memory. But there is another reason this little man's hunt is so special to me, you see; I really didn't mind "carrying" that little boy turkey hunting on this long ago hunt, because that shivering little boy way back in 1973 is my little brother Marty.

Old Joe

Deep within the Missouri Ozarks, an old Willys Jeep rattles its way across the pasture heading toward the creek ford hidden by heavy fog hugging the valley. From bouncing headlights, frost glistens across wet meadow grass as we leave only tracks behind to tell of our passing.

With the smelly mixture of burning oil and hot exhaust steam spewing, the motor groans as it churns through the gravel bottom of a deep, clear Ozarks stream. Once through the low-water crossing, we turn right onto an old two track-logging road, a road that generations of my family and others have traveled, a road that no one knows is how old.

The old Jeep lurches from side to side across ancient ruts originally cut by horse-drawn wagons as we follow the rough trail to where the road forks at the base of the mountain. Turning right at the fork, as we drop into the valley, we are greeted with a series of washouts and mud holes, as the Jeep's dim headlights reflect off sheets of ice, and light dances across treetops during the roughest stretch of our journey.

With a quick downshift and punch of the accelerator, the '46 Willys lurches forward, the lockout hubs doing their job as we bounce and churn, breaking through ice that conceals several deep, rutted mud holes.

Once we are through the steep timbered valley, the four-wheel-low gears sing as we climb upward on a twisting, turning, narrow, rock-strewn two-track that eventually leads us to government ground, and up to the peak of one of Missouri's highest mountains.

On this frosty early April morning way back in '65, my dad's youngest brother, my Uncle Lee, is the veteran hunter driving this old Jeep. Uncle Lee is my favorite uncle and the black sheep of the family, quite a colorful character, known far and wide for his wild sense of humor, and who is legendary for pulling practical jokes, especially in a hunting camp.

Uncle Lee was late meeting me on this morning of turkey hunting, and with a straight face he explained he was reading stories at the old folks' home, then spent some of his night at the old feed store playing cards and drinking root beer. But the real reason he is late, was his late-night trip to the library to expand his vocabulary. But the inside of the Jeep is filled with a honky-tonk odor of stale beer and cigarette smoke mixed with cheap perfume—all tell a very different story.

Uncle Lee's favorite hunting buddy, ole Joe, is supposed to be hunting with us this morning but is missing in action and nowhere to be found. So when I ask, Uncle Lee explains that ole Joe will drive his Jeep and join us later up on the mountain just before daylight.

Ole Joe is definitely yet another interesting Ozarks character; he drives a rusted-out '49 Chevy pickup truck with a "spider-webbed" windshield, broken more than four years ago from rocks falling from a Tiff truck. Ole Joe never laces his boots, his pants zipper is always at half-mast, and I have never seen his flannel shirt tucked in.

He wears a John Deere baseball cap, always on backwards, long before it was in style as it is today. Ole Joe chews about a can of Copenhagen a day, everyone else's; he smokes cigars and Lucky Strike cigarettes whenever he can mooch them. With Uncle Lee and Joe in a hunting camp, you are in for a wild ride of fun and nonstop laughter.

As we continue on our early morning journey, the old road is steep as we traverse rocky glades toward our final destination. This morning we are hunting one of my uncle's favored places, the saddle of a lower ridge that separates two steep mountains, a place he has taken many mountain turkeys over the years.

The Jeep's climb is headed toward a summit with a parking place known as the "icebox." The icebox is on an open area next to the old road on the main ridge marked with the remains of an old-time icebox someone dumped on the mountain bench years before.

As we crest the ridge, we drive right past the old icebox. So, I ask Uncle Lee why we didn't stop and park. As the old Jeep sputters to a stop about seventy yards past the icebox, he pauses and says, "Boy, you are old enough now to learn a few of life's many lessons. When Joe gets here, this morning, just watch, listen and learn."

Our old deer and turkey hunting rock camp fire pit near the icebox.

Then as we climb from the Jeep, he speaks once more, "Boy, this morning's lesson is one that I'll teach you about what happens to someone who messes with you. Ole Joe messed with the wrong guy this time, so if you can dish it out, you have to be able to take it."

Making our way on foot back down the dark road toward the icebox, we stop just across from the pullover, then he tells me, "Now be real quiet, just follow me and do what I say."

After a short walk, we pause next to a big oak. "I want you to stay right here," Uncle Lee says, pointing to the rear base of the big tree just across the road from the icebox.

Lying on the ground next to the tree, it's cold, very cold, but it shouldn't be long now as I watch moonlight dance as it filters down through the timber. Finally there is a hint of daylight in the eastern sky, just as the full moon begins to slip below the horizon of the mountain.

I clearly hear a Jeep coming up the old logging road long before I can see the headlights. It is pretty quiet on this unseasonably cold early morning ridge. A distant owl hoots, and the whip-poor-will's song is slowing as the groaning of the four-wheel-drive churning its way up the mountain closes the distance.

Lying low against the base of a huge oak, I can now see headlights below the ridge bouncing up and down through the trees. Cresting the ridge, the Jeep downshifts, and brake lights glow as the Jeep pulls in next to the icebox to park. After the motor is silent and headlights are dark, once again all is quiet, with the exception of the ever-slowing ticking sounds of a cooling engine.

My uncle gives the "shhh" signal with his finger to his lips, then whispers for me not to move, be real still, and very quiet. The Jeep door slowly opens, and the dark shape of a person steps out into the dark world. The shadowlike figure, with his back to us, lights up a cigarette as he pours a coffee from a Thermos into his cup on the hood of the Jeep.

The long, relaxed puffs on the cigarette create a red glow and the only light for miles, and a target for my Uncle Lee, who is quietly stalking toward the unsuspecting ole Joe, reminiscent of a mountain lion on a hunt as he closes the distance to his prey.

The obscure human outline then pours a second cup of coffee, takes a sip, then sets the coffee cup down on the hood of the old Jeep. After a long pull on the cigarette, he turns, facing away with one hand on his hip for an early morning nature call, just as my uncle reaches the unsuspecting victim from behind.

Uncle Lee strikes quickly, without mercy, pushing forward with great force, emitting loud, deep growling sounds as he locks his arms around him, violently lifting him off the ground, shaking his body, while growling and biting across his shoulders like a crazed animal.

The sounds of a grown man screaming like a schoolgirl echo across the mountain, a sound that will haunt me forever. As a thirteen-year-old boy, I believe I have just witnessed death for the first time.

The smells of coffee and urine fill the morning air as the now-limp, quivering body collapses to the ground in a fetal position sobbing pile, and my uncle is standing over him laughing hysterically like a man gone mad.

Uncle Lee strikes his lighter, lights a cigarette, takes a puff, and then lowers his burning lighter closer to his victim to cut the darkness and admire his work. Then in a loud voice, "So how did you like that? That ought to teach ya to mess with me."

Uncle Lee is leaning over, ever closer, still holding his lighter, and his words abruptly stop. Suddenly, Uncle Lee stands straight up, turns, and runs back toward the road and me.

On his way back to his Jeep, I will never ever forget those words screamed on that long-ago morning as Uncle Lee ran past me with his lip-clenched cigarette in full glow.

"Run boy, it ain't Joe! Wrong guy, wrong guy. Run boy, run, *wrong guy!*"

The Game Warden

The Ozarks hills and hollers are a display of color from the redbud, wildflowers, and blooming dogwood trees. Old Man Winter has reluctantly released his grip after a long, cold, snowy season. Mud holes and ponds are full of spring peepers reciting their springtime music, and morel mushrooms push their spongy heads up through the leaf-covered forest floor.

My 1975 turkey hunting camp is located on a logging road at the junction of the old Banner Road, eight miles from any paved road and deep within the national forest. Camp setup is high on a long ridge, for easy access to hunting areas and so as not to disturb gobblers that might be roosted at the heads of hollers.

After many years of turkey hunting in this area of the Ozarks, with much thought, planning, and consideration, we decided on this location as the best possible place to set up our camp, our home for the next several weeks. From this long ridgetop our guides and hunters are able to cover a lot of ground quickly, as well as set up on gobbling buck turkeys down the adjoining finger ridges, without climbing up the steep, bottomless hollows.

A huge fire pit sits in the middle of the road surrounded by old wooden chairs borrowed from the Council Bluff church house. Just under the hill is an old pond with ample water for coffee making, washing dishes, and taking our weekly baths. Several military-style olive drab tents are set up just off the roadbed. One is the cook tent, the other for supplies and our "camp cook" quarters, complete with a table for strategy meetings.

Times have changed; these are modern times, and in addition to the tents we have a 1964 Chevy pickup truck with a big over-the-cab camper. We pulled this through deep mud holes up the eight-mile logging road.

A couple of smaller tents are on other side of the logging road for our guests. On the cook table in the center of camp are a Coleman stove and a Coleman lantern. The lantern has a "wick" called a mantle, which makes a much brighter light than the old kerosene lanterns hanging on tree limbs around camp.

We're waiting for the arrival of our clients for a three-day guided turkey hunt. Yes, times have changed, a skilled turkey hunter today can make a hundred dollars guiding, sometimes more if he receives a tip. Besides making money by calling turkeys, there are additional benefits as a successful big-city hunters may reward his guide with shotgun shells, a knife, or a woodland camouflage shirt, a coveted prize that very few have.

My guides are seasoned hunters, Ozark veterans of many springtime battles with public-ground gobblers. Billy is my main guide, Butch is a little rough with people but a very good guide, and Tom is one of the best turkey hunters in the Ozarks. Uncle Lee guides for me on occasion, when he is in camp, but he left two nights ago to buy a case of beer and ice, and is still missing.

Just before dark, I walk from camp to roost turkeys. My destination is a big ridge that overlooks a deep valley of old fields and timbered spur ridges of an old abandoned farm. Choruses of whip-poor-wills begin their late evening serenade as a beautiful Ozarks sunset slowly disappears behind the western hills as I cup my hands and call like a barred owl.

The excited response of hooting owls answering my call generates a throaty gobble from the roost of old tom turkey near the split-rail fence in Hop Holler. Other gobblers on the roost down the valley join in with a good-night call that echoes across the hollows and hills. I quietly leave my evening listening post; I am more than satisfied with the results of putting several turkeys to bed and always enjoy the peaceful walk back to camp on the faded two-track road.

The evening meal is spread out on the table when Billy finally pulls his Jeep into camp; a pickup truck follows close behind. The plan was for the hunters to park their truck at the paved road, load the Jeep with gear, and for Billy to drive them back to our camp on the rutted road. It is obvious by the look on Billy's face as walks past me that we are in for a great time with the new clients.

Billy says one of the hunters, a loud, obnoxious person, refused to leave his truck out at the main road. Besides, his brand new four-wheel-drive truck could run circles around any old Jeep. I watch our new hunters walk into the light of camp; they are wearing sandals and Bermuda shorts and are very much under the influence of alcohol. I escort them into the tent for a private meeting at the table to discuss the rules of their guided hunt. This loudmouth guy's first words to me were: "I already called my taxidermist; we both must have a wild turkey to complete our trophy rooms, and I am paying, so I expect results."

I am so glad my guides did not hear this conversation; my guys are Iron County boys, not just veteran turkey hunters, but a rough bunch, always the last men standing in a fight. If my guys were pushed and possibly lost it, neither one of these guys would be conscious the next morning for anything, much less a turkey hunt.

Our new guests also refuse to sit down to dinner with us; they sit next to the fire with weird-looking girlie drinks with little umbrellas, and continue drinking late into the night. Things have changed on this first morning of the hunt, we will not be hunting the roosted gobblers an easy walk from camp. The plan for the next morning is quite simple; we will hunt the roughest parts of these hills, and my guides will take these egotistical big shots for a little nature walk. Three-thirty in the morning comes early in turkey camp, especially for our guests. All the guides are just begging to take these late-night, hung-over drinkers hunting.

After the first morning's hunt, Billy returns with his hunter. This guy looks bad; he is stripped down to his T-shirt and is dragging his unloaded gun by the barrel and is about fifty yards behind his guide. Billy has an evil smile on his face as he passes me and says, "The turkeys were really tough today." Loudmouth did not make it back for another hour, guide Tom looked quite happy and very refreshed as loudmouth crawled into his tent and collapsed in his bed.

With our hunters taking a much-needed nap, I overhear Tom telling the other guys how this gobbler was determined to come to the call. Tom would tell his hunter the bird was not coming, get up and leave, only to have the gobbler follow them to the next setup. All were dying laughing when Tom said he had to finally stand up behind his positioned hunter and wave his arms in the air to finally convince the turkey to leave.

The second day of their hunt is pretty much the same and I feel they learned their lesson, and I am obligated with paying hunters to get them a turkey. So on the last morning of their hunt, Butch and I decide take our hunters north, to a really good place not as steep, with rolling hills and a lot of easy walking roads, 6,000 acres of Tiff mining ground.

In some of the older areas of the Tiff mining ground, hand-dug test holes from the 1930s and 1940s are everywhere. These test holes look very much like grave sites. To keep with the Ozarks tradition and folklore, we tell our hunters the sunken holes and rock mounds are where my relatives buried a game warden and a "revenuer" in 1946 or maybe 1956.

Butch's hunter kills a bird; my hunter, ole loudmouth, got close but didn't close the deal.

We load up hunters, gear, and turkey for the drive to town and the checking station. After checking the turkey, we pull into the local bar for a cold drink and lunch, time to introduce our hunters to some of the local folks.

We enter through doors into a world filled with smoke and George Jones singing a love song from an ancient jukebox. The floor is hundred-year-old oak plank wood, stained with blood and tobacco juice. Sawdust is scattered on the floor in front of the bar. The wall behind the bar is covered with turkey beards and buck racks, a pot-bellied stove sets in the corner, and groups of rough-looking men are playing cards at big tables.

Butch and I grab a table close to the door as our hunters stand in the doorway with mouths open and wide eyes as they survey the room filled with miners, farmers, and local turkey hunters. Most are shirtless, wearing bib overalls; many have huge arms and long, thick, nasty looking beards.

Someone pulls the plug from the jukebox and the room falls silent as everyone in the tavern is staring silently at the two strangers standing in the door. Stanley is the first to speak. With a loud booming voice he yells, "Hey, Panhandle, get Ray and his friends some beers!"

What our guests do not know is that I work at the mines and turkey hunt with most of these guys. The jukebox is wailing once more, and we have long-neck beers four deep in front of us as turkey hunting stories run rampant with Stanley, Sonny, and my cousin Wayne joining us at the table.

On our late afternoon return to camp we drive all backwoods roads and we stop along a logging road a few miles from camp to hunt for mushrooms; our hunters are better now, much more relaxed, and seem to be enjoying their trip. We walk up on another Tiff test hole, and one of the hunters laughs out loud and quickly says, "I bet somebody buried the game warden there."

After dark back in camp we are sitting around the campfire after a huge meal of fresh fried turkey breast, morel mushrooms, baked potatoes, baked beans, and cathead biscuits. Everyone is full and a little tired on this last evening of the hunt as we all sit and stare silently into the fire.

Billy suddenly stands up, and on full alert, walks away from camp, stops, and listens intently. Quickly returning to the fire, he looks at me and says, "Sounds like someone is walking up the road toward camp." My guides grab their guns, quietly loading as they slip into the darkness, leaving the two hunters, Marty, and me in camp.

A few minutes later I catch movement in the road as a shadow of a man's outline walks into the faint firelight. He is a man who looks to be in his mid- to late thirties, wearing bib overalls, a faded woodland camouflage shirt, and a brown-and-white feed store ball cap.

I ask the stranger, "Can I help you?"

He walks closer into the firelight. "Good evening, how you all doing?" he says.

I look the guy right in the eye and say, "Why don't you knock it off? Why don't you just ask us for our tags, why not just drive into camp and check us? Why play dress-up? I know you are a game warden."

"Okay," he says, "Let's see some identification and some turkey tags."

"Whoa, whoa now, how about some identification from you first?" I reply. The man promptly takes out a badge and holds it in the firelight. Our hunters stand up quickly and dig for their drivers' licenses and turkey tags and then hand them to the game warden.

I walk toward the guy and say, "We don't need any damn turkey license, why don't you just leave and mind your own business?"

The stranger comes right back with, "How would you like to go to jail?"

I respond, "We aren't doing anything wrong, you come sneaking in here acting like a big shot. Go to hell."

The game warden and I are now face to face in a heated argument, with our hunters trying to separate us. The warden walks quickly back out to the road, turns, and yells for me to come out there and we will settle this, and I'm going to jail whether I like it or not.

I march toward the road as Bill and Butch come back into camp to keep the hunters back. As I step past the fire, Marty slaps a .32 caliber handgun into my hand for everyone to see.

Out in the road we go at it, arguing at first, then the hunters hear the unmistakable sounds of fists landing, then I yell, "Don't do it, don't go for your gun!" Then three quick shots ring out.

The game warden is now on the ground and flopping in the road. The hunters' faces are ghostly white. They're trembling with sweat pouring from their faces while the guys calmly unload their guns. Grabbing a shovel, they're whistling as they walk down the road toward the now very still game warden.

Marching back into camp, I say, "I didn't want it to come to this, but he asked for it."

Then I tell Marty to help drag the guy down into the woods. Marty, while sitting in his chair making a bologna sandwich, calmly says, "No way, I had to help drag the last one off."

Loudmouth grabs me by the shirt, screaming, "Tell me you didn't shoot that man, please tell me you didn't shoot him!"

I yell, "I didn't want to, but yeah I did, right here!" as I point to my forehead. Loudmouth runs a little farther out in the road and sees my guys dragging the body into the woods. All the while his buddy is frantically throwing their gear in their truck, and Loudmouth looks like he may pass out, grabs his lit Coleman lantern, and throws it in his truck.

The hunter's truck roars to life. Loudmouth is standing in the road trembling with his mouth open, gasping for air when Butch says, "Hey, what about those guys? They seen it all."

"Yeah," says Billy, "they saw everything. Hell, we're already digging a hole anyway." That's all it takes. The hunter's truck roars off, throwing dirt and rocks with Loudmouth running like a madman behind and jumping in the bed of the truck.

As the sound of the roaring truck disappears into the distance, a loud cheer roars up from camp. Laughter is deafening, and our fake play-actor game warden is now standing next to the fire with tears running down his face, laughing so hard he is about to pee his pants. The entire camp yells loudly as everyone raises a drink to toast our unfortunate victims of one of the cruelest practical jokes in the history of hunting our Ozarks camps.

You know, Hollywood may be a place they give out awards for acting, but if there ever were a cast and crew that deserved an Academy Award, it was that ragged bunch of turkey hunters in the Missouri Ozarks way back in 1975 in a turkey camp on an old ridgetop where the eight-mile road meets the old Banner Road.

The Big-City Hunter

Back in Missouri's early years of turkey hunting, hunters traveled from great distances to the Ozarks to experience springtime wild turkey hunting. Missouri's wild turkey restoration program was in full swing, with live-trapped wild turkeys relocated throughout the Ozarks. Missouri's turkey hunting season was fairly new with the first spring season since 1935 opening in 1960.

The successful turkey relocation program and recent turkey season have provided much-needed additional revenue in rural areas. Hunters from across the state, as well as out of state, pump a ton of money into the economy of small towns in southern Missouri during hunting season. My Uncle Lee was not one to look a gift horse in the mouth. He was one of the first to figure out how to make a dollar from turkey hunting. Very few of the new turkey hunters traveling to the Ozarks knew much, if anything, about how to hunt or call these wild creatures.

My uncle was a very good turkey hunter, known far and wide for his calling ability. He grew up around wild turkeys; there were always wild turkeys in the hills around Grandpa's farm. In fact, some of the very first live trapping of turkeys took place in the hills of the farm. He killed big gobblers in each of the first five seasons, as well as luring birds into the gun for friends and family.

Out of a small group of Ozarks resident hunters who guided out-of-area novices or "foreigner turkey hunters" as they were called by locals, Uncle Lee was one of the fortunate few who could get $20, in advance. On many occasions strangers

This is a photo of my Uncle Lee in 1975 with a bow-killed gobbler.

would stop by the old store to request help after little success on their own. "Wild Bill," the man who ran the local gas station and check station, would send hunters to my Uncle Lee every spring turkey season.

On a warm, sunny springtime afternoon, a stranger drives a brand new, shiny 1966 dark blue Cadillac up the rutted road to the farm. The man is in his late forties, he is short and a bit heavy; he's wearing new hunting clothes and brand new hunting boots. His name is Jim Smith, from north Missouri, from up around Kansas City. Jim is an upland bird hunter, a quail hunter, and his gun is a fancy gold-and-silver over-and-under 20-gauge, an open choke bird gun.

"Wild Bill" sent him over to meet Uncle Lee to see if he would guide him for a turkey hunt. Jim's plan is to fulfill his dream to kill a wild turkey and have it mounted for his trophy room. Jim explains that he is willing to pay $20 for the hunt and give him another $30 if he kills a turkey. My uncle does not want this one to get away, so he agrees with a handshake as he takes the man's money—a crisp, brand new $20 bill.

Grandma invites the stranger into her home for a big supper: corn on the cob, pork chops, mashed potatoes, gravy, and homemade bread. After a great meal, Uncle Lee has Jim follow him down the valley to the head of Dry Fork Holler to my great uncle Mont's cabin, where they will put him up for the night.

At dusk Uncle Lee hikes up to Clinton Ridge, high above the old cabin, to roost one very valuable wild turkey. Right at dark at the edge of an Ozarks glade, he hears the unmistakable sounds below him, turkeys flying up, and then hears what he is waiting for: the wingbeats of a gobbler that roosts at the edge of the glade. He cups his hands around his mouth and hoots a perfect "who cooks for you, who cooks for you all" of the barred owl, and the gobbler rifles back a reply. Uncle Lee is smiling as he quietly slips back down the mountain to the valley below.

Early the next morning, the men are trying their best to wake up after a late night around the campfire. The cabin is warm from a wood stove and filled with the soft glow of a large ceiling beam-hanging kerosene lamp. In a sleepy stupor, Jim struggles to get dressed as his guide prepares the morning breakfast.

Hunter and guide gulp fresh coffee and devour a big plate of biscuits and gravy. After breakfast Uncle Lee picks up Jim's little 20-gauge, turning it over in his hands. He offers the use of his personal 10-gauge, but Jim declines and says he is fine with his gun and knows it well.

Stepping outside, Uncle Lee strikes a wooden match and lights the old kerosene lantern. As the hunters depart into the cool early morning air, they walk along to a chorus of whip-poor-wills, hoot owls, and a gurgling stream, the age-old song of an Ozarks turkey hunter.

They make the long walk all the way across the dew-laden old field to the base of Clinton Ridge before they speak for the first time since leaving the cabin. Uncle Lee explains his plan for the morning.

"Jim, we are going to have to climb a ways." He pauses and then begins again, "You have to be very quiet. When we get to where we're going you have to sit very still and only move when I tell you."

Jim nods his head as they turn and begin the steep, rough climb up the ridge and on toward the gobbler roosted on the glade far above them.

The city hunter is breathing heavily as he labors to keep up with his guide. When they arrive just short of the glade and the sleeping gobbler, Uncle Lee tells his hunter, "I'll tote the gun from here. Move very slowly."

Holding up the lantern, the guide says, "Set down against that big pine tree," as the lantern goes out. Their world goes dark, very dark, as they wait for daylight.

As the soft orange glow of first light finally appears in the eastern sky, Lee whispers in his hunter's ear, "Now you have to sit still. Raise your left knee and rest the gun barrel, keep your head up until I tell you to shoot." As he slides the small gun to Jim, he's thinking about their chances.

This open glade is the right choice for an open shot, but with Jim's bird gun, the gobbler will have to be very close, real close. That presents the next problem; he hopes during the excitement of the hunt, he can keep this new turkey hunter from moving too much because he could really use that extra $30.

Just after the first songbirds awake, and the hens below the glade speak first. The soft tree calls signal the beginning of a new day, and a different gobbler sounds off below their setup as an owl hoots somewhere down the ridge.

Uncle Lee whispers to his hunter, "Remember, don't move, sit still, and do not shoot until I tell you." The guide takes a big breath then hoots like a great horned owl. The booming gobble is close, right in front of the hunter. The veteran guide carefully scratches out a couple of soft yelps on his weathered box call; the gobbler's reply cuts him off.

Turkeys are now gobbling all across the ridge as the hunter is breathing heavily and shaking uncontrollably. The gobbler roosted on the glade is gobbling nonstop, at the crows, owls, other turkeys, and the love call from a weathered Ozarks box call. Then, all is quiet on the ridgetop as the big tom pitches and glides down, landing about seventy yards out in the open glade in full strut.

"Don't move," Lee whispers as he scratches out a quick series of yelps. The gobbler folds up, and starts their way.

With the early morning sun now peeking over the horizon from behind the hunters, soft morning light reflects off the colorful plumage of the Ozarks gobbler. Jim is really breathing heavily now and drawing large, doughnut-size circles with the gun barrel.

Jim frantically whispers, "I can kill him."

Lee is right behind his shoulder and whispers, "He's too far, you can't kill 'im, sit still."

Jim whispers again, "I tell you I can kill him."

"You can't kill 'im, sit still," replies Uncle Lee.

Now my uncle is thinking, this guy is shaking so bad, the barrel is going in circles, the bird is now a little less than fifty yards, he has dropped out of strut, his head straight up in an alert posture, peering into their setup as he begins to sidestep. Something has to give; this bird is going to spook at any time. He has done all he can do; he will just have to lose the extra money. Oh well, this guy has had a hell of a show.

The bird suddenly stops and putts, so Uncle Lee pokes Jim in the ribs with his three middle fingers and says, "Okay, kill 'im."

The gun roars. At the sound of the shot the gobbler collapses, slamming to the ground, not so much as a quiver, graveyard dead, one little turkey feather in the air slowly floating to the ground as the gunshot echoes across the valley. The big-city hunter collapses into a heap of total exhaustion.

Uncle Lee slowly stands up, pulls off his hat and scratches his head and says, "Holy cow, I have never seen anything like that, man you hammered him, come on, let's go get your turkey." Uncle Lee pulls his now-smiling hunter to his feet and takes the gun.

As they walk across the glade to claim their prize, breaking the gun open, he asks, "Jim, what in the world are you shootin' in this thing?" Breathing heavily, Jim stops walking, and with a huge smile looks right into my Uncle Lee's eyes and says:

"Deer slugs—why do you ask?"

The Bronze Gobbler "Ole Copper"

After crossing the creek by stepping from rock to rock, I climb the steep creekbank and make my way across a dew-laden pasture to a logging road entrance at the corner of the field. Finding the opening, I briskly walk up the old logging road that leads past the old Sutterfield sawmill.

From the old mill pond across the holler, a spring peeper serenade fills the morning air, as I continue my early morning journey up the valley to the head of Sawmill Holler. At the base of the mountain, I leave the old road behind, turning east at the big rock outcropping. From there, the real work begins, as I climb straight up the face of this Ozark mountain.

On the last morning of the 1969 Missouri spring turkey season in the Ozark Mountains, I'm climbing up the rugged, rock-strewn west side of Pruitt Mountain, out of breath, breathing like a steam engine, and pretty much turned around—some would probably use the word "lost."

It's 3:30 AM when I stop to rest on a rock ledge; I must keep climbing if I am to arrive at my destination before first light. I pause only long enough to replenish the air in my aching lungs and for my legs to stop burning. My 1950 GMC pickup is now far below, all the way down at the base of the mountain. I'm climbing this mountain for one last chance at a rare bronze "copper-colored" gobbler.

I wipe the sweat from my face with my faded T-shirt, shake my cheap plastic, two-cell, gas station flashlight, and continue my climb straight up, with only dim light to show me the way. My destination is the pine and rock ridge and a saddle that lies between Pruitt and Logan Mountains, home of the copper gobbler.

The majestic bronze gobbler has eluded my every attempt this season; I blew an opportunity when I missed a ten-yard shot at the gobbler on the second day of the season. If missing wasn't enough, I painfully watched the copper gobbler set his wings and sail out of my dreams, as a wrist-size center-punched sapling crashed to the ground right in front of me.

Ray's 1950 GMC parked by the old church near the holler.

This Missouri spring turkey season has been a rough one for me, one this sixteen-year-old turkey hunter will not soon forget. I've bumped turkeys, missed turkeys, and just plain scared off more gobblers than anytime during my young turkey hunting career.

Before the turkey season I entered my dollar in the "jackpot" for the biggest turkey at Pine Valley gas station and local hunter hangout. I should have entered a dollar in a jackpot for spooking birds or missing multiple times in a row. I would've won hands down.

After seven days of unproductive turkey hunting, I was forced to return home near St. Louis for several days because of school, but I managed to talk my dad into allowing me get up at midnight, drive by myself, and return to the Ozarks for this last day, and my last chance at the bronze gobbler.

By the time I finally make it up to the main ridge, the edge of a huge orange ball is just starting to peek over the top of Buford Mountain as false dawn's orange streaks the eastern skyline and the whip-poor-will completes its early morning serenade. I quickly cross the first glade to the timbered saddle and walk the narrow ridge that leads to a glade where the bronze gobbler struts and gobbles, announcing to the world he is king.

With this new dawn, a morning mist rises from the hills, and from somewhere across the steep valley a booming gobble of the mystical Ozarks Ghost greets a new day. But I have to pause once more to take in the beauty of early morning's first golden sunlight filtering through blooming dogwood trees, creating a sea of white across a green mountainside.

For me there is nowhere like the Ozarks during first light in the springtime with the aroma of blooming wildflowers and sound of spring water rushing through granite "shut-ins" on its journey down the mountainside.

Moving quickly, but quietly, I move on and finally arrive on the Pruitt side of the narrow ridge. I also realize I'm close to where I need to set up, because I clearly hear water from the rock shut-ins tumbling down the mountain, just as thunder begins to rumble in the distance. Pausing to catch my breath and locate a good tree for my setup, I hear the

False dawn's orange streaks the eastern skyline.

A morning mist rises from somewhere deep in the holler.

"Just as I arrive . . . the morning sunlight quickly disappears behind dark clouds."

whip-poor-will finish its early morning song and the turkeys begin gobbling all across the hills and the hollers.

But just then, the morning sunlight quickly disappears behind dark clouds, thunder rumbles, and a light fog begins to cloak the mountaintop. I owl hoot, a turkey rifles back a reply just beyond the glade, and I quickly close the distance as thunder rumbles and heavy fog settles in, blanketing the mountaintop.

Moving toward the gobbling, I pray it's Ole Copper. I set up against a huge tree with the jagged rock outcroppings of shut-ins to my left. Out in front, a faded logging road disappears below the hill, to my right, and this narrow bench drops straight down; this is a near perfect setup.

Just as I prepare to call with my box call, beautiful hen music floats from across the deep granite ravine from the ridge just above the glades. The hen yelping is "real hen" in tone and has that perfect up-and-down yelping cadence to it, something I have only heard real wild hens ever make.

The woods come alive as gobblers near and far enthusiastically respond to the yelping hen. One gobbler is quickly closing the distance, in fact gobblers are moving toward the calling hen from three sides. The seductive hen turkey goes silent, yet the gobbling moves ever closer to where the last hen sounds called

Dogwoods blossoms create a sea of white.

The woodlands around the shut-in come alive.

out for springtime love, and now all is quiet but a few songbirds.

Suddenly, from across the ravine, a boom goes off like stick of dynamite. The shotgun blast startles me—no, scares the living hell out of me—along with the sound of flopping turkey and the beating of wings and breaking of limbs as others near the scene take flight. I didn't know there was another hunter within miles of me. I actually thought the voice across the ravine was a real hen calling.

Sitting listening to the sounds of a flopping turkey, all the while trying to regain my composure, I see a gobbler on set wings glide from across the deep shut-in directly toward me, then with cupped wings and turning to my left, the heavy bird drops to the ground, snapping small limbs as he lands. I shift to my left, quickly standing up as I pull my gun to my shoulder. I am not going to pass up a "gimme" with the season I'm having. The bronze gobbler will have to wait until next year. Just as the gobbler stands up with a shifting of feathers and ready to leave, I aim and pull the trigger, a miss, then as the bird runs faster and pitches into flight, I miss twice more.

All is quiet now with the exception of cows mooing far away in the pastures at the base of the mountain, and as thunder increases rumbling across the hills, I pick up my gear as well as my pride. It's time for the long, painful walk back down the mountain. I turn to leave and as I stumble on the steep hillside, the early morning soft orange light filters through the fog, creating a strange eerie glow across the mountain.

Pausing, I just happen to look across the steep ravine through the fog and catch movement. I'm straining to see through the fog, when in an opening on the glade about seventy yards or so across, an older man appears with a full beard, wearing bib overalls, and an old faded brown felt hat. He has a big gobbler slung over his shoulder and a shotgun cradled in the crook of his arm.

He seems to be looking across the ravine toward me and is now pointing up the mountain, toward the northeast. None of this makes any sense and

The old-timer appears through the fog, shotgun cradled, and turkey slung over his shoulder.

seems just a little strange. Why would the old hunter point up the mountain? So, I turn to go down the mountain, but the old-timer stops, turns, and once again points across the mountain to the northeast, then waves as if to say good-bye. The thunder intensifies as he walks off into the fog, and turkeys are gobbling nonstop in every direction, unlike anything I have ever heard before.

The old man walking toward the summit also seems strange, because the only way off this remote mountain from here is straight down. Then higher on the hillside, in a brief opening in the fog, I see the old-timer again as he continues climbing toward the top of the mountain.

Thunder now becomes much more intense as a strange, eerie-looking wide beam of sunlight shines down from dark clouds, through the fog, and to the ground at the highest point of the mountain.

As thunder gradually subsides and gobbling grows silent, the fog lifts, and beautiful sunlight floods across the mountain. I hesitate, rethink my departure, and look toward the northeast.

I stop on the next hillside to make one last call before going back down the mountain. I yelp on my box call and hear a gobble across the glade to the northeast, the same direction the old man had just pointed.

Quickly moving forward about seventy-five yards, I pause to listen as the turkey gobbles again, but much closer now, so I scramble to find a tree, plop down, and stroke the old box again. The booming gobble is now slightly to my right, almost to the old roadbed. I quickly adjust and point my gun down the road.

Yelping again as I scratch the leaves with my hand, I now clearly hear drumming and the buzz of wings dragging in the leaves. I turn slowly to the left as I follow the sounds with my gun barrel.

The drumming sounds are close as I'm shaking uncontrollably, then I see movement to the left of the road just under the hill. My heartbeat quickens as the gobbler's head and the top of his fan appear just under the rise.

I voice yelp, the bird drops out of strut, comes up over the edge of the ridge, and sprints right toward me, his bronze body rocking from side to side. I clutch my dad's old Browning, say a quick prayer, cover the neck with the bead, and pull the trigger.

The roar of the shotgun echoes across miles of hills and hollers, then all is quiet. I stand up slowly on wobbly legs, totally exhausted, both mentally and physically. One final wing flop, and all is still. My entire body is trembling with emotion as tears well up in my eyes, and I cannot believe I'm standing over the copper-colored bronze gobbler.

He is a beautiful bronze bird, the prettiest wild turkey I have ever seen. He has long, curved, razor-sharp spurs and a thick, long, bushy "paintbrush" beard. The bronze wild Ozarks gobbler is one I will never match in all my years of turkey hunting.

The mountain is quiet now with the exception of a few songbirds and a squirrel barking as if to scold me for intruding into his world. I take a deep breath, pause, and reflect on this unbelievable, very strange morning.

I walk toward the old roadbed that will lead me down the mountain, when I happen to notice turkey feathers blowing lightly across the ground; a few more steps and I find a pile of feathers where a hunter's gobbler fell.

I adjust my load and move on, then just above where I saw the old turkey hunter, I see a makeshift blind of pine tree limbs. I walk over for a quick look at his setup. I see where the old man was sitting against the tree.

A little farther past the tree I spot something lying in the leaves. I step across the homemade blind to find one of the prettiest box calls I have ever laid

"He is a beautiful bronze bird, the prettiest wild turkey I have ever seen . . ."

There's nowhere quite like the Ozarks.

my hands on. It has an engraved gobbler on the lid and a smoothly finished exterior. I pull the lid across the calling edge, and the sweet music of a perfect hen comes from within. This is without question the call I heard from across the ravine.

As I turn this work of art over in my hands, I notice notches on the bottom of the call with dates and names of mountains: Logan, Pruitt, Johnson, and Buford. Near the bottom edge are the initials, O. R. S.; this call belongs to Orville Sutterfield, and he must be the old-timer I saw standing across the shut-ins.

I now realize the old turkey hunter, who very easily could have killed Ole Copper, helped a young hunter fulfill his dream as he took a lesser bird and directed this boy to where Ole Copper gobbles and struts.

The walk down the mountain is easier and much more enjoyable than the nightmarish early morning climb. I carefully place the gobbler in the front seat, load my gear, and throw gravel as I head toward the paved road and on to town.

The old gas station is full of hunters as I pull past the gas pumps to park in front of the store. I lift the gobbler from the cab and walk inside the station. Hunters are abuzz with talk about the fog, the strange light, and how wild turkeys were rocking to the thunder with unbelievable gobbling this morning on Johnson, Bell, Buford, and Pruitt Mountains.

Most are gathered around the scale as hunters check in their turkeys; Floyd is in the lead with a twenty-three-pound gobbler from Clinton Ridge. But my copper gobbler weighs in at twenty-four and a half pounds, huge for a mountain bird, and easily wins the jackpot, and on the very last day of the season.

Wild Bill asks to hear my story of this morning's hunt. I tell it in its entirety and with great gusto, leaving nothing out. But when I tell about the old turkey hunter pointing to the northeast, Wild Bill abruptly interrupts me and says what I'm saying just cannot be true. So I pull out the box call to show him and place it on the table. The entire room falls silent.

With a somber expression, Wild Bill leans forward and softly whispers "Ray—Orville Sutterfield, at eighty-one years old, climbed Pruitt Mountain early yesterday morning to turkey hunt his favorite place on the mountain. When he didn't return, your Uncle Lee went up on the mountain and found him, dead in his blind, still at the base of his favorite tree, his final gobbler lying on the ground right out in front of him."

20

The Future of Turkey Hunting

FROM JUST UNDER A RISE, LESS THAN TWENTY YARDS AWAY, the loud, throaty rattle of the turkey's love call caused my startled young hunter to press back tight against me. Sitting on a small folding stool, a trembling little Sarah was facing the wrong direction. So I picked up seat and all, and quickly turned Sarah to face the oncoming feathered thunder gut.

We were in southern Missouri as part of one of my organized youth turkey hunts. I was hunting with little Sarah and a group of great kids who were experiencing turkey hunting and the outdoors for the first time. This youth hunt, as well as the many others I've organized over the years, was not all about the kill, but was much more about the overall total outdoor experience.

It's very important that during their first hunt kids get to experience the total package of what turkey hunting is all about, so around 9:30 AM I gathered up all the kids and drove them into town to a local café for a big breakfast.

Our hunts and programs introduced countless kids to hunting and the outdoors.

Over many, many years, I have introduced countless kids to hunting, and I
find the experience pretty much the same
with all my youth hunts. There is a completely wonderful, warm feeling in sharing the outdoors with all those wonderful little people. I've hunted with kids all
across America, and I also find it interesting that in many states turkey hunting is
as new to the grownups attending the
hunt as it is to the kids.

A diversity of great kids attend our
youth hunts, some of them from broken
homes, a few without any fathers in their
homes, one without either parent at all in
his life, as well as several physically challenged kids.

Today's kids represent tomorrow's
turkey hunting future.

I love all of them. I wish I could hug, smooch, and squeeze the stuffing out
of every one of these kids, and I did just that years ago, during these hunts, but
it's really a shame that in today's world one has to be very careful with showing any affection toward kids—or to anyone else for that matter.

It really didn't used to be that way. Teachers, Sunday school teachers, car-
egivers, babysitters, and even turkey guides
could hug and show kids a whole bunch of
love, something that way too many kids in
today's world too often go without.

It's really sad the many negative things
some kids experience during their young lives,
but giving them your time and just a little of
your attention, and taking kids hunting, really
revives them and they become much more
excited about life.

It's really sad how many negative things some kids
experience during their young lives, but by giving
them your time, just a little of your attention,
and by taking them hunting, it can really revive
them and get them much more excited about life.

Kimi Sabati with her first Hawaiian gobbler.

But there is a downside to all this, in that in the last few years I've found it more and more difficult to even locate kids to invite and to take hunting. In today's world, there's just so much competition for young people's attention, and time with computers, games, malls, television, movie theaters, and theme parks often takes precedence.

Through today's organized youth hunts we all try our best to build positive attitudes and create wonderful memories for every youngster we encounter. We convey to young hunters that there is so much more to hunting than just killing a turkey; it is really about the total experience.

Many needed life lessons are a part of the experience during youth hunts, such as how to work and communicate effectively with others, building confidence and self-esteem, how to humbly accept success, as well as deal with failure and disappointment, for instance if they miss a shot at a turkey.

I am a very fortunate person. I have so many wonderful turkey hunting memories and I feel it is my obligation to pass along to others what I have learned and experienced in my lifetime, especially to our future generations of turkey hunters.

All those wonderful little people just need a little direction, a whole lot of love, and someone to help them build their own special memories of turkey hunting and a big fat gobbler to call their very own. Yes indeed, it is without question part of my destiny to pass along my hunting experience to our future generations of turkey hunters.

Any chance of turkey hunting in the future rests in the small hands of today's youth hunters. This is why it is so important to introduce young people, but even more important to introduce their families, guardians, whoever, to continue their new hunting experience long after their first youth hunt.

But it is just as important to introduce new hunters of all ages to the outdoors and hunting for the sake of our future. Today, we are losing hunter numbers at an alarming rate, with hunting license sales down nationwide. Education, youth hunts, and positive hunting role models all help. But as hunters, we must do more than enlist new hunters. We all must be positive

This youth hunt in southern Missouri is among the many I've organized over the years, with the focus always being on the overall outdoor experience.

ambassadors of our sport of hunting and also of gun ownership.

As hunters and gun owners, we must address misguided, heavily funded, anti-hunting, animal rights, and gun control groups spewing misinformation, telling outright lies, all in an organized mass media blitz to outlaw hunting and ban firearms. Their motives are not just the manifestation of saving innocent little animals from big bad hunters, as they claim, but to make a ton of money from people who believe their rhetoric and are willing to donate millions of dollars, not just to fund their groups, but to pay six-figure salaries to their founders and animal rights executives.

As an American citizen, gun owner, and hunter, I've never, ever been more concerned for the future of owning a gun, hunting itself, and our overall free-doms in this country as I am now. As a member of the outdoor media and a national hunting spokesperson, I work with the hunting public on a national level, and have done so in the hunting industry for more than thirty years. And I have battled anti-hunting protesters, anti-gun groups, and their ridiculous rhetoric for almost as many years.

I work with the outdoor writers/outdoor media, U.S. Sportsmen's Alliance, the NRA, NWTF, and many other national hunting organizations. I have extensive media training as a professional communicator, and now have years of experience battling misinformation and extensive scrutiny and false

accusations by anti-gun/anti-hunting groups and the media.

Because of my extensive travels, media contacts, and national hunting

Television is a powerful medium. Those of us fortunate enough to appear before the millions of hunters who view television programs have a moral responsibility to represent hunting in an honest and ethical manner.

Ray, at one of his many seminars, preaching the gospel of sound wildlife management.

organization affiliations, I experience, hear, and see so much more than anyone could ever imagine, especially so much more than a "local" citizen who works and lives only within their local community. Many times, protesters have spat on me, harassed me, protested and picketed, called me a baby killer, a Bambi killer, and a murderer during many of my national seminar presentations for conservation groups and for outdoor industry national conventions.

One of the reasons is the slanted opinion and selective coverage of the mainstream media's propagation of hunting and guns as evil, while only covering the protesters and their message, and never hunting, or gun-positive messages.

A perfect example is from the NRA annual meetings several years ago, where media coverage, especially television news, focused on a dozen sign-carrying anti-gun protesters, and totally ignored over a thousand pro-gun sign holders just across the street. Not to mention the thousands upon thousands of honest, law-abiding, gun-owning citizens inside the convention center, as well as positive pro-gun messages, gun safety training, self-defense, and hunting seminars.

I traveled extensively for many years as part of the NRA Great American Hunters tour, as a seminar speaker on white-tailed deer and turkey hunting programs. In every city, local TV camera news reporters shoved a microphone in my face, plying me with these questions: "Why do you believe citizens should own machine guns?"; "Why do you teach children to kill?"; "Is it right to teach children to use guns and arm them with deadly weapons?"

Hunting's first line of defense has always been the trappers, and the National Trappers convention is yet another example of unfair media coverage—and, I might add, with much more aggressive protesting. Just like the NRA, news coverage is always on the side of protesters, not any positive messages of what's proven, sound wildlife management, the number of jobs provided by the outdoor industry, the fur industry, and the importance of this income for rural areas.

However there is usually surprisingly little protest during the NWTF's convention. Apparently turkeys are considered ugly by many nonhunters, and without that big, brown-eyed Bambi, cute-and-cuddly effect for animal rights groups to take to the public, to raise money, apparently turkey hunters are not worthy of protest.

Over the years I've also been harassed by airport security, interrogated because of traveling with a firearm, and most recently, on my return from both Africa and Old Mexico, was treated like a common criminal for returning to my own country, as an American citizen, and traveling with a legal firearm. I have way too many instances to list here of being detained, missing flights, and being called a "killer of innocent animals" by airport and security personnel.

Today, I have never seen such an all-out assault on America's law-abiding, hardworking, honest, hunting gun owners as these past few years. I do not and never will understand why honest gun owners are in effect blamed for some maggot's crime and then punished for legally owning guns, all under the false pretense of keeping guns out of the hands of criminals.

Our hunting world is under attack just as extensively as are gun owners. Bills are introduced weekly by anti-hunting groups to ban hunting. Many are successful, like dove hunting in Michigan and bear hunting in Maryland. Deer overpopulation problems in suburban areas are addressed with untested birth control and sharpshooters, while hunters are lambasted as losers, country bumpkins, and as unsafe and unsuccessful in controlling overpopulation, and sound wildlife management is ridiculed as a joke made up by hunters.

It is without question how successful the media, news anchors, and anti-gun/anti-hunting groups have done such a convincing job of portraying guns as evil, gun owners as criminals, and hunting as a blood sport perpetuated by backwoods slobs. Hollywood, movie stars, TV sitcoms, movies, politicians, and even many school systems hammer, openly oppose guns and hunting every day, and millions of our American public believe this crap, lies, and false accusations.

Today's audiences are hungry for information. Sometimes hunting is every bit as new to adults as it is to youth.

The unfortunate thing is that there are many hunters and gun owners who still claim that "they do not want to take our guns." Just remember that gun owners said that same thing in Germany in 1939, and more recently in Australia as well. But it was already too late for their citizens, when complete gun confiscation by the government took place. The fact is, we are already under massive gun control, the Second Amendment is under attack, and there are already thousands of laws in place to harass gun owners, but that do absolutely nothing to stop criminals and gun crimes.

In spite of the Second Amendment, your personal property—your guns— are restricted, through permits, waiting periods, and government registration. You are required to take a class and get a permit in order to carry your gun to protect yourself and your family. None of these gun control laws has ever stopped a criminal from committing a gun crime; these laws only affect gun owners who have never committed any crime with guns.

You are restricted on magazine capacity, type of gun you can own, and type of ammo you can use for whatever purpose. It is a nightmare to purchase a gun, involving filling out a stupid questionnaire. As if anyone is going to say, "Yep, I am unstable, I am on drugs, I committed a crime with a gun." What happened to our freedom? How and why can anyone tell you what to do with your right to own a gun? And what does any of this have to do with keeping guns out of the hands of criminals?

You better enjoy your hunting seasons, enjoy your time hunting with your family and friends, enjoy your favorite hunting gun, because of naive hunters and gun owners within our own ranks, because of a "lemming attitude." In spite of so many nonbelievers, without question, and sooner than you may believe, all will be taken from you. From my personal experience over the last thirty years, today's well funded anti-hunting and anti-gun groups' unbelievable evolution and growing public acceptance to end gun ownership and ban all hunting, all hunters and gun owners' way of life and our very hunting future in America is in deep trouble.

Something you never hear in the mainstream media is that hunters are the greatest conservationists on the planet; hunters' dollars have paid for the lion's share of wildlife management for today's flourishing wildlife populations for all to enjoy. As much as anti-hunting groups disagree, hunting is the greatest wildlife management tool ever implemented to save wildlife across the world, even with the extensive loss of habitat due to the expansion of mankind destroying wildlife's home.

Hunters are the greatest conservationists, providing a revenue stream that helps ensure sound wildlife management.

Hunters must be on the offense and not the defense. Hunters have nothing to apologize for. Hunters do in fact kill critters, but it is for the benefit and good of all wildlife. You should always carry yourself in public in a positive way for hunting, and spread the gospel of positive, sound wildlife management, the many benefits of hunting, and always share with others what you have learned so that they too can experience a positive, fun, and great time with hunting and enjoying the outdoors.

However, I must tell you, much of the evidence anti-hunting groups utilize to claim that hunting is "bad" comes directly from within our own hunting ranks. Hunters are sometimes their own worst enemies, with almost nonstop infighting between gun hunters, dog hunters, and bowhunting and crossbow hunting. It is the unethical behavior of many hunters, while in the eye of the general nonhunting public, especially on outdoor television shows, who act like some stupid booger-eating inbred, giving all hunters a bad name, that is killing our sport.

Outdoor television is a powerful medium, and those of us fortunate enough to have earned the privilege to represent millions of hunters on television have a moral responsibility to represent hunting in an honest and ethical manner and with uncondi-tional respect for all of God's creatures.

So many of today's over-the-top TV show "kill cel-ebrations" show absolutely no

A positive image fostered through ethical behavior and suitable role models, as well as continuing to educate the public, will help to defuse virulent messages from anti-hunting/anti-gun groups and their protests.

respect whatsoever for a fallen critter. For the sake of our hunting future, our hunting fraternity, outdoor television producers and viewers alike must make a commitment to represent hunting in a positive light, to pass on our hunting heritage, and to share with others what we have learned.

I have a great example, which took place during a recent outdoor media camp from an actual outdoor TV show, airing recently on a major outdoor network. While dragging my gear through the lodge, I noticed several of our guys pointing and laughing in front of a large, big-screen TV. I paused to watch the screen, as a Rio Grande gobbler was madly scooping corn from under a large tripod feeder, all to the driving beat of reverberating rock music.

Returning to the big room, after storing my bags and camera gear, I saw this Texas turkey show explode with a show opener of driving music, thunder rolling, lighting flashing, and graphics flying across the screen.

Suddenly, as rock music screams, two camo-clad dudes walked out of thick fog all bowed up, arms crossed tightly, and with angry, black-painted glaring faces, as if they had just faced off with someone who stole their girlfriends at the dance.

The show announcer's booming voice came up, telling the world how great these guys are, real killers, and all one hundred of their titles of self-proclaimed accomplishments, and none of that fancy editing on this show, no fancy camera work, no re-creations, no cutaways—this is real, as it happens, real hunting, and it is all about them, without any positive message about hunting or any hint of educational value for the viewer.

Next, our two TV show wannabe heroes, in a logo-covered truck with their headshot photos painted on the side, went racing down a gravel road with dust flying, as they passed a carload of scantily dressed young women waving madly as they roared past.

They raced up a long driveway, slid sideways to a quick stop, and jumped from the truck, high-fives flying, as they met their outfitter. Then the music built, as the show cut to our hunters and a cameraman stuffed inside a small blind, chirping loudly, with what I think was supposed to be turkey calling.

Suddenly one of the camo-clad trio barked out, "Take 'em!" A shotgun roared, and the Texas-corn-eating gobbler went down in a pile of feathers and corn. The scene erupted into wild celebration and victorious laughter, as the camera violently jerked in every direction as they all rushed out of the blind, where host, guide, and cameraman alike danced wildly and then jumped into a human pile.

Now, not that there's anything wrong with showing a little emotion after a successful hunt, and of course hunters should be proud of their successes—it's all part of the overall hunting achievement. But screaming *yes, yes, yes,* with clenched teeth, tears on their faces, and wild fist-pumping with fake emotion, on the edge of insanity, all seems a bit uncalled for.

Finally, they all settled down behind the now expired, corn-eating turkey, high-fived some more, as backslapping and fist-bumping filled the big screen, as today's standard "outdoor TV" phrases resonated from the large speakers, "Did you see that?"; "Great shot!"; "What a hunt!"; "What a bird!"; "Unbelievable!" all repeated over and over.

Then the host paused, staring into the camera with tears running down his face, and thanks the high-fence ranch, the outfitter, the guide, the camouflage company, the gun company, the blind company, the feeder company, the game call company, the truck company, the ATV company, the ammo company, and their mothers for giving birth to such skilled turkey hunters.

Next, a shaky handheld camera pulled out to show yet another session of nonstop handshaking and backslapping, as our TV hero host throttled the bird in a chokehold while shoving its open corn-filled beak and bloody noggin right into the camera lens.

With the host stumbling through a weak attempt of a hunt recap, with inaudible "whispering" and a complete annihilation of the English language, he interjected, "That's what I'm talking about," "what a hunt," and "I'll tell you what," over and over and over again.

Walking toward the camera carrying the turkey, the host then engaged with the camera lens in a futile effort of his very weak attempt to describe everything the viewer did not see, as he uncaringly tossed the now unimportant turkey off camera, with a resounding thud, and his face filled the TV screen with yet another round of senseless, insane babbling.

I said to our guys, "What has happened to outdoor television? This isn't anything like the old *American Sportsman* hunting show." Just then, the next week's preview came up, again with blaring rock and roll music. The preview showed this little black-and-white spotted Porky the Pig under the same feeder, madly vacuuming up the corn. Yep, same guys, same blind, same time next week.

Unfortunately, there are way too many TV shows like this one today. It seems as if TV hunters or "hosts" only care about themselves. The host radiates an "it's all about me" attitude. These types seem to have little regard for wildlife, or for sharing knowledge with others, or leading by example, only worrying about TV show face time, in an egotistical attempt to become television superstars.

Unfortunately, when it comes right down to some of today's programming, way too many viewers believe that because it's on television, it's the right way to do things, that this is how they should react to a kill, and how they should hunt. They have a tendency to copy everything they see and hear, and then take it to the woods with them.

There is something very important missing from this TV show: the lack of any hint of respect for the animal. There is not a splinter of reverence for a fallen animal, something that was instilled within me from the very beginning of my hunting career since I was a very small boy. The killing of an animal is such a small part of the hunt, of the total experience. It is the final step in hunting, and not the entire story, and it certainly should not be the main focus of any hunting show. We must portray hunting in an honest and ethical way as it happens each and every time we take any game animal.

Actually, as hunters, all of us have a huge responsibility to demonstrate hunting as it really is, as a crucial wildlife management tool, a wholesome family activity, and a very valuable part of our American heritage. We must exemplify the reasons we hunt, not make excuses, but explain through our television programs why the taking of an animal is so much more than just killing.

So it is up to all of us, and we better do something about these types of totally ridiculous and unrealistic representations of hunting on today's outdoor television shows, because if we do nothing about it, those well-funded, very determined anti-hunting groups will most certainly be more than happy to do it for us.

With anti-hunting/animal rights groups, with their large war chests of money, it is difficult to fight them as an individual, so it is important to join and support the ranks of organized hunting, conservation, and pro-firearms organizations. The U.S. Sportsmen's Alliance, The National Wild Turkey Federation,

Organized youth hunts build positive attitudes and create wonderful memories.

and the National Rifle Association are just a few. Please review the information below, and join in our fight to save and protect our precious shooting and hunting heritage.

National Wild Turkey Federation, Post Office Box 530, Edgefield, SC 29824-0530.
Phone: 1-800-THE-NWTF (843-6983) or (803) 637-3106
Email: info@nwtf.net

The author's daughter, Sara, after a turkey hunt on Johnson Mountain.

The NWTF is the leader in upland wildlife habitat conservation in North America. A nonprofit organization dedicated to conserving the wild turkey and other wildlife and preserving our hunting heritage, the NWTF and its volunteers work closely with state, federal, and provincial wildlife agencies and other partners.

Through these dynamic partnerships, the NWTF and its members have helped restore wild turkey populations throughout North America, investing more than $372 million to conserve 17 million acres of critical wildlife habitat.

The NWTF also brings new conservationists and hunters into the fold through outdoor education programs and dedicated NWTF

Writer Kimberly Hiss with a Rio she took in Nebraska in December 2009. Hiss wrote her story, which appeared in the December 2010 issue of Oprah's *O* Magazine—yet another sign that turkey hunting is gaining acceptance everywhere.

volunteers introduce about 100,000 people to the outdoors through these pro grams every year.

To become a member of the NWTF, join a committee or start a chapter, visit www.nwtf.org or call 800-THE-NWTF. The NWTF is also at www.facebook.com/theNWTF.

Brent Lawrence, NWFT Public Relations Director, with a Merriam's gobbler he took in the Clearwater Mountains of Idaho. With more than half a million members in fifty states and sixteen foreign countries, the National Wild Turkey Federation has been instrumental in the comeback of the wild turkey. PHOTO BY JOHN HAFNER/JOHN HAFNER PHOTOGRAPHY.

All hunters have a huge responsibility to represent hunting in a positive, ethical way, as a crucial wild life management tool, a wholesome family activity, and a valuable part of our American heritage.